Workbook for

Auto Fundamentals

How and Why of the Design, Construction, and Operation of Automobiles. Applicable to All Makes and Models.

by

Martin W. Stockel

Martin T. Stockel

James E. Duffy

Chris Johanson

Publisher

The Goodheart-Willcox Company, Inc.

Tinley Park, Illinois

INTRODUCTION

The workbook for **Auto Fundamentals** provides a thorough study guide for the text. It highlights important information, improves understanding, and simplifies the contents of the textbook.

The workbook contains many unique features designed to make your learning easier and more interesting. It has two major types of exercises—**Chapters** (in-text activities) and **Jobs** (in-shop activities).

Each workbook chapter serves as an "open book" review and study guide for a textbook chapter. You are led through the text page by page, making sure you cover the most essential material.

The questions and illustrations are organized by subject. The workbook is organized to correlate with the order of the textbook material.

The illustrations in the workbook correspond to those in the text. Some of the problems require that you identify and draw the missing components.

The **Jobs** section also corresponds to the contents of the textbook. They give easy-to-follow instructions and will give you experience in developing the basic skills you will need to service and repair an automobile.

The workbook will be a valuable learning tool to you as you study auto mechanics.

Martin W. Stockel

Martin T. Stockel

James E. Duffy

Chris Johanson

CONTENTS

Instructions for Answering Workbook Questions

Each chapter in the workbook correlates to the same chapter in the textbook. Before answering the questions in the workbook, study the assigned chapter of the text and answer the end-of-chapter questions while referring to your text. Then, review the objectives at the beginning of each workbook chapter. This will help you to review the important concepts covered in the chapter. Try to complete as many questions as possible *without* referring to your text. Then, use the textbook to complete the remaining questions.

A variety of questions are used in the workbook, including multiple choice, identification, completion, short answer, and matching. The question sequence corresponds to the sequence of the material in the chapter. Following are examples of completed workbook questions.

Multiple Choice

1. Technician A says that alloy steel tools are useless for many jobs. Technician B says that quality tools are heat treated. Who is right?
   (A) A only.
   (B) B only.
   (C) Both A and B.
   (D) Neither A nor B.

1. _____(B)_____

2. Impact wrench drive sizes run from 1/4″ to _____.
   (A) 1″
   (B) 2″
   (C) 3″
   (D) 4″

2. _____(A)_____

Completion

3. Polished tools are easy to _____.

3. _____(clean)_____

4. Always keep your tools _____ and clean.

4. _____(orderly)_____

Identification

5. Identify the parts of the hacksaw pictured below.

   (A) _____Adjustable frame_____
   (B) _____Handle_____
   (C) _____Blade tensioner_____
   (D) _____Blade_____

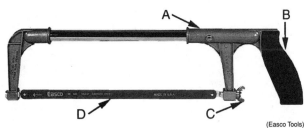

(Easco Tools)

Short Answer

5. Define *starting punch*.

_____ It tapers to a flat tip, used for starting to punch out pins, rivets, etc. _____

Matching

Match the terms on the right with the descriptions on the left.

6. Opens to let fuel-air mixture enter cylinder.

7. Air pressure at sea level.

8. Formed when an enclosed area has air pressure lower than outside air pressure.

9. Forms a vacuum pump in the engine.

10. A vacuum pump is formed in the engine by the action of the _____ as it moves down in its cylinder.

(A) Piston and cylinder
(B) Valve
(C) Intake valve
(D) Flywheel
(E) 14.7 lb. per square inch
(F) Vacuum
(G) Piston
(H) Ports

6. ___C___

7. ___E___

8. ___F___

9. ___A___

10. ___G___

Instructions for Completing Workbook Jobs

The jobs in the workbook are designed to supplement the material in the text by outlining various hands-on activities. Before beginning any job, read through the entire assignment and discuss the procedure with your instructor. It is also important to read the related chapters in the text and to review all pertinent safety information before you begin.

Some of the jobs may take more than one class period to complete. When this occurs, be sure to inform your instructor so that your project can be stored properly until you are able to resume.

As you complete each numbered step in a job, place a check mark in the corresponding box. This will help you keep track of your progress. When you finish an entire job, have your instructor inspect your work and initial your completed job sheet.

Name _____

Date _____ Period _____

Instructor _____

● Score _____ Text pages 11–26

1

Building an Engine

Objectives: After studying Chapter 1 in the textbook, and completing this section of the workbook, you will be able to:

- Identify the basic parts of an engine.
- Explain engine operating principles.
- Describe the function of the major parts of an engine.
- Describe the four-stroke cycle sequence.

Tech Talk: The engine in a modern vehicle may seem to have little in common with engines of 50 or 75 years ago. Surprisingly, however, the basic parts of today's engines are almost identical to those used on our first "horseless carriages." In fact, a one cylinder lawn mower engine uses the same fundamental components as a multi-cylinder automotive engine. If you understand the principles of the engine presented in Chapter 1, you understand the principles of every piston engine.

Instructions: Read the general instructions on pages 5–6 for answering the workbook questions. Then, as you study Chapter 1 of the text, answer the following questions in the spaces provided.

What Is an Engine?

1. An engine is a group of _____ _____ assembled to convert the energy of a burning fuel into a more usable form of energy.

1. _____

2. Define *internal combustion engine.* _____

_____

3. Gasoline is made by refining _____.
   (A) coal
   (B) crude oil
   (C) oxygen

3. _____

4. Since gasoline is a mixture of carbon and hydrogen, it is often termed a(n) _____.

4. _____

5. To burn, gasoline must be mixed with _____.
   (A) oxygen
   (B) nitrogen
   (C) argon
   (D) hydrocarbons

5. _____

6. To make gasoline burn more rapidly, it must be broken into
   _____ particles.
   (A) large
   (B) smaller

6. _____

7. The crankshaft changes up and down or _____ motion of
   the piston into a more readily usable _____ motion.

7. _____

   _____

8. Identify the indicated parts and draw arrows depicting part motion.

   (A) _____

   (B) _____

   (C) _____

   (D) _____

   (E) _____

   (F) _____

   (G) _____

   (H) _____

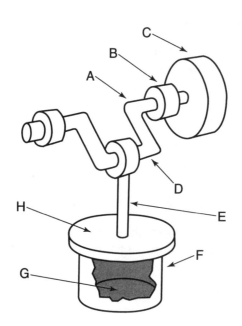

Basic Parts of an Engine

9. The _____ is the container or mounting for the other engine
   parts.
   (A) cylinder
   (B) crankcase
   (C) block
   (D) None of the above.

9. _____

10. The _____ is the hole in the block that holds the piston.   10. _____
    (A) cylinder
    (B) camshaft
    (C) port
    (D) None of the above.

11. Define *connecting rod.* _____

    _____

    _____

12. Define *main bearings.* _____

    _____

13. The lower portion of the engine block is called the _____.   13. _____
    (A) camshaft
    (B) flywheel
    (C) crankcase
    (D) head

14. Define *piston pin.* _____

    _____

    _____

15. The upper cylinder area is called the _____ chamber.   15. _____
    (A) crankshaft
    (B) combustion
    (C) exhaust
    (D) intake

16. The cylinder head is a _____ top fastened in place with   16. _____
    bolts or studs and nuts.
    (A) permanent
    (B) flexible
    (C) removable
    (D) None of the above.

17. _____ are the passages in and out of the cylinder for fuel   17. _____
    mixture and exhaust flow.

18. _____ open and close engine cylinder head ports.   18. _____

19. What is the purpose of the valve guide? _____

    _____

    _____

    _____

    _____

20. The _____ _____ hold the engine valve closed.   20. _____

21. Draw the missing portions in the illustration below and identify the indicated parts.

(A) _____

(B) _____

(C) _____

(D) _____

(E) _____

(F) _____

(G) _____

(H) _____

(I) _____

(J) _____

(K) _____

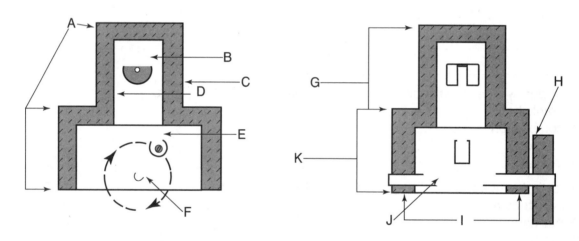

22. Draw the missing portions in the illustration below and identify the indicated parts.

    (A) _____

    (B) _____

    (C) _____

    (D) _____

    (E) _____

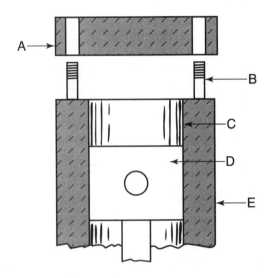

Four-Stroke Cycle

Match the terms on the right with the descriptions on the left.

23. Opens to let fuel-air mixture enter cylinder.

24. Air pressure at sea level.

25. Formed when an enclosed area has air pressure lower than outside air pressure.

26. Forms a vacuum pump in the engine.

27. A vacuum pump is formed in the engine by the action of the _____ as it moves down in its cylinder.

(A) Piston and cylinder
(B) Valve
(C) Intake valve
(D) Flywheel
(E) 14.7 lb. per square inch
(F) Vacuum
(G) Piston
(H) Ports

23. _____

24. _____

25. _____

26. _____

27. _____

28. Identify the valve related parts in the following illustration.

(A) _____

(B) _____

(C) _____

(D) _____

(E) _____

(F) _____

(G) _____

(H) _____

(I) _____

(J) _____

(K) _____

(L) _____

(M) _____

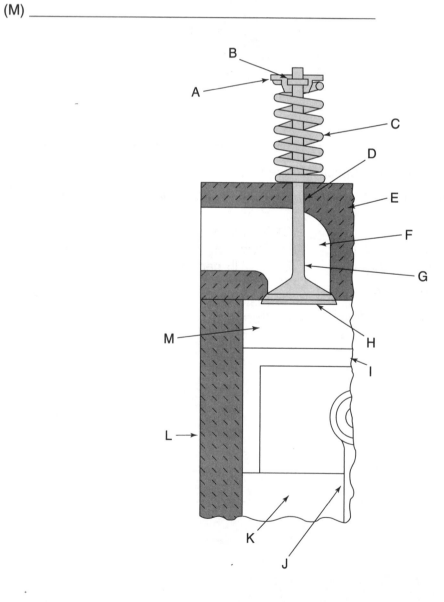

The Intake Stroke

29. During the intake stroke, the _____ and _____ mixture is down into the cylinder.

29. _____

   _____

30. The intake stroke requires _____ turn of the engine crankshaft.

30. _____

31. Before labeling the illustrations, draw the valves in their proper positions. Also, draw the fuel mixture as it enters and is compressed in the cylinder.

   (A) _____

   (B) _____

   (C) _____

   (D) _____

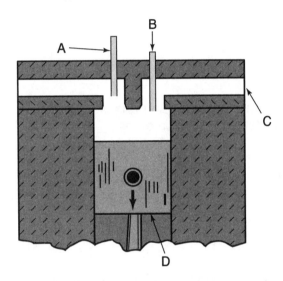

The Compression Stroke

32. _____

32. During compression, the piston is moving _____ in the cylinder.
   (A) upward
   (B) downward

33. _____

33. During the compression stroke, the fuel and air mixture is _____ in the cylinder.

34. _____

34. The compression stroke requires _____ turn of the crank for completion.
   (A) 1/2
   (B) 1
   (C) 1 and 1/2
   (D) 2

35. _____

35. The compression ratio is the _____ of the cylinder at the bottom of its stroke compared to its _____ at the top of its stroke.
   (A) volume, capacity
   (B) capacity, volume
   (C) volume, volume

   _____

The Power Stroke

36. The stroke that supplies energy to rotate the crankshaft is the _____ stroke.
    (A) compression
    (B) power
    (C) exhaust
    (D) intake

36. _____

37. As the piston reaches the top of the compression stroke, the mixture is broken into _____ _____ and heated up.

37. _____

38. A spark is provided inside the combustion chamber by means of a _____.

38. _____

39. The high voltage that causes the spark is produced by the _____ system.
    (A) compression
    (B) ignition
    (C) charging
    (D) fuel

39. _____

40. Both valves are _____ and the expanding gases force the piston down which results in the rotation of the _____.
    (A) closed, crankshaft
    (B) open, crankshaft
    (C) closed, camshaft
    (D) None of the above.

40. _____

41. In what position are the valves in the following illustration?
    (A) open
    (B) closed

41. _____

42. In what direction does the piston travel in the following illustration?
    (A) down
    (B) up

42. _____

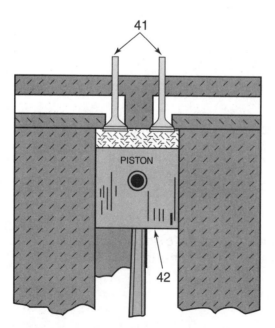

43. The valves in the following illustration are _____.

43. _____

44. The piston in the following illustration travels _____ by the force of exploding fuel mixture.

44. _____

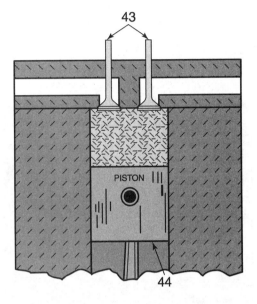

The Exhaust Stroke

45. When the piston reaches the bottom of the power stroke, the _____ valve opens.
    (A) intake
    (B) exhaust
    (C) Neither valve.

45. _____

46. The spinning crank forces the piston _____ through the cylinder blowing the _____ out of the cylinder.

46. _____
    _____

47. The intake valve is _____ during the exhaust stroke.

47. _____

48. The four half turns in the intake, compression, power, and exhaust strokes, gives two complete turns, or _____ of the crankshaft.

48. _____

49. The intake, compression, power, and exhaust cycles are often referred to as the _____ cycle.

49. _____

50. Identify the valves, their positions, and the direction in which the piston is traveling in the following illustration.

(A) _____

(B) _____

(C) _____

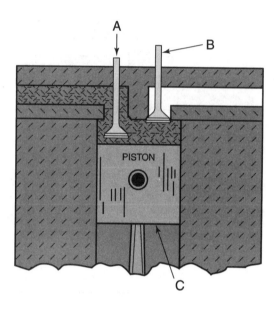

Camshaft

Match the terms on the right with the descriptions on the left.

51. The camshaft has a bump or eccentric which is called a(n) _____ machined on the shaft.

52. The distance and time the valve is opened can be controlled by the _____ of the cam.

53. The cam follower or _____ rides on the cam lobe separating the lobe from the valve stem or push rod.

54. The essential parts of the valve system are commonly referred to as the _____.

55. The _____ must turn at one-half crank-shaft speed.

56. One way to turn the camshaft is by gears and a _____.

(A) belt
(B) valve train
(C) output shaft
(D) camshaft gear
(E) cam lobe
(F) height and shape
(G) crankshaft
(H) valve lifter
(I) intake valve

51. _____

52. _____

53. _____

54. _____

55. _____

56. _____

57. Identify the parts of the camshaft illustrated below.

   (A) _____

   (B) _____

   (C) _____

   (D) _____

   (E) _____

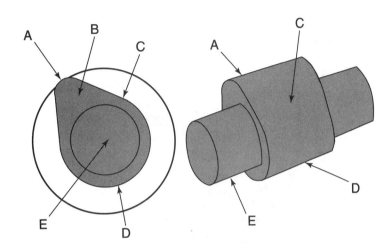

58. Draw the missing parts and identify all of the indicated parts in the following illustration.

   (A) _____

   (B) _____

   (C) _____

   (D) _____

   (E) _____

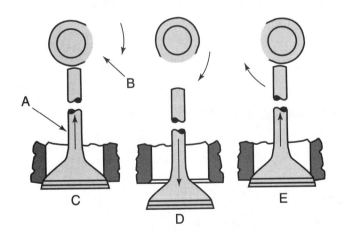

59. Identify the valve timing components in the following illustration.

(A) _____

(B) _____

(C) _____

(D) _____

(E) _____

(F) _____

(G) _____

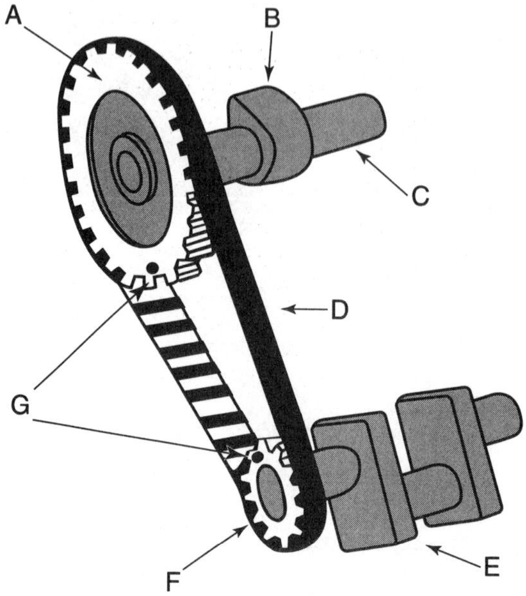

Timing the Valves

60. Getting the valves to open at the right time is called valve
_____.
(A) lift
(B) duration
(C) timing
(D) None of the above.

60. _____

61. Punch marks on the camshaft gear and crankshaft gear are
called _____ marks.
(A) timing
(B) piston
(C) gauge
(D) None of the above.

61. _____

62. When the piston reaches _____ on the exhaust stroke, the
flank of the cam lobe will again be touching the intake lifter.
(A) right or left dead center
(B) top capacity (TC)
(C) bottom dead center (BDC)
(D) top dead center (TDC)

62. _____

63. The only difference between the intake and exhaust timing
is that you start by placing the piston on _____ .
    (A) uppermost capacity (UC)
    (B) right or left dead center
    (C) bottom dead center (BDC)
    (D) top dead center (TDC)

63. _____

The Flywheel

64. The flywheel is attached to the end of the _____.

64. _____

65. The flywheel is caused to spin by the _____ stroke and will
continue to spin because it is heavy.

65. _____

66. When the crankshaft is coasting, it cannot slow down as
quickly because the flywheel _____ keeps it spinning.
    (A) velocity
    (B) compression
    (C) power
    (D) camshaft
    (E) crankshaft

66. _____

67. Identify the indicated parts in the drawing below.

    (A) _____

    (B) _____

Basic Engine Completed

68. The basic engine described in Chapter 1 of the text will run
if _____ is added.
    (A) fuel
    (B) spark
    (C) oil
    (D) All of the above.

68. _____

69. What types of equipment are operated by one-cylinder engines? _____

_____

70. What is the major difference between a multi-cylinder
engine and the engine built in Chapter 1?
    (A) The basic parts are different.
    (B) The basic parts do a different job.
    (C) There are more of the same basic parts.
    (D) There are fewer of the same basic parts.

70. _____

2

Design, Construction, Application of Engine Components

Objectives: After studying Chapter 2 in the textbook, and completing this section of the workbook, you will be able to:

- Describe engine part design.
- Explain the construction of engine components.
- Define the purpose of each engine part.
- Identify engine part variations.

Tech Talk: A good auto mechanic not only understands engine operating principles, but also engine design and construction aspects. The competent mechanic will know why a piston is made of aluminum instead of cast iron or why the surface of a connecting rod bearing is made of soft rather than hard material. These kinds of facts give the mechanic a "body of knowledge" which can be used during the service and repair of a car.

Instructions: Read the general instructions on pages 5–6 for answering the workbook questions. Then, as you study Chapter 2 of the text, answer the following questions in the spaces provided.

The Engine Block

1. All of the following statements about a modern engine block are true, EXCEPT:
   (A) the block is a rigid foundation for other engine parts.
   (B) the cylinders are in the block.
   (C) the valves are in the block.
   (D) the block supports the crankshaft and camshaft.

1. _____

2. Name the parts indicated in the typical block construction illustrated below.

(A) _____

(B) _____

(C) _____

(D) _____

(E) _____

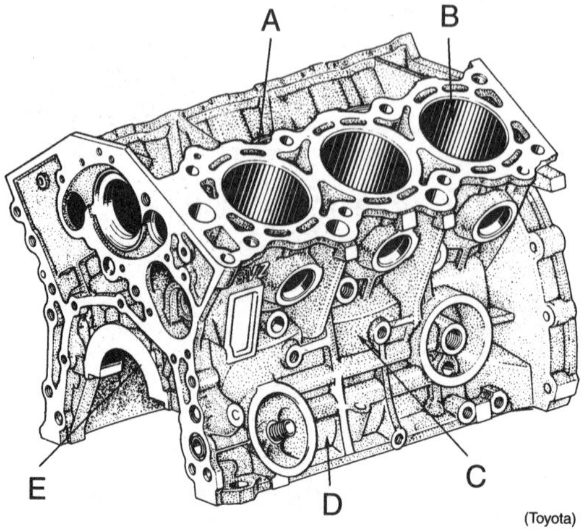

(Toyota)

Cylinders

3. Define *cylinder*. _____

_____

4. A good cylinder will not vary in diameter more than _____
   (A) .0005″ (0.013 mm)
   (B) .004″ (0.012 mm)
   (C) .010″ (0.026 mm)
   (D) None of the above.

4. _____

5. A page in your textbook is about _____ thick.
   (A) .0005″ (0.013 mm)
   (B) .004″ (0.012 mm)
   (C) .010″ (0.026 mm)
   (D) None of the above.

5. _____

6. The cylinder acts as a guide for the _____ and acts as a container for taking in, compressing, firing, and exhausting the fuel mixture.

6. _____

7. Steel cylinder sleeves are usually used in _____ engine blocks.

7. _____

8. A cylinder sleeve is a round, _____-like liner.

8. _____

9. Technician A says that on some aluminum engines, a worn
cylinder sleeve can be replaced by pulling it out of the block.
Technician B says that a sleeve can sometimes be installed
to repair a worn or cracked cylinder in a cast iron engine.
Who is right?
(A) A only.
(B) B only.
(C) Both A and B.
(D) Neither A nor B.

9. _____

Pistons

10. Define *piston*. _____

_____

_____

11. The piston slides up and down in the _____.
(A) cylinder head
(B) valve guide
(C) cylinder
(D) None of the above.

11. _____

12. The piston moves down in the cylinder producing a _____
which draws the fuel and air into the engine.

12. _____

13. When the fuel mixture is fired, pressure is transmitted to the
_____ of the piston.
(A) bottom
(B) side
(C) top
(D) None of the above.

13. _____

14. Pistons are usually made of _____ because of its light
weight.

14. _____

15. When a piston tips or flops sideways in the cylinder and
makes a knocking sound, it is termed piston _____.

15. _____

16. A piston will _____ when it gets hot.
(A) crack
(B) expand
(C) contract
(D) None of the above.

16. _____

17. A cam ground piston is egg or elliptical shaped when _____
and round when _____.
(A) hot, cold
(B) cold, hot

17. _____

_____

18. The top of a piston can reach a temperature of above _____.

18. _____

19. The head of a piston is usually _____ than the skirt.   19. _____
    (A) smaller
    (B) wider
    (C) thicker
    (D) None of the above.

20. Identify the indicated parts in the illustration below.

    (A) _____

    (B) _____

    (C) _____

    (D) _____

    (E) _____

    (F) _____

    (G) _____

    (H) _____

    (I) _____

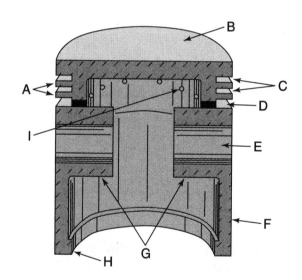

21. Using a ruler, draw the missing portion of the hot and cold pistons illustrated below.

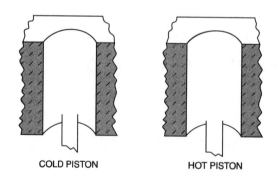

COLD PISTON   HOT PISTON

Piston Rings

22. The piston alone cannot _____ pressure in the engine cylinder.

22. _____

23. To prevent the burning fuel mixture from leaking into the bottom of the engine, _____ are installed on the piston.

23. _____

24. A piston ring is built so that it must be compressed or _____ to enter the cylinder.

24. _____

25. The space between the ends of the piston ring is called the piston ring _____ .

25. _____

26. A general rule for piston ring gap clearance is to allow _____ per inch of cylinder diameter. A four inch cylinder would require a ring gap of approximately _____.

26. _____

27. Leakage past the piston rings is commonly called _____.

27. _____

28. Label the parts indicated in the illustration to the right.

(A) _____

(B) _____

(C) _____

(D) _____

(E) _____

(F) _____

(G) _____

(H) _____

(I) _____

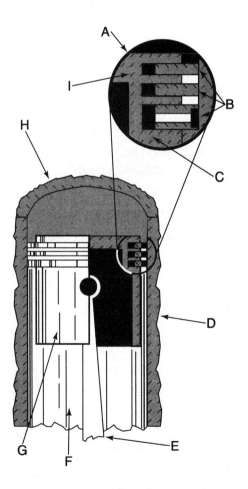

29. Draw the arrows showing piston ring pressure and identify the parts indicated in the illustration below.

(A) _____

(B) _____

(C) _____

(D) _____

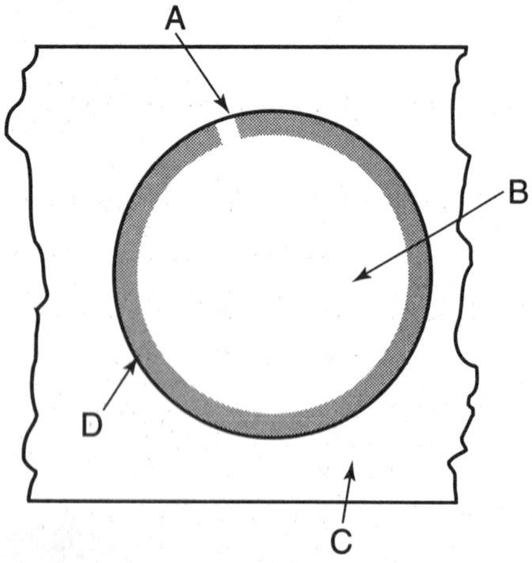

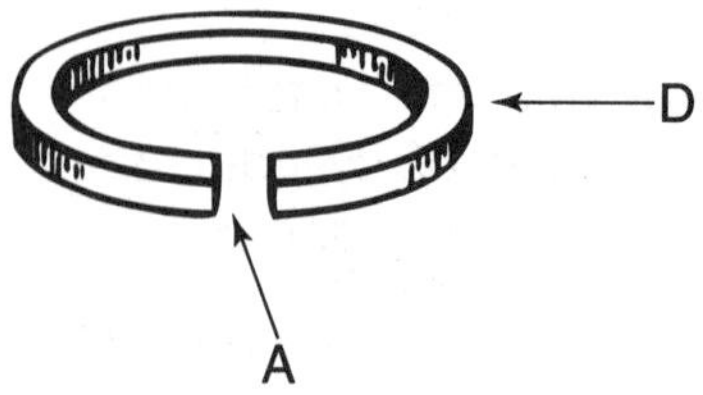

Types of Rings

30. The two types of piston rings are the _____ and oil rings.

30. _____

31. Most engines use three rings on each piston: two compression rings and one oil _____ ring.

31. _____

32. Compression rings are designed to prevent leakage between the piston and the _____ .

32. _____

33. The oil control ring is used to _____

_____

_____.

34. Why are all oil control rings slotted? _____

_____

_____

35. Some piston rings designed for use in worn cylinders use _____ _____ to force the rings out against the cylinder wall.

35. _____

36. If a cylinder is worn, the top of the cylinder is normally _____ than the bottom.

36. _____

37. When installing new rings, the cylinder must have a certain degree of roughness so that the rings will _____.
    (A) expand
    (B) wear-in
    (C) None of the above.

37. _____

38. Compression rings are often coated with _____.   38. _____
    (A) graphite
    (B) phosphate
    (C) molybdenum
    (D) All of the above.

39. Compression rings are very brittle. They must be installed   39. _____
    on the piston carefully to avoid _____.

40. Thin oil rings are usually made of _____.   40. _____

41. Draw the missing oil and arrows showing oil flow in the illustration below and identify the indicated
    parts.

    (A) _____

    (B) _____

    (C) _____

    (D) _____

    (E) _____

    (F) _____

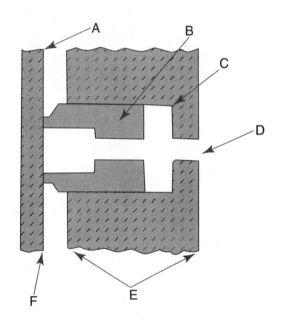

42. Identify the parts indicated in the drawing below.

(A) _____

(B) _____

(C) _____

(D) _____

(E) _____

(F) _____

(G) _____

(H) _____

(I) _____

(J) _____

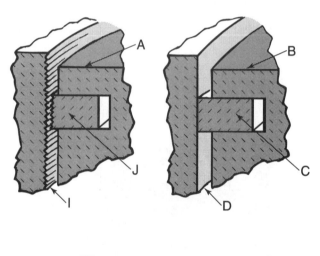

Piston Pins

43. Define *piston pin*. _____

_____

_____

44. All of the following statements about piston pins are true, EXCEPT:

44. _____

    (A) a piston pin can be secured to the rod by a press fit.

    (B) a free-floating pin makes use of snap rings in each piston boss.

    (C) most piston pins are solid for extra strength.

    (D) piston pins are usually case-hardened.

45. Identify the parts indicated in the illustration below.

    (A) _____

    (B) _____

    (C) _____

    (D) _____

    (E) _____

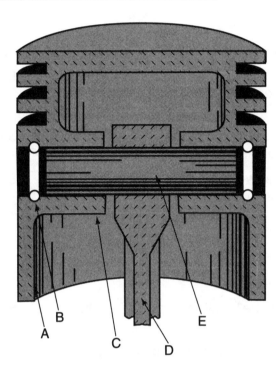

Connecting Rods

46. Define *connecting rod.* _____

_____

_____

47. The upper end of the connecting rod has a small hole in it
for the _____.

47. _____

48. The lower end of the connecting rod must be _____ so that
it can be installed on the crankshaft journal.
    (A) removed
    (B) installed
    (C) flexible
    (D) None of the above.

48. _____

49. The top of the rod and the connecting rod cap are bolted
together and if removed, they should be _____.
    (A) replaced
    (B) numbered
    (C) cleaned
    (D) None of the above.

49. _____

50. Turning the connecting rod cap around so that the numbers do not line up could cause the rod bore to be _____. This could lock the rod on the crankshaft.

50. _____

51. In making connecting rods, the upper and lower halves are bolted together and the holes are _____ to an accurate size.

51. _____

52. Connecting rods are generally made of _____ .
    (A) carbon steel
    (B) alloy steel
    (C) wrought iron
    (D) cast iron

52. _____

53. The customary shape of the rod uses _____ construction.

53. _____

54. The lower end of the connecting rod uses a precision _____ that fits between the connecting rod and the journal of the crankshaft.

54. _____

55. The rod bearing or insert is held in place by a _____ that fits into a notch in the connecting rod.

55. _____

56. The connecting rod bearing will protrude one or two thousandths of an inch above the connecting rod. This is called _____ and it causes the bearing to fit tightly in the rod.
    (A) bearing height
    (B) clearance height
    (C) crush height
    (D) None of the above.

56. _____

57. Some bearings have steel shells with a thin _____ babbitt lining.

57. _____

58. Identify the parts indicated in the illustration on the right.

    (A) _____

    (B) _____

    (C) _____

    (D) _____

    (E) _____

    (F) _____

    (G) _____

    (H) _____

    (I) _____

    (J) _____

(Jaguar)

59. Indicate the numbers that would be stamped on each cap and identify the illustration parts.

(A) _____

(B) _____

(C) _____

(D) _____

(E) _____

(F) _____

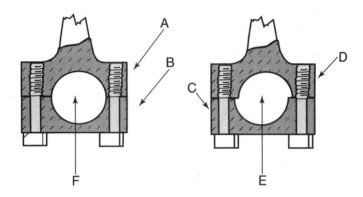

60. Identify the parts indicated in the illustration below.

(A) _____

(B) _____

(C) _____

(D) _____

(E) _____

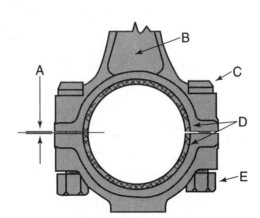

Crankshaft

61. Define *crankshaft.* _____

    _____

    _____

62. The function of the crankshaft is to convert _____ motion of the piston into a rotary motion to power the car.

    62. _____

63. The crankshaft is held in position by a series of _____ _____.

    63. _____

64. The main bearings (precision _____) are similar to connecting rod bearings in construction but are usually larger.

    64. _____

65. One of the main bearings must control the _____ (forward and backward movement of the crankshaft).

    65. _____

66. The _____ bearing has flanges on the edges that rub against a ground surface on the edge of the journal.
    (A) piston
    (B) thrust
    (C) main
    (D) None of the above.

    66. _____

67. The crankshaft of a V-8 engine has four _____ with two connecting rods bolted to each.
    (A) weights
    (B) inserts
    (C) throws
    (D) None of the above.

    67. _____

68. Many crankshafts use counterbalances or _____ to prevent vibration.
    (A) weights
    (B) bearings
    (C) throws
    (D) None of the above.

    68. _____

69. A vibration damper or _____ _____ is attached to the front of the crankshaft to stop any winding motion and smooth out engine operation.

    69. _____

70. The balance shaft is installed to _____ vertical and torsional vibrations from the crankshaft.

    70. _____

71. Why is the crankshaft drilled? _____

    _____

    _____

72. All bearing surfaces are precision ground and highly _____ to increase bearing life.

    72. _____

73. A timing gear, chain, or belt sprocket is installed on the front of the crankshaft. It is secured with a metal _____ that ride in a slot in the shaft end.

    73. _____

74. Identify the parts of the crankshaft and main bearings in the illustration below.

(A) _____

(B) _____

(C) _____

(D) _____

(E) _____

(F) _____

(G) _____

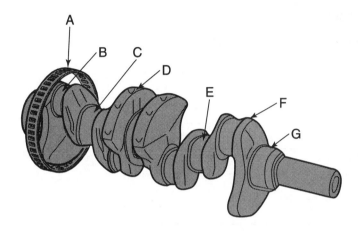

75. Draw the arrows and dots showing the flow of oil through the engine crankshaft and identify the parts indicated.

(A) _____

(B) _____

(C) _____

(D) _____

(E) _____

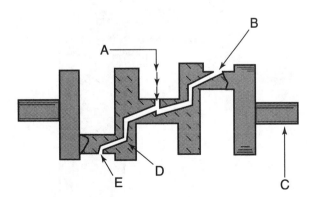

Flywheel

76. A heavy flywheel bolts to the _____ of the crankshaft to smooth engine operation.
    (A) side
    (B) front
    (C) rear
    (D) None of the above.

76. _____

77. The outer rim of the flywheel has a large ring with gear _____ cut into it so that the starting motor can crank and start the engine.

77. _____

78. When an automatic transmission is used, the _____ _____ works with the flywheel.

78. _____

79. Identify the indicated parts of the flywheel illustrated below.

    (A) _____

    (B) _____

    (C) _____

    (D) _____

    (E) _____

    (F) _____

    (G) _____

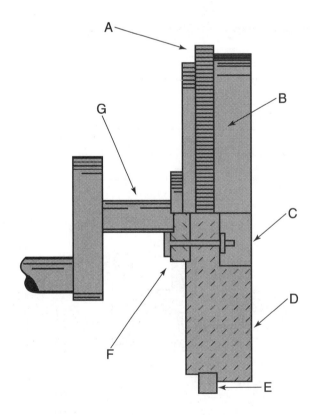

● Camshaft

80. An engine camshaft is used to _____

_____.

81. Most automobile engines use _____ camshaft(s).   81. _____

82. A camshaft has a series of support _____ along its length   82. _____
which hold the camshaft in place.

83. A camshaft turns at _____ crankshaft speed.   83. _____
    (A) one-third
    (B) twice
    (C) one-half
    (D) None of the above.

84. A gear cut into the camshaft is often used to drive the _____.   84. _____
    (A) distributor
    (B) oil pump
    (C) water pump
    (D) Both A and B.

85. An additional cam or eccentric may be ground on the   85. _____
camshaft to drive a _____.

86. The camshaft gear can be made of _____ or a special   86. _____
pressed _____.   _____

87. A gear or chain setup is commonly used in cam-in- _____   87. _____
engines.

88. Identify the parts indicated in the following illustration.

(A) _____

(B) _____

(C) _____

(D) _____

(E) _____

(F) _____

(G) _____

(H) _____

(I) _____

(J) _____

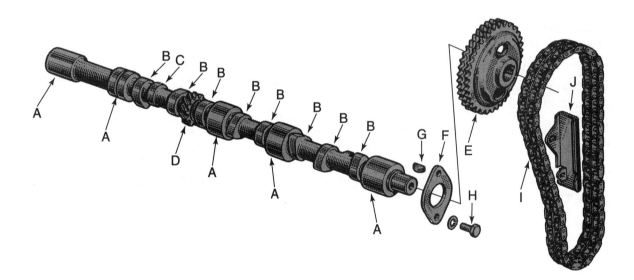

89. Identify the parts indicated in the following illustration.

(A) _____

(B) _____

(C) _____

(D) _____

(E) _____

(F) _____

(G) _____

(H) _____

(I) _____

(J) _____

(K) _____

(L) _____

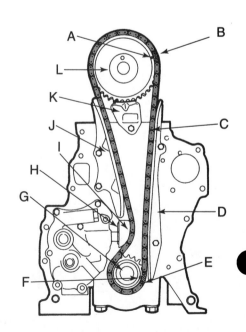

Valves

90. Modern engines may have _____ valves per cylinder.
    (A) 2
    (B) 3
    (C) 4
    (D) All of the above.

90. _____

91. Exhaust valves are made of heat resistant metal. To prevent burning, they must give off heat to the valve _____ and valve _____ .

91. _____
    _____

92. Two common valve seat angles are _____ .

92. _____

93. A _____ degree difference may be ground between the valve face and the valve seat for fast break-in.
    (A) one
    (B) two
    (C) three
    (D) four

93. _____

94. Valve seats can be _____ or _____ into the cylinder head.

94. _____
    _____

95. The valve face and valve seat must make perfect _____ if leakage is to be prevented and the engine is to run efficiently.

95. _____

96. The valve guide can be a(n) _____ part of the cylinder head or it can be pressed into an existing hole in the cylinder head.

96. _____

97. Normal guide-to-stem clearance is approximately _____.
    (A) .001″–.002″ (0.02 mm – 0.05 mm)
    (B) .002″–.003″ (0.05 mm – 0.08 mm)
    (C) .003″–.004″ (0.08 mm – 0.11 mm)
    (D) None of the above.

97. _____

98. Identify the parts indicated in the following illustration.

(A) _____

(B) _____

(C) _____

(D) _____

(E) _____

(F) _____

(G) _____

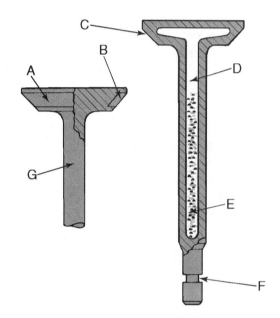

99. Identify the parts indicated in the following illustration.

(A) _____

(B) _____

(C) _____

(D) _____

(E) _____

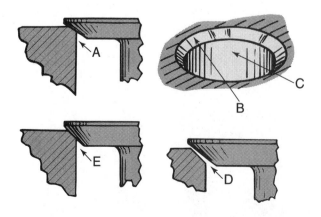

Lifters

100. _____ valve lifters are usually made of cast iron. They require some means of adjustment, normally an adjustable rocker arm.

101. The solid lifter must be adjusted periodically to maintain correct valve _____ .

102. To reduce weight, some mechanical-type lifters are _____.

103. The hydraulic lifter serves the same function as a mechanical lifter. However, it is oil filled and is _____ and operates with no valve clearance.

104. Hydraulic lifters are very _____ during operation and do not make the tapping sound common to mechanical lifters.

105. To reduce carbon buildup, the valve can be designed to be turned. This cleans the valve and seat by a _____ action.

106. Roller lifters are often used in modern engines to _____.
    (A) reduce wear
    (B) increase friction
    (C) increase speed
    (D) None of the above.

107. Technician A says that the intake and exhaust valves are both open for longer than it takes the piston to make a stroke. Technician B says that the valve timing is the same for all engines. Who is right?
    (A) A only.
    (B) B only.
    (C) Both A and B.
    (D) Neither A nor B.

108. The cylinder head holds the _____.
    (A) spark plugs
    (B) valves
    (C) pistons
    (D) Both A and B.

109. Oil pans can be made of _____.
    (A) plastic
    (B) stamped steel
    (C) aluminum
    (D) All of the above.

100. _____

101. _____

102. _____

103. _____

104. _____

105. _____

106. _____

107. _____

108. _____

109. _____

110. Draw arrows indicating oil flow and oil under pressure and identify the parts indicated in the illustration below.

(A) The valve is _____.

(B) _____

(C) The valve is _____.

(D) _____

(E) _____

(F) _____

(G) _____

(H) _____

(I) _____

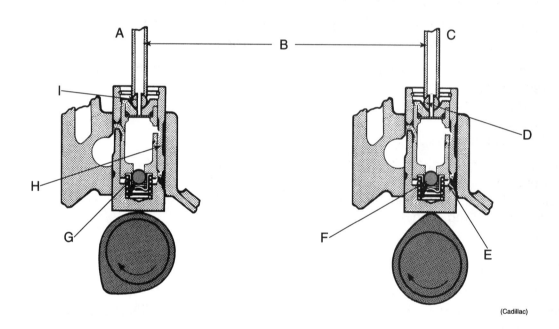

(Cadillac)

Timing Gear Cover

111. The timing gears or chain must be covered to prevent _____

_____

_____.

112. The timing cover contains an oil _____ that fits around the crankshaft to prevent oil leakage.

112. _____

113. Timing covers can be made from _____.
    (A) thin steel
    (B) plastic
    (C) cast iron
    (D) All of the above.

113. _____

114. Identify the parts indicated in the illustration below.

(A) _____

(B) _____

(C) _____

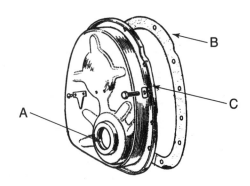

Gaskets

115. In an engine where machined parts fit together, gaskets   115. _____
     are used to make the joints tight and to prevent the leak-
     age of _____.
     (A) oil
     (B) water
     (C) gasoline
     (D) All of the above.

116. The cylinder head gasket must seal in the _____ of the   116. _____
     cooling system and must also contain the _____ of the
     expanding fuel mixture.   _____

117. Cylinder head gaskets are usually made of _____

     _____.

118. Gasket material is somewhat resilient (soft and springy)   118. _____
     and will adapt to part _____ and _____ (due to heating
     and cooling cycles) without leakage.   _____

119. Most important, a gasket must conform to _____ in the   119. _____
     surfaces of mating parts.

120. Identify the following gaskets.

(A) _____

(B) _____

(C) _____

(D) _____

(E) _____

(F) _____

(G) _____

(H) _____

(I) _____

(J) _____

(K) _____

(L) _____

(M) _____

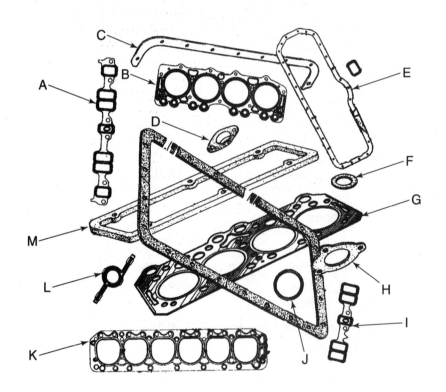

Name _____

Date _____ Period _____

Instructor _____

Score _____ Text pages 55–72

3

Engine Classification, Parts Identification

Objectives: After studying Chapter 3 in the textbook, and completing this section of the workbook, you will be able to:

- Compare four-stroke and two-stroke cycle engines.
- Explain the different engine classifications.
- Describe the operating principles of a rotary type engine.
- Identify the parts of various engine types.

Tech Talk: Chapter 3 covers basic engine theory and the production of multicylinder engines. Engine classification and types of engines will be discussed. An experienced automotive technician can glance at an engine and describe a long list of engine facts. For example, a race car technician might say, "This is a V-8 427 SOHC hemi with two-fours, roller rockers, no push rods or lifters, and 606 stock horses." To the technician, this "shop talk" has meaning. If you want to learn the language of an automotive technician, get to work studying this chapter!

Instructions: Read the general instructions on pages 5–6 for answering the workbook questions. Then, as you study Chapter 3 of the text, answer the following questions in the spaces provided.

Cycle Classifications

1. On a four-stroke cycle engine, it takes _____ crankshaft revolutions to complete the entire cycle.
   (A) 1
   (B) 2
   (C) 3
   (D) 4

1. _____

2. The average two cycle gasoline engine uses all of the following, EXCEPT:
   (A) a reed valve.
   (B) a turbocharger.
   (C) ports in the cylinder walls.
   (D) a spark plug.

2. _____

3. On a two cycle engine, oil is mixed with the gasoline to provide engine _____.

3. _____

Valve Location

4. Define *L-head engine*. _____

   _____

   _____

5. Define *I-head engine*. _____

   _____

   _____

   _____

6. An I-head engine is commonly called a(n) _____ engine.   6. _____

7. With a push rod type valve train, movement of the push rod   7. _____
   is transferred in the opposite direction by the _____.

8. When the camshaft is mounted overhead (above the   8. _____
   valves), _____ are not required.

9. The engine illustrated below is a(n) _____ head type.   9. _____

10. Identify the parts indicated in the following illustration.

   (A) _____

   (B) _____

   (C) _____

   (D) _____

   (E) _____

   (F) _____

   (G) _____

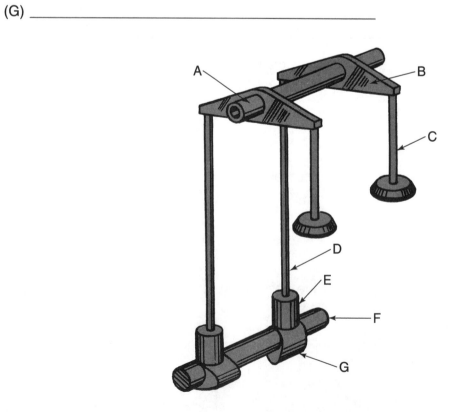

11. Identify the parts indicated in the illustration below.

(A) _____

(B) _____

(C) _____

(D) _____

(E) _____

(F) _____

(G) _____

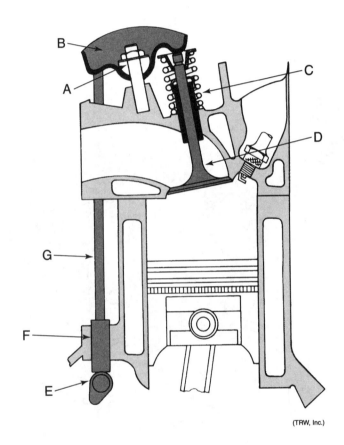

(TRW, Inc.)

12. Identify the parts indicated in the illustration below.

(A) _____

(B) _____

(C) _____

(D) _____

(E) _____

(F) _____

(G) _____

(H) _____

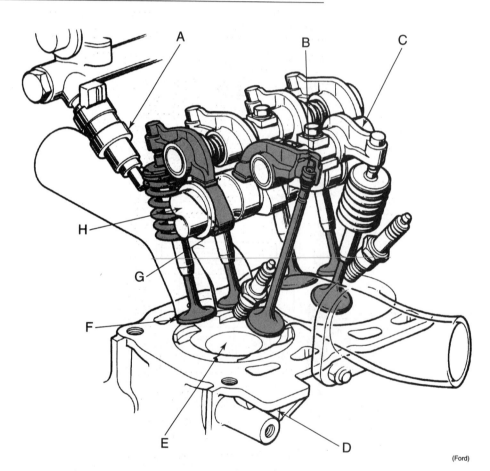

(Ford)

13. Identify the parts on the overhead camshaft engine illustrated below.

(A) _____

(B) _____

(C) _____

(D) _____

(E) _____

(F) _____

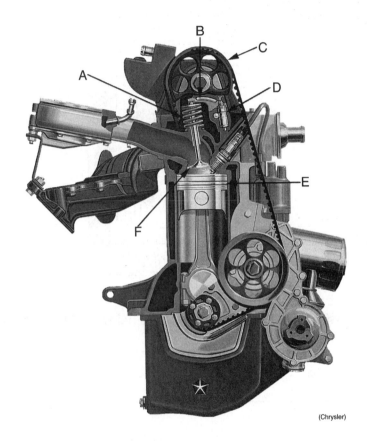

(Chrysler)

Overhead Valve Adjustment

14. The adjusting screw in the push rod end of the rocker arm is turned in or out until the recommended clearance exists between the _____ and the rocker arm.

14. _____

15. There is no valve clearance or play between valve train parts when _____ are used. Typically, the only adjustment is the initial setting after the valve train has been disassembled.

15. _____

16. Some engines make the initial valve adjustment setting with adjustable rocker arms, while others use _____ of precise length that provide proper setting.

16. _____

17. Technician A says that detonation is an explosion occurring after the spark plug fires. Technician B says that preignition can be caused by the production of two flame fronts in the combustion chamber. Who is right?
    (A) A only.
    (B) B only.
    (C) Both A and B.
    (D) Neither A nor B.

17. _____

18. Draw normal combustion in the figure below and label the actions in the engine.

    (A) _____

    (B) _____

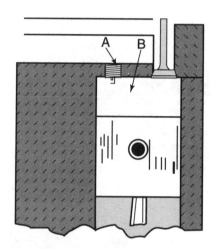

19. Draw abnormal combustion or detonation in the figure below and label the actions in the engine.

    (A) _____

    (B) _____

    (C) _____

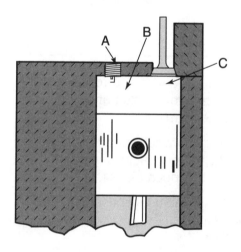

Combustion Chamber Design

20. A combustion chamber's _____ and _____ is very important to the operation of an engine.

20. _____
    _____

21. Compression ratios of around _____ were used for many years.

21. _____

22. Current practice has lowered compression ratios to around _____ to aid emission controls.

22. _____

23. The squish area produces _____ in the combustion chamber.
    (A) heat transfer
    (B) turbulence
    (C) detonation
    (D) cooling

23. _____

24. Combustion chambers which produce the "squish" effect are the _____ and the wedge.

24. _____

25. The illustration below shows a(n) _____ combustion chamber.

25. _____

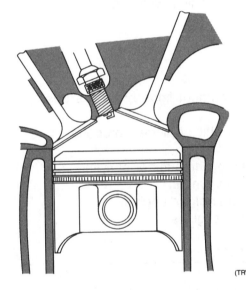

(TRW, Inc.)

Cylinder Classification

26. Define *in-line engine*. _____

    _____

27. The inclined engine is an in-line engine with the _____ slanted to one side.

27. _____

28. Define *V-type engine*. _____

    _____

    _____

29. The size of the block of a V-type engine permits a(n) _____ in vehicle length with no effect on passenger room.
    (A) increase
    (B) reduction
    (C) Neither A nor B.

29. _____

30. The short heavy crankshaft in the V-type engine is more _____ to torsional vibration.

30. _____

31. Define *horizontal-opposed engine*. _____

_____

_____

_____

32. A horizontal opposed engine has a(n) _____ overall height.
    (A) lower
    (B) even
    (C) higher
    (D) None of the above.

32. _____

33. _____ refers to the sequence in which cylinders fire.
    (A) Cylinder order
    (B) Piston order
    (C) Firing order
    (D) None of the above.

33. _____

34. All of the following statements about firing order are true, EXCEPT:
    (A) firing order is the order in which cylinders produce power.
    (B) firing order is determined by the number of cylinders and crankshaft throw arrangement.
    (C) firing orders start at the rear of the engine.
    (D) firing orders vary between engines.

34. _____

Cooling and Fuel Classifications

35. Automobile engines may be classified as being either air or _____ cooled.

35. _____

36. Air-cooling is simple and has no _____ to leak or freeze in cold weather.

36. _____

37. Gasohol is a mixture of gasoline and _____.

37. _____

38. The majority of automobile and light truck engines use _____ as a fuel.

38. _____

39. The same basic type of engine can operate on gasoline or _____.
    (A) LNG
    (B) CNG
    (C) LPG
    (D) All of the above.

39. _____

Engine Mounting

40. Some motor mounts are _____ filled, while others are solid _____ .

40. _____

41. The three point mounting is usually used on _____ wheel drive vehicles.

41. _____

Alternative Engines

42. A two-stroke diesel engine has all of the following parts, EXCEPT:
    (A) intake valve.
    (B) exhaust valve.
    (C) supercharger.
    (D) piston.

42. _____

43. Identify the parts of the diesel engine illustrated below.

43. _____

   (A) _____

   (B) _____

   (C) _____

   (D) _____

   (E) _____

   (F) _____

   (G) _____

   (H) _____

   (I) _____

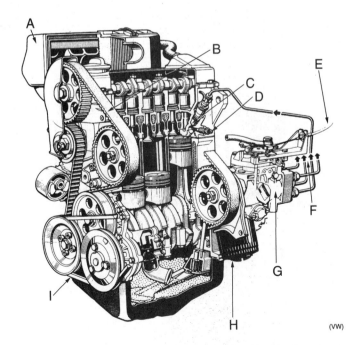

(VW)

44. Identify the parts of the rotary engine illustrated.

(A) _____

(B) _____

(C) _____

(D) _____

(E) _____

A
E
B
C
D
(NSU)

45. The illustration above shows the rotor in the _____ position.

45. _____

46. On a Miller-cycle engine, the _____ valve is held open for a longer time than with other engines.

46. _____

47. Most natural gas engines are gasoline engines with a modified _____ system.
    (A) ignition
    (B) valve
    (C) cooling
    (D) fuel

47. _____

New Technologies

48. Identify the parts of the hybrid vehicle shown below.

(A) _____

(B) _____

(C) _____

(D) _____

(E) _____

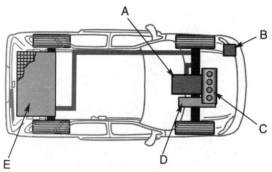

A
B
C
D
E

49. Identify the parts of the V-6 engine illustrated below.

(A) _____

(B) _____

(C) _____

(D) _____

(E) _____

(F) _____

(G) _____

(H) _____

(I) _____

(J) _____

(K) _____

(L) _____

(M) _____

(N) _____

(O) _____

(P) _____

(Q) _____

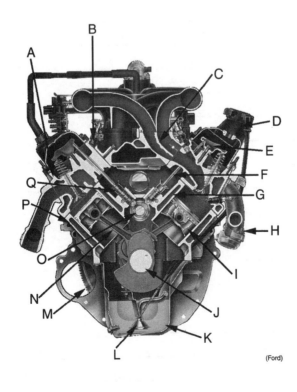

(Ford)

50. Identify the parts of the overhead cam engine illustrated on the facing page.

(A) _____

(B) _____

(C) _____

(D) _____

(E) _____

(F) _____

(G) _____

(H) _____

(I) _____

(J) _____

(K) _____

(L) _____

(M) _____

(N) _____

(O) _____

(P) _____

(Q) _____

(R) _____

(S) _____

(T) _____

(U) _____

(V) _____

(W) _____

(X) _____

(Y) _____

(Z) _____

(AA) _____

(AB) _____

(AC) _____

(AD) _____

(AE) _____

(AF) _____

(AG) _____

(AH) _____

(AI) _____

(AJ) _____

(AK) _____

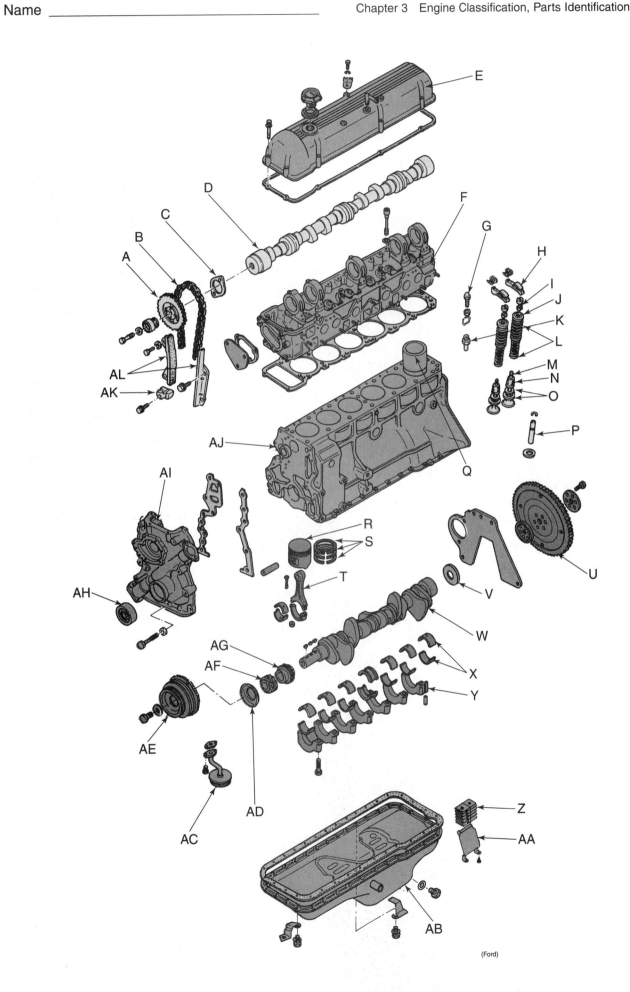

(Ford)

4

Safety, Lab Procedures

Objectives: After studying Chapter 4 in the textbook, and completing this section of the workbook, you will be able to:

- Identify the major types of accidents and their causes.
- Identify the consequences of accidents.
- Explain how to dress safely in the shop.
- Identify personal protective equipment.
- Explain how to identify and correct unsafe conditions in the shop.
- Identify unsafe work procedures.

Tech Talk: Preventing accidents helps everybody—the technician, the shop owner, the customer, and the general public. Dressing safely, working safely, and maintaining a safe shop are the most effective practices you can maintain. The safety precautions covered in this chapter are intended to teach you good safety habits for use in class as well as during your career. Various types of unsafe shop conditions and work practices are examined as well as ways to correct or avoid them. Accidents are also costly for the employer as well as the employee. Even a minor accident can cause direct and hidden costs. Always make sure that you do all repair procedures as safely as possible.

Instructions: Read the general instructions on pages 5–6 for answering the workbook questions. Then, as you study Chapter 4 of the text, answer the following questions in the spaces provided.

1. _____ are unplanned events that can occur without anyone intending for them to happen.

1. _____

2. Long-term exposure to some types of chemicals can cause _____ .

2. _____

3. Accidents are often caused by a series of unsafe _____ or unsafe conditions.

3. _____

4. A _____ light bulb should not be substituted for a rough service bulb in a drop light.

4. _____

5. All of the following statements about the results of accidents are true, EXCEPT:
   (A) some accidents can kill.
   (B) you cannot lose your job because you cause accidents.
   (C) even minor accidents can be painful.
   (D) an accident can keep you from working.

5. _____

6. The technician who dresses _____ is usually a safe worker.

6. _____

7. Which of the following could get caught in moving parts?
   (A) Long hair.
   (B) Ties.
   (C) Loose sleeves.
   (D) Jewelry.
   (E) All of the above.

7. _____

8. If jewelry is caught between a _____ terminal and ground, severe burns could result.

8. _____

9. The danger of falling parts or tools make _____ protection necessary.
   (A) eye
   (B) respiratory
   (C) foot
   (D) All of the above.

9. _____

10. The illustration below is an example of wearing proper _____ protection.

10. _____

(Deere & Co.)

11. Asbestos can damage your _____.

11. _____

12. When should the technician wear rubber gloves? _____

_____

13. _____ is the number one accident preventer.

13. _____

14. A(n) _____ workbench reduces the possibility that critical parts will be lost in the clutter.

14. _____

15. _____ tools that are oily or dirty before putting them away will extend the life of the tool.

15. _____

16. Technicians and customers can slip on floors coated with _____.   16. _____
    (A) oil
    (B) antifreeze
    (C) water
    (D) All of the above.

17. Knowing the layout of your shop and the location of its _____ will help you keep your head and extinguish a shop fire.   17. _____

18. Name the class of fire extinguisher needed to extinguish the type of burning material listed below.

    (A) Wood _____

    (B) Gasoline _____

    (C) Paper _____

    (D) Electrical equipment _____

    (E) Oil _____

19. Why should you never put water on a gasoline fire?   _____

    _____

20. The most that the technician can expect from a fire extinguisher is to _____ the fire.   20. _____

21. When a fire starts, which of the following should you do FIRST?   21. _____
    (A) Attempt to extinguish the fire.
    (B) Open all windows and doors.
    (C) Call your insurance company.
    (D) Call the fire department.

22. When servicing any shop equipment, be sure that it is _____.   22. _____

23. Before working with any unfamiliar chemical read the appropriate _____.   23. _____

24. A sealed shop, or a sealed room in the shop, can permit the _____ of exhaust fumes or chemical vapors which can be fatal.   24. _____

25. Overhead lights should be _____ and centrally located.   25. _____

26. Do not _____ the ground prong of a three-prong plug.   26. _____

27. Strict waste disposal guidelines are established and enforced by the _____.   27. _____
    (A) EPA
    (B) MSDS
    (C) OSHA
    (D) None of the above.

28. Some companies specialize in recycling _____ wastes.   28. _____

29. What are work procedures? _____

    _____

30. Always make sure that repairs are done right to avoid an   30. _____
    _____ .

31. Ultimately, noticing and correcting safety problems is up to   31. _____
    _____ .
    (A) the Environmental Protection Agency (EPA)
    (B) the Occupational Health and Safety Administration
        (OSHA)
    (C) the shop owner
    (D) you

Name _____

Date _____ Period _____

Instructor _____

Score _____ Text pages 81–100

5

Tool Identification and Use

Objectives: After studying Chapter 5 in the textbook, and completing this section of the workbook, you will be able to:

- Identify the most common automotive tools.
- Describe commonly used measuring tools.
- Describe commonly used test equipment.
- Select the correct tool for a given job.

Tech Talk: Most professional auto mechanics buy tools that have a lifetime guarantee. If a tool breaks or is damaged in service, the tool manufacturer will replace it free of charge. Some tool guarantees replace a tool if the chrome plating begins to peel or flake. In the long run, a mechanic has made a wise investment by purchasing fine quality tools.

Instructions: Read the general instructions on pages 5–6 for answering the workbook questions. Then, as you study Chapter 5 of the text, answer the following questions in the spaces provided.

1. Technician A says that alloy steel tools are useless for many jobs. Technician B says that quality tools are heat treated. Who is right?
   (A) A only.
   (B) B only.
   (C) Both A and B.
   (D) Neither A nor B.

1. _____

2. Polished tools are easy to _____.

2. _____

3. Always keep your tools _____ and clean.

3. _____

Hammers

4. To prevent marring or damage to parts, a _____ or _____ tipped hammer should be used.

4. _____

_____

5. Identify the hammers pictured below.

   (A) _____

   (B) _____

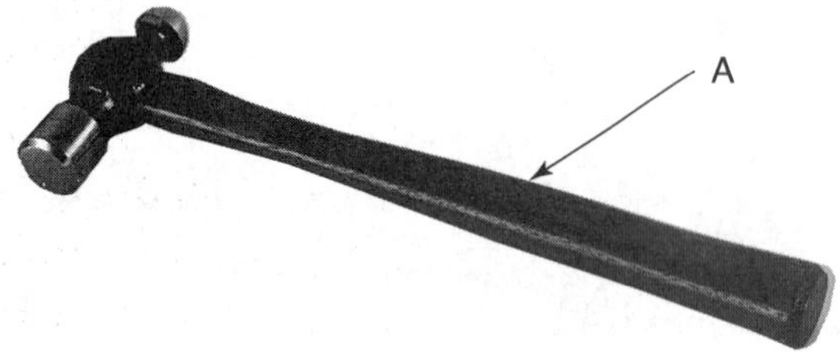

A

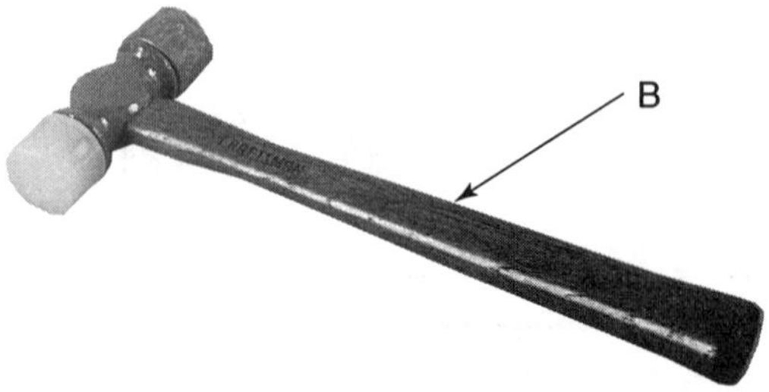

B

Chisels

6. Several types of _____ are needed for cutting rusted or stripped bolts, and other metal parts.

6. _____

7. The _____ chisel is used for general cutting.

7. _____

Punches

8. Define *starting punch*. _____

   _____

   _____

9. Define *drift punch*. _____

   _____

   _____

10. Define *aligning punch*. _____

   _____

   _____

11. A center punch is commonly used to _____

   _____

   _____.

12. Identify the tools pictured below and the parts indicated.

   (A) _____

   (B) _____

   (C) _____

   (D) _____

   (E) _____

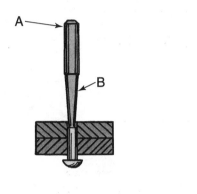
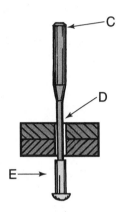

Files

13. A single-cut file has _____

   _____

   _____.

14. A double-cut file has _____

   _____

   _____.

15. A rotary file is designed to be used with a hand-held drill or   15. _____

   _____ _____.

16. Identify the parts of the file illustrated below.

(A) _____

(B) _____

(C) _____

(D) _____

(E) _____

(F) _____

(G) _____

(H) _____

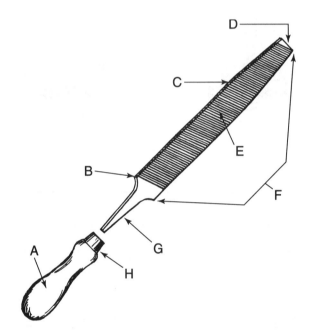

17. Identify the file shapes illustrated below.

(A) _____

(B) _____

(C) _____

(D) _____

(E) _____

(F) _____

(G) _____

(H) _____

(I) _____

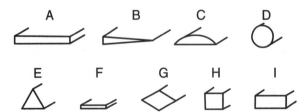

Drills

18. A hand-held drill can be operated by electricity or _____.

18. _____

19. The _____ drill is the most common.
    - (A) 1/4"
    - (B) 3/8"
    - (C) 1/2"
    - (D) 3/4"

19. _____

20. Using a drill press ensures that the hole will be properly _____ and sized.

20. _____

21. Drill bits do the actual _____ when drilling holes.

21. _____

22. Carbon steel bits require frequent _____.

22. _____

23. Reamers are used to enlarge and shape _____.

23. _____

24. A reamer should *not* be used to make _____ cuts in metal.
    - (A) deep
    - (B) shallow
    - (C) smooth
    - (D) accurate

24. _____

Impact Wrenches

25. An impact wrench is necessary when work must be done _____.

25. _____

26. A impact wrench can be operated by _____ or _____.

26. _____

    _____

27. Heavy-duty impact _____ should be used with an impact wrench.

27. _____

28. Impact wrench drive sizes run from 1/4" to _____.
    - (A) 1"
    - (B) 2"
    - (C) 3"
    - (D) 4"

28. _____

Hacksaws

29. A hacksaw is commonly used for _____

_____.

30. A 14 teeth inch per blade should be used on _____.
    - (A) iron
    - (B) soft steel
    - (C) rails
    - (D) All of the above.
    - (E) None of the above.

30. _____

31. An 18 teeth per inch blade should be used on _____.
    (A) brass
    (B) copper
    (C) medium tubing
    (D) None of the above.

31. _____

32. A 24 teeth per inch blade should be used on _____.
    (A) brass
    (B) copper
    (C) medium tubing
    (D) All of the above.

32. _____

33. A 32 teeth per inch blade should be used on _____.
    (A) light angle iron
    (B) iron pipe
    (C) thin sheet metal
    (D) None of the above.

33. _____

34. Identify the parts of the hacksaw pictured below.

    (A) _____

    (B) _____

    (C) _____

    (D) _____

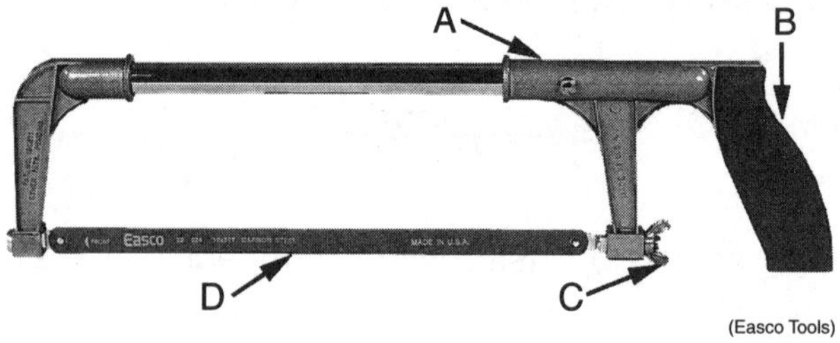

(Easco Tools)

Vise

35. A vise is a _____ device.

35. _____

36. To protect a part from marring or damage while in the vise, place special _____ or _____ covers over the jaws.

36. _____
    _____

37. The working parts of the vise should be _____ occasionally.

37. _____

38. Never use a vise as an _____.

38. _____

Taps

39. A tap is used to cut _____ threads.

39. _____

40. Each size tap will have to be provided in both _____ and _____ thread types, as well as metric sizes.

40. _____
    _____

41. The _____ type tap is used to cut threads completely through a hole with no bottom.

41. _____

42. The _____ type tap is used to cut to the bottom of a blind hole.

42. _____

43. The _____ type tap is used to cut partway through a hole.

43. _____

44. The _____ type tap is the most versatile and commonly used tap.

44. _____

45. The _____ type tap handles the small diameter, fine thread jobs.

45. _____

46. Identify the four types of taps illustrated below.

(A) _____

(B) _____

(C) _____

(D) _____

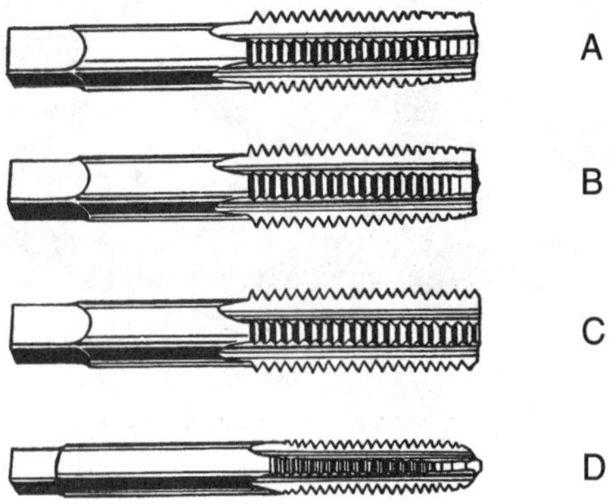

Dies

47. Dies are used to cut _____ threads.

47. _____

48. Most dies are adjustable to enlarge or reduce the _____ of the threaded area.

48. _____

49. Dies and taps should be lightly _____ to increase tool life.

49. _____

Cleaning Tools

50. Identify the cleaning tools illustrated below.

(A) _____

(B) _____

(C) _____

(D) _____

(E) _____

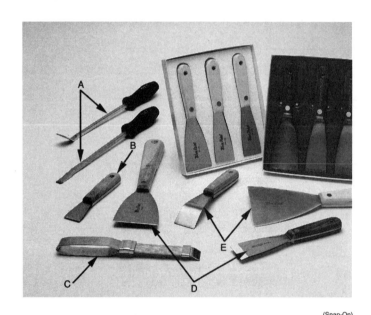

(Snap-On)

Pliers

51. Identify the pliers illustrated below.

(A) _____

(B) _____

(C) _____

(D) _____

(E) _____

(F) _____

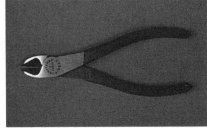
A

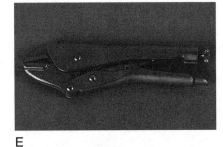
B

C

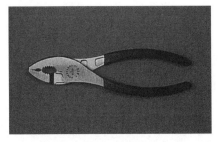
D

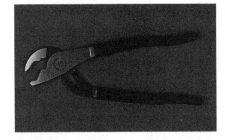
E

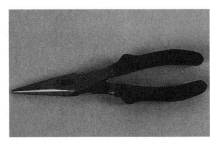
F

Screwdrivers

52. Identify the point configurations for screw heads used in the typical automobile.

(A) _____

(B) _____

(C) _____

(D) _____

(E) _____

(F) _____

(G) _____

(H) _____

A

B

C

D

E

F

G

H

Wrenches

53. The modern technician must have a wide variety of _____ and _____ wrenches.

53. _____

_____

54. A box end wrench grips the nut on _____ sides.

54. _____

55. For general use, the _____ point box configuration works well. It allows the wrench to be removed and replaced without a long swing of the wrench.

55. _____

56. A _____ point wrench is useful for stubborn or rounded nuts.

56. _____

57. Open end wrenches grab the nut or bolt head on _____ flats.

57. _____

58. The head of the open end wrench is offset at an _____ and can be flipped over in tight places to free the handle of an obstacle.

58. _____

59. The combination wrench is a very convenient and efficient tool since the box end can be used for both breaking loose and for _____ tightening.

59. _____

60. The open end of a combination wrench is for _____ removal and installation of fasteners.

60. _____

61. Technician A says that the adjustable wrench is useful for odd-size bolts or nuts. Technician B says that the adjustable wrench tends to slip. Who is right?
    (A) A only.
    (B) B only.
    (C) Both A and B.
    (D) Neither A nor B.

61. _____

62. Some adjustable wrenches are _____ and adjust themselves to the work.

62. _____

63. Torque is a measure of fastener _____.

63. _____

64. Torque wrenches are available in _____ pound and _____ pound versions.

64. _____

_____

65. Metric torque wrenches measure torque in _____ meters.

65. _____

Sockets and Ratchets

66. A socket wrench is convenient and, in most instances, _____ than other wrenches.

66. _____

67. Sockets are available in _____ point, _____ point, and other specialized openings.

67. _____

_____

68. A _____ drive is for small work in difficult areas.
    (A) 3/4″
    (B) 1/2″
    (C) 1/4″
    (D) None of the above.

68. _____

69. When torque requirements are not too high, the _____ drive is used.

69. _____

70. The _____ drive is for all-around service.
   (A) 3/4″
   (B) 1/2″
   (C) 1/4″
   (D) None of the above.

70. _____

71. The _____ drive is for very large bolts and nuts requiring high torque settings.
   (A) 3/4″
   (B) 1/2″
   (C) 1/4″
   (D) None of the above.

71. _____

72. The _____ socket is designed to reach over a stud bolt.

72. _____

73. _____ or universals are used when working at an angle.

73. _____

74. Sockets should be kept clean and stored on _____ according to _____.

74. _____

    _____

75. The _____ is used for fast installation. It can be turned or twisted rapidly.

75. _____

76. _____ handles or breaker bars allow the socket to be turned with great force.

76. _____

77. The _____ bar will vary the length of the socket setup to reach difficult areas.

77. _____

78. The _____ handle allows the user to either tighten or loosen a bolt without removing the handle.

78. _____

79. Identify the following tools. Study each tool closely.

   (A) _____

   (B) _____

   (C) _____

   (D) _____

   (E) _____

   (F) _____

   (G) _____

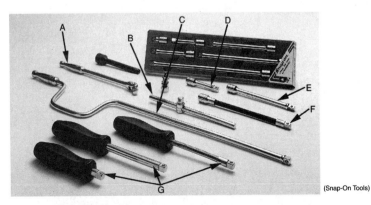

(Snap-On Tools)

Special Tools

80. Define *slide hammer puller.* _____

_____

_____

81. For soldering automotive wiring, an _____ soldering iron works well.

81. _____

82. For large soldering jobs, a _____ is used.

82. _____

83. _____ should *not* be used when soldering electrical wiring.
    (A) Acid core solder
    (B) Rosin core solder
    (C) Soldering iron
    (D) Soldering tip

83. _____

Measuring Tools

84. A metric micrometer will be calibrated in _____ instead of inches.
    (A) meters
    (B) centimeters
    (C) millimeters
    (D) decameters

84. _____

85. Inside calipers can be used to measure the _____ of a hole.

85. _____

86. Caliper reading can be determined by holding the caliper on a _____ rule.

86. _____

87. Dividers are made like calipers but have _____ shanks and pointed ends.

87. _____

88. A dial indicator reads the _____ in thousandths of an inch.

88. _____

89. Dial calipers can take inside, outside, and _____ measurements.

89. _____

90. Feeler gauges can be used to record _____ between two surfaces.

90. _____

91. Identify the parts of the micrometer.

   (A) _____

   (B) _____

   (C) _____

   (D) _____

   (E) _____

   (F) _____

   (G) _____

(Central Tools)

Electrical Testers

92. Analog gauges indicate the electrical reading with a _____ or pointer.

92. _____

93. A digital tester indicates the reading by displaying a _____.

93. _____

94. Technician A says that a test light can be used to check exact electrical values. Technician B says that a test light can be used to test for the presence or absence of electricity. Who is right?
   (A) A only.
   (B) B only.
   (C) Both A and B.
   (D) Neither A nor B.

94. _____

95. Electrical resistance is measured by an _____.

95. _____

96. Resistance is the opposition to current _____.

96. _____

97. Technician A says that polarity is important when using a voltmeter. Technician B says that polarity is important when using an ohmmeter to test some electronic components. Who is right?
   (A) A only.
   (B) B only.
   (C) Both A and B.
   (D) Neither A nor B.

97. _____

98. A unit which combines several electrical testers into one housing is called a _____.

98. _____

99. Tachometers measure _____ speed.

99. _____

Pressure Gauges

100. Negative air pressure is usually called a _____.

100. _____

101. The oil pressure gauge can be used to check the pressure in all of the following units, EXCEPT:
    (A) engine lubrication.
    (B) intake manifold.
    (C) power steering.
    (D) automatic transmission.

101. _____

102. The fuel pressure tester measures the pressure developed by the _____ pump.

102. _____

103. Identify the parts indicated on the compression gauge illustrated below.

    (A) _____

    (B) _____

    (C) _____

    (D) _____

    (E) _____

(Lisle Tools)

Other Diagnostic Equipment

104. Exhaust gas analyzers can be used to measure all of the following, EXCEPT:
    (A) unburned hydrocarbons.
    (B) carbon monoxide.
    (C) oxides of nitrogen.
    (D) hydrogen.

104. _____

105. A vehicle _____ combines the functions of several test instruments, including a multimeter, an oscilloscope, an exhaust gas analyzer, and a scan tool.

105. _____

Name _____

Date _____ Period _____

Instructor _____

Score _____ Text Pages 101–108

6

Engine Tests and Measurements

Objectives: After studying Chapter 6 in the textbook, and completing this section of the workbook, you will be able to:

- Recall engine measurement formulas.
- Solve basic engine measurement problems.
- Develop an understanding of engine ratings.

Tech Talk: Do you know the difference between an engine's brake horsepower and its net horsepower? Does the size of an engine include the space above the piston at TDC? Is one horsepower really the pulling power of a horse? Everyone has heard the word horsepower, but very few people understand exactly what it means. The science of engine testing and measurement is very complicated and, in its true sense, lies in the realm of engineering. Nevertheless, it is important that you should be familiar with the basic formulas, terms, and their computation.

Instructions: Read the general instructions on pages 5–6 for answering the workbook questions. Then, as you study Chapter 6 of the text, answer the following questions in the spaces provided.

Horsepower

1. Define *work*. _____

   _____

   _____

2. The amount of work done can be computed by multiplying the _____ a body moved by the weight of the body.

   2. _____

3. Define *one foot pound*. _____

   _____

   _____

4. Horsepower is the _____ at which work can be done.

   4. _____

5. The formula for horsepower is:

   _____

   _____

6. The ability to perform 99,000 foot-pounds of work in one minute is the same as _____ horsepower.

   6. _____

75

7. Identify the parts indicated in the illustration below.

(A) _____

(B) _____

(C) _____

(D) _____

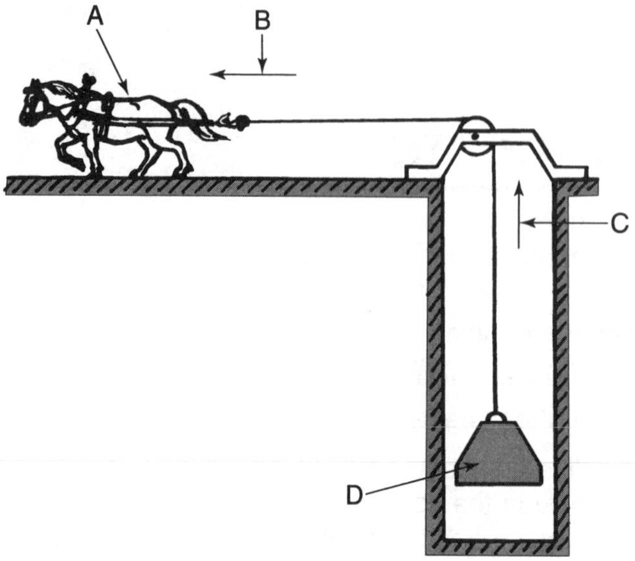

8. Engine thermal efficiency is the measurement of how much of the energy in the _____ fuel is converted to useful horsepower.

8. _____

9. Heat in the combustion chamber is lost to the _____ system.
   (A) cooling
   (B) exhaust
   (C) lubrication
   (D) All of the above.

9. _____

10. Fuel heat value is rated in _____ per pound.

10. _____

11. In the average engine, _____ of the engine power is lost to friction.
    (A) 10%
    (B) 25%
    (C) 32%
    (D) 85%

11. _____

12. The practical engine efficiency is the percentage of the potential energy in the fuel to reach the _____.
    (A) combustion chamber
    (B) exhaust system
    (C) drive wheels
    (D) All of the above.

12. _____

13. Define *indicated horsepower.* _____

_____

14. Define *brake horsepower*. _____

    _____

    _____

15. A chassis dynamometer measures brake horsepower at the   15. _____
    _____.
    (A) crankshaft
    (B) flywheel
    (C) drive wheels
    (D) All of the above, depending on the manufacturer.

16. The net horsepower of an engine is the resulting value with   16. _____
    all of the _____ installed on the engine.

17. Net horsepower is an informative rating because it shows   17. _____
    that actual engine horsepower is produced in _____ usage.

18. Frictional horsepower losses increase with engine _____.   18. _____

19. Identify the parts indicated on the schematic of the engine dynamometer pictured below.

    (A) _____

    (B) _____

    (C) _____

    (D) _____

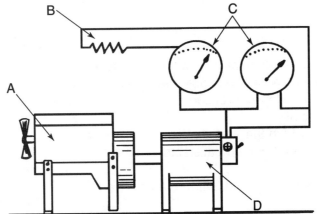

Torque

20. Torque is a _____ action.   20. _____

21. Engine torque increases with engine speed up to the point   21. _____
    where the engine is drawing in the _____ amount of fuel
    mixture, after all factors are considered.
    (A) maximum
    (B) minimum
    (C) Either A or B.
    (D) None of the above.

22. Technician A says that torque will drop off as volumetric efficiency increases. Technician B says that volumetric efficiency drops off as engine speed is increased. Who is right?
    (A) A only.
    (B) B only.
    (C) Both A and B.
    (D) Neither A nor B.

22. _____

23. Name some ways that volumetric efficiency can be increased. _____

_____

_____

_____

Engine Size and Compression

24. Piston displacement refers to _____

_____

_____.

25. What is the formula for calculating engine size when the bore and stroke are known?

_____

26. The bore is the _____ of the cylinder.

26. _____

27. Compression ratios range from _____ to slightly over 11:1 for gasoline engines.

27. _____

28. Diesel compression ratios range from _____ to 22.5:1.

28. _____

29. All of the following statements about why compression ratios are not increased on all engines are true, EXCEPT:
    (A) modern fuels will not allow decreased compression beyond a certain point.
    (B) the temperature at which the air-fuel mixture will ignite itself limits the amount it can be satisfactorily compressed.
    (C) detonation or knocking will occur when the compression ratio is too high.
    (D) emission control has required that compression ratios be lowered from 10 or 11:1 to about 8:1.

29. _____

Name _____

30. Match the terms on the right with the letters in the illustration below.

(A) _____
(B) _____
(C) _____
(D) _____
(E) _____
(F) _____

Additional water
Bottom dead center
Top dead center
Original water

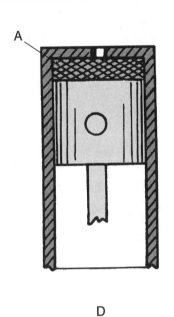
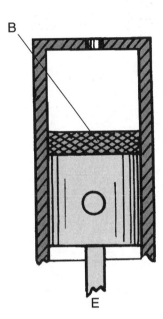
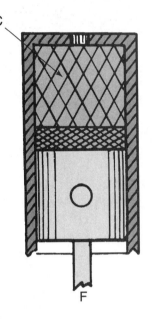

Name _____

Date _____ Period _____

Instructor _____

Score _____ Text pages 109–120

7

Electrical System Fundamentals

Objectives: After studying Chapter 7 in the textbook, and completing this section of the workbook, you will be able to:

- Explain the principles of electricity and electronics.
- Name the values used to measure electricity.
- List the basic types of electrical circuits.
- Explain the effects of magnetism.
- Explain how diodes work.
- Explain how transistors work.
- Explain the construction of an integrated circuit.

Tech Talk: In the last few years, electronic components have taken over the operation of most vehicle systems. Today's automotive technician must have a working knowledge of electricity and electronics to service and repair these components. This chapter covers basic electricity and electronics; study it thoroughly.

Instructions: Read the general instructions on pages 5–6 for answering the workbook questions. Then, as you study Chapter 7 of the text, answer the following questions in the spaces provided.

Basic Electricity

1. The accepted theory regarding electricity is termed the _____.

1. _____

2. Electricity is produced by a flow of _____ from one area to another.

2. _____

3. The area with surplus electrons is referred to as _____ and the area in short supply, the _____.

3. _____

_____

4. Conventional theory says that electrons flow from _____ to _____.

4. _____

_____

5. Define *matter.* _____

_____

_____

6. Atoms that exist in their pure state are called _____.

6. _____

7. The center of the atom is made up of _____.
   (A) electrons
   (B) protons
   (C) neutrons
   (D) Both B and C.

7. _____

8. The outer orbits of some atoms (conductors) contain _____
   _____ which can move from one atom to another, producing electricity.

8. _____

   _____

9. The following illustration depicts the basic structure of an atom. Identify the parts indicated.

   (A) _____

   (B) _____

   (C) _____

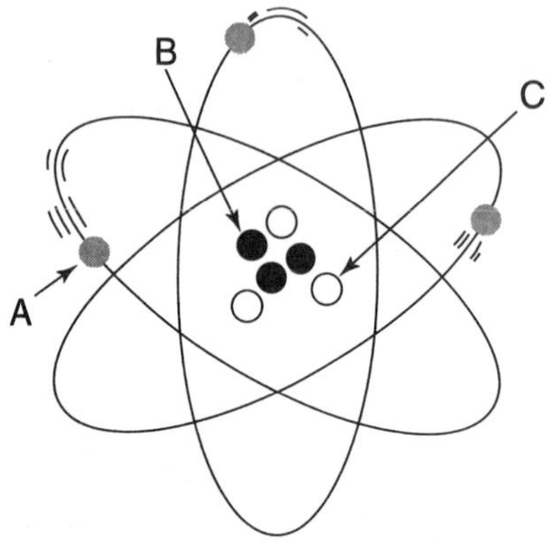

10. Identify the two types of atoms illustrated below.

    (A) _____

    (B) _____

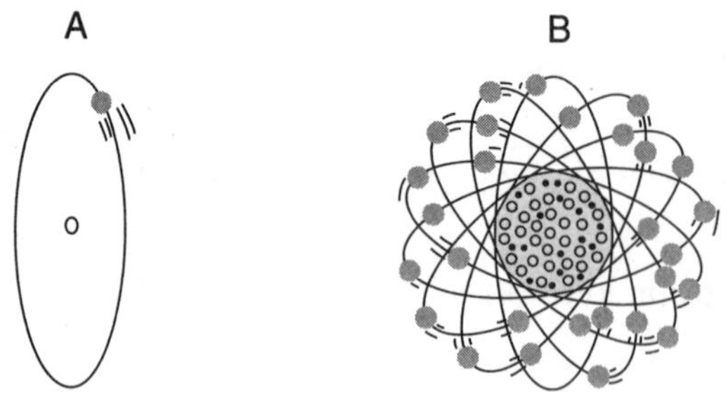

Electrical Current

11. Define *current.* _____

    _____

    _____

12. The amount of current flow is measured in _____.

12. _____

13. Before current will flow through a conductor, there must be a surplus of electrons at the other end and a _____ at the other.

13. _____

14. Electron flow in a circuit is from _____ to _____.

14. _____

_____

15. When electricity flows through the filament of a lightbulb, the filament will _____

_____ .

16. Current is the same as _____.
    (A) electrical flow
    (B) electrical pressure
    (C) opposition to flow
    (D) All of the above.

16. _____

17. The following drawing illustrates a schematic of a simple circuit using a battery as the source. Draw the electrons as they flow through the batteries and circuits and identify the parts and actions.

    (A) _____

    (B) _____

    (C) _____

    (D) _____

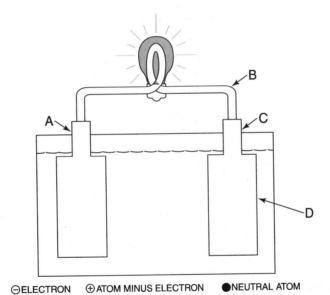

⊖ELECTRON   ⊕ATOM MINUS ELECTRON   ●NEUTRAL ATOM

18. Draw the electrons as they flow through the batteries and circuits and identify the parts and the actions in the illustrations below.

(A) _____

(B) _____

(C) _____

(D) _____

● NEUTRAL ATOM
⊖ ELECTRON
⊕ ATOM MINUS ELECTRONS

Voltage

19. A difference in electrical potential, or pressure, at each end of a wire is called _____.

19. _____

20. Initial voltage in the vehicle is supplied by the _____ when the engine is not running, and by the _____ when the engine is running.

20. _____

_____

21. When current flows through a conductor, it meets some _____.

21. _____

22. As electrons attempt to flow through a resistance, _____ is produced.

22. _____

23. Such things as lights and _____ make use of the resistance of a poor conductor.

23. _____

24. A large diameter conductor will offer _____ resistance than a smaller one.

24. _____

25. Resistance is measured in _____.

25. _____

26. If an atom has more than _____ electrons in its outer shell, it will make a good insulator.

26. _____

27. What are some examples of materials that make good insulators? _____

_____

_____

28. Draw the missing wires to the ammeter and load and identify the parts indicated.

(A) _____

(B) _____

(C) _____

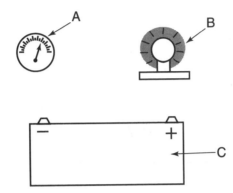

29. Draw the missing wires to show a voltmeter connection and identify the parts indicated.

(A) _____

(B) _____

(C) _____

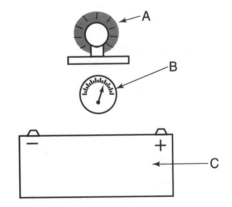

30. Draw the missing wires to show an ohmmeter connection and identify the parts indicated.

(A) _____

(B) _____

(C) _____

(D) _____

Electrical Circuits

31. A circuit consists of _____

_____

_____.

32. For current to flow in a circuit, the circuit must be _____.   32. _____

33. Define *simple circuit.* _____

_____

_____

34. A series circuit consists of _____

_____

_____.

35. Total resistance in a series circuit will determine the _____   35. _____
flow.

36. If amperage flow is checked at several points in a series   36. _____
circuit, all readings will _____.
(A) be the same
(B) vary
(C) alternate in strength
(D) None of the above.

37. As voltage drops in a series circuit, the current flow _____.   37. _____
(A) varies between units
(B) remains the same throughout
(C) is interrupted
(D) None of the above.

38. If voltage drop in a series circuit is _____, the electrical circuit can malfunction.

38. _____

39. _____ _____ is controlled by using the proper size wires, ample source voltage, proper insulation, and clean connections.

39. _____

40. All of the following statements about one device failing in a parallel circuit are true, EXCEPT:
    (A) the others will still function.
    (B) the total resistance is less than any one device's.
    (C) it will cause the entire circuit to fail.
    (D) equal voltage is applied to all electrical devices.

40. _____

41. Total resistance in a parallel circuit is _____ the resistance of any one device.
    (A) more than
    (B) less than
    (C) equal to
    (D) None of the above.

41. _____

42. Equal _____ is applied to all electrical devices in a parallel circuit.

42. _____

43. Draw the missing wires showing a simple circuit.

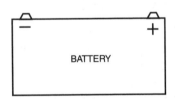

44. Draw the missing wires showing a series circuit.

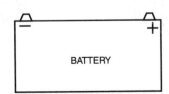

45. Draw the missing wires showing a parallel circuit.

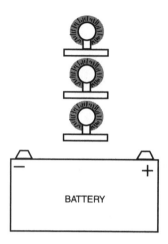

Series-Parallel Circuit

46. A series-parallel circuit must have at least _____ electrical devices.

46. _____

47. Current flow in a series-parallel circuit is determined by the _____ resistance.

47. _____

48. Voltage drop in a series-parallel circuit will be the drop across the parallel circuit, plus that of any series _____ unit.

48. _____

49. Draw the missing wires showing a series-parallel circuit and identify which units are in series and which are in parallel.

(A) _____

(B) _____

(C) _____

(D) _____

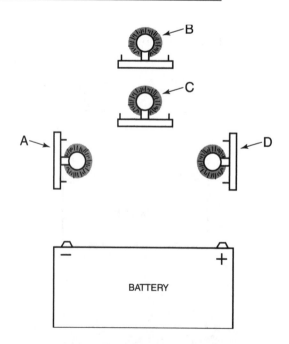

Vehicle Chassis as a Ground Wire

50. The vehicle chassis can act as a _____ wire.

50. _____

51. Most modern vehicles have a _____ ground.

51. _____

52. A ground symbol in a wiring diagram indicates that the _____ is grounded to the chassis.

52. _____

53. The following drawing depicts the use of a vehicle frame as one wire in a circuit. Draw the missing wires and arrows showing flow and identify the parts indicated.

(A) _____

(B) _____

(C) _____

(D) _____

(E) _____

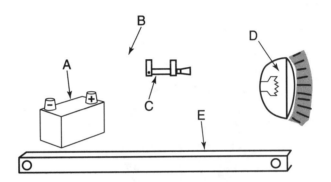

54. In the drawings below, the top figure shows the ground wire intact. The bottom figure has replaced the ground wire with a _____.

54. _____

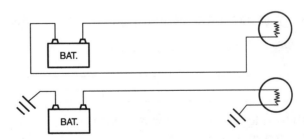

Ohm's Law

55. Ohm's law can be expressed in three basic forms:

   (A) Amperes equals _____

   _____.

   (B) Volts equals_____

   _____.

   (C) Ohms equals _____

   _____.

56. Ohm's law can be used to find an unknown electrical factor when _____

   _____.

57. Identify the letters missing from the Ohm's law pie chart.

   (A) _____

   (B) _____

   (C) _____

Magnetism

58. A material is magnetized by lining up the magnetic _____.   58. _____

59. Define *magnetic lines of force.* _____

   _____

   _____

60. If two bar magnets are shoved together with unlike poles on   60. _____
   the approaching ends, the magnets will _____.
   (A) repel each other
   (B) snap together
   (C) snap apart when released
   (D) None of the above.

61. Like poles of two magnets will _____ each other.   61. _____

62. Magnetic lines of force will follow _____ more readily than
_____.
   (A) metal, air
   (B) air, metal
   (C) plastic wires, metal
   (D) None of the above.

62. _____

_____

63. Technician A says that magnetism can be used to create
electricity. Technician B says that electricity can be used to
create magnetism. Who is right?
   (A) A only.
   (B) B only.
   (C) Both A and B.
   (D) Neither A nor B.

63. _____

64. A wire wound into a _____ to create a stronger magnetic
field is called an electromagnet.

64. _____

65. An electromagnet has north and south poles which can be
changed by reversing the _____ of current flow.

65. _____

Basic Automotive Electronics

66. Semiconductors are sometimes conductors, and sometimes _____.

66. _____

67. Technician A says that a diode allows current to flow in only
one direction. Technician B says that a Zener diode allows
current to flow when a certain voltage is reached. Who is
right?
   (A) A only.
   (B) B only.
   (C) Both A and B.
   (D) Neither A nor B.

67. _____

68. Alternators contain diodes to change _____ current to
_____ current.

68. _____

_____

69. A transistor is a solid state electronic _____ device.

69. _____

70. Transistors have no _____ parts to wear out.

70. _____

71. Which of the following transistor terminals has the smallest
current flow?
   (A) Emitter.
   (B) Base.
   (C) Collector.
   (D) Varies with the type of transistor.

71. _____

72. A transistor which is designed to carry a heavy current load
is called a _____ transistor.

72. _____

73. An integrated circuit (IC) contains _____.
   (A) resistors
   (B) transistors
   (C) diodes
   (D) All of the above.

73. _____

74. A single IC can operate a vehicle's _____.
    (A) alternator
    (B) ignition system
    (C) fuel injectors
    (D) All of the above.

74. _____

75. The following illustration indicates current flow through a PNP transistor. Identify the components indicated.

(A) _____

(B) _____

(C) _____

(D) _____

(E) _____

(F) _____

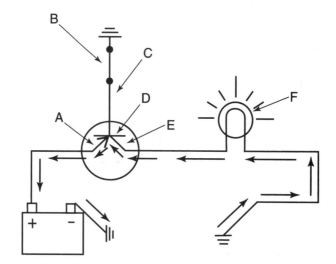

Name _____

Date _____ Period _____

Instructor _____

Score _____ Text pages 121–140

8

Ignition Systems

Objectives: After studying Chapter 8 in the textbook, and completing this section of the workbook, you will be able to:

- Explain why battery voltage must be increased.
- Describe the primary circuits of an ignition system.
- Describe the secondary circuits of an ignition system.
- Describe the construction of major ignition system components.
- Summarize the basic function and operating principles of ignition system parts.
- List the differences between a contact point and an electronic ignition system.
- Explain the action of spark advance mechanisms.
- Explain how a distributorless ignition system operates.

Tech Talk: An ignition system has two jobs: to increase battery voltage and to send this voltage to the right spark plug at the right time. If any ignition system component is not functioning properly, engine performance will be reduced. This chapter covers the theory, design, and construction of the ignition system and how its components are combined to produce, control, and distribute the spark.

Instructions: Read the general instructions on pages 5–6 for answering the workbook questions. Then, as you study Chapter 8 of the text, answer the following questions in the spaces provided.

Ignition Systems

1. Why must the battery voltage be increased to fire the spark plug? _____

_____

_____

2. If you touch a spark plug and are shocked, the chance of actual damage is slight because the _____ is low.

2. _____

3. House current has enough power to _____ you.

3. _____

4. The two separate ignition circuits are the _____ and _____.

4. _____

_____

Primary Circuit

5. The ignition primary circuit consists of all of the following, EXCEPT:
   (A) a battery and an ignition module.
   (B) a coil primary winding.
   (C) an ignition switch.
   (D) spark plug wires.

5. _____

6. The wires of an ignition system are covered with a thin layer of insulating material to prevent _____.

6. _____

7. When it is discharging, the battery changes electricity into _____ energy.

7. _____

8. The ignition switch receives current from the _____ and sends it to the _____ system when the key is turned to the ON position.

8. _____
   _____

9. Some resistors are _____ types, while others are calibrated resistance wires.

9. _____

10. Most modern electronic ignition systems have _____ resistors.
    (A) 1
    (B) 2
    (C) 3
    (D) no

10. _____

11. The following illustration depicts a steering column-mounted ignition switch. Identify the parts indicated.

    (A) _____

    (B) _____

    (C) _____

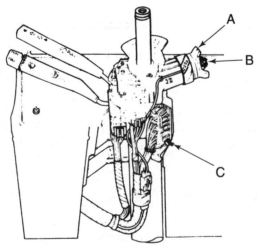

(Ford)

Ignition Coil

12. The ignition coil is connected with a special laminated _____ to increase field strength.

12. _____

13. Many thousands of turns of very fine _____ wire are wound around the central core.

13. _____

14. Several hundred turns of heavier copper wire are wrapped around the secondary windings and they form the _____ windings of the ignition coil.

14. _____

15. When the ignition switch is turned on, _____ flows through the primary winding.

15. _____

16. All of the following is true about coil operation, EXCEPT:
    (A) current flow prevents the build up of a magnetic field.
    (B) a strong magnetic field is produced.
    (C) the magnetic field will collapse into the laminated iron core.
    (D) the magnetic field surrounds the secondary and primary windings.

16. _____

17. Self-induction does not affect the _____ winding operation but can cause arcing on contact point systems.

17. _____

18. The high voltage produced by the secondary windings exits the high tension coil terminal and is directed to the _____.

18. _____

19. The cutaway illustration on the right depicts an ignition coil. Identify the parts indicated.

(A) _____

(B) _____

(C) _____

(D) _____

(E) _____

(F) _____

(G) _____

(H) _____

(I) _____

(J) _____

(K) _____

(L) _____

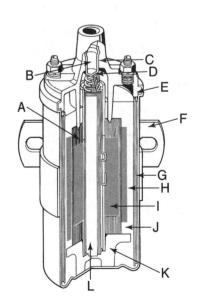

Methods of Current Interruption

20. For efficient coil operation, the current flow through the _____ _____ must be interrupted instantly.

20. _____

21. Define *flashover*. _____

_____

22. Technician A says that older contact point systems could produce up to 100,000 volts. Technician B says that high voltages are needed to fire leaner mixtures on modern vehicles. Who is right?
    (A) A only.
    (B) B only.
    (C) Both A and B.
    (D) Neither A nor B.

22. _____

23. The contact points used on older vehicles were a simple mechanical way of _____ the coil primary circuit.
    (A) installing
    (B) testing
    (C) making and breaking
    (D) All of the above.

23. _____

24. The movable arm on a set of points is pushed outward by the distributor _____ _____.

24. _____

25. The breaker arm contacts the distributor cam by means of a fiber rubbing _____. A special high temperature lubricant is used to prevent undue wear.

25. _____

26. The point breaker arm is insulated from ground so that it will *not* allow current flow unless the points are _____.

26. _____

Contact Point Dwell

27. Cam angle or dwell refers to the number of _____ the distributor cam rotates while the points are closed.

27. _____

28. The longer the breaker points are _____, the greater the time the ignition coil has to build the high voltage.

28. _____

29. If breaker point gap is lessened, dwell is _____.

29. _____

30. The following drawing depicts the *dwell* of a distributor cam. Identify the position of the breaker points and the parts indicated.

(A) _____

(B) _____

(C) _____

(D) _____

(E) _____

(F) _____

(G) _____

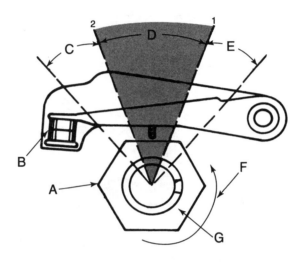

Condenser

31. The condenser provides a place for the primary current to flow when the points are _____.

31. _____

32. Most condensers are constructed of two sheets of thin _____ that are separated by layers of insulation.

32. _____

33. If a condenser was not used, the _____ in the primary circuit would arc across the points, consuming the coil's energy.

33. _____

34. Identify the parts indicated on the hermetically sealed condenser illustrated below.

(A) _____

(B) _____

(C) _____

(D) _____

(E) _____

(F) _____

(G) _____

(H) _____

(I) _____

(J) _____

(K) _____

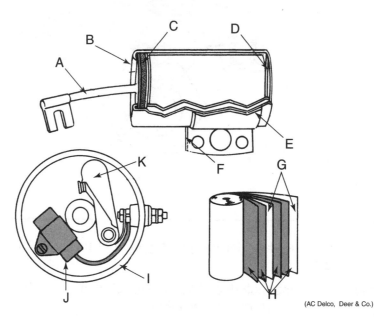

(AC Delco, Deer & Co.)

Electronic Ignition

35. Some ignition modules are installed on the _____ to protect it from heat.
    (A) firewall
    (B) inner fender
    (C) rear quarter panel
    (D) Both A and B.

35. _____

36. Ignition modules are installed in or on all of the following, EXCEPT:
    (A) on the distributor body.
    (B) in the distributor.
    (C) as part of the coil assembly.
    (D) on the steering column.

36. _____

37. The electronic ignition module contains the _____.
    (A) triggering device
    (B) power transistor
    (C) coil
    (D) All of the above.

37. _____

38. Currently used triggering devices include _____.
    (A) Hall effect
    (B) magnetic
    (C) optical
    (D) All of the above.

38. _____

39. Triggering devices can be operated by the rotation of the _____.
    (A) camshaft
    (B) distributor shaft
    (C) crankshaft
    (D) All of the above.

39. _____

40. The rotating tooth assembly of a magnetic pickup is called the _____ or trigger wheel.

40. _____

41. The stationary tooth assembly of a magnetic pickup is called the pickup coil or _____.

41. _____

42. The air gap between the pickup coil and reluctor teeth prevents _____ contact and eliminates wear.

42. _____

43. All of the following statements about the Hall effect switch are true, EXCEPT:
    (A) it is a thin wafer of semiconductor material.
    (B) a magnet is located opposite the sensor.
    (C) a shutter is placed between two magnets.
    (D) there is an air gap between the sensor and magnet.

43. _____

44. The optical sensor contains all of the following parts, EXCEPT:
    (A) a photo sensitive diode.
    (B) a rotor plate.
    (C) a light emitting diode.
    (D) a permanent magnet.

44. _____

45. The following drawing depicts the internal parts of a distributor. Identify the parts indicated.

(A) _____

(B) _____

(C) _____

(D) _____

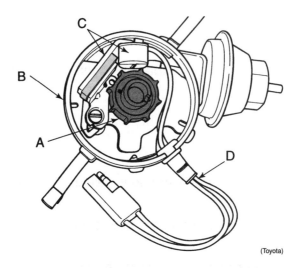

(Toyota)

46. Identify the parts indicated on the Hall-effect sensor illustrated below.

(A) _____

(B) _____

(C) _____

(D) _____

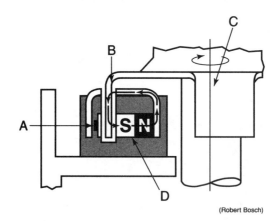

(Robert Bosch)

47. Identify the parts indicated on the optical sensor illustrated below.

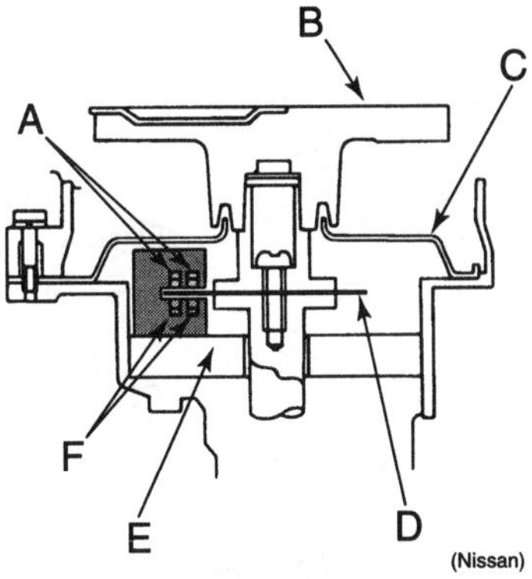

(A) _____

(B) _____

(C) _____

(D) _____

(E) _____

(F) _____

(Nissan)

Distributorless Ignition System

48. A distributorless ignition system can have all of the following parts, EXCEPT:
(A) a distributor.
(B) coils with two discharge terminals.
(C) a second sensor on the camshaft.
(D) a crankshaft position sensor.

48. _____

49. A distributorless ignition system uses sensors which can determine the engine speed and the position of each _____.

49. _____

50. Technician A says that all distributorless ignition systems have more than one ignition coil. Technician B says that all distributorless ignition systems have more than one position sensor. Who is right?
(A) A only.
(B) B only.
(C) Both A and B.
(D) Neither A nor B.

50. _____

51. Define *a waste spark system.* _____

_____

_____

52. The following diagram illustrates one possible arrangement of components for a distributorless ignition system. Identify the parts indicated.

(A) _____

(B) _____

(C) _____

(D) _____

(E) _____

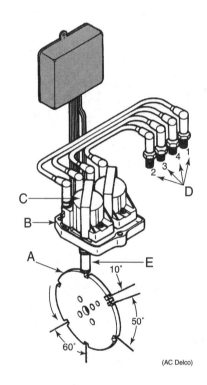

(AC Delco)

Spark Plug Construction

53. A spark plug is made up of three major parts:

(A) _____

(B) _____

(C) _____

54. Spark plug gap is the space between the plug _____.   54. _____

55. Electrons will flow more easily from a _____ to a _____ one.   55. _____

_____

56. Spark plug insulators must resist _____

_____

_____.

Name _____

57. If a spark plug runs too cold (low heat range), it could collect _____ and become fouled.

57. _____

58. If a spark plug runs too hot (high heat range), it could cause _____ of the fuel mixture.
   (A) bubbling
   (B) fouling
   (C) preignition
   (D) None of the above.

58. _____

59. The heat range of a spark plug is determined by the _____ and length of the insulator.

59. _____

60. The center electrode, surrounded by the insulator, is placed in a steel _____.

60. _____

61. Identify the parts indicated on the spark plug illustrated below.

   (A) _____
   (B) _____
   (C) _____
   (D) _____
   (E) _____
   (F) _____
   (G) _____
   (H) _____
   (I) _____
   (J) _____

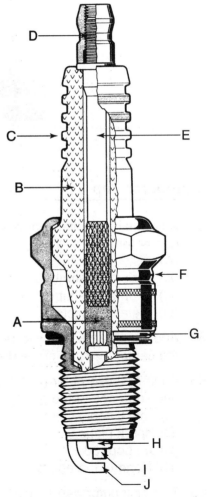

(Bosch)

62. The following diagram illustrates the heat path for cold and hot spark plugs. Identify the spark plug types as well as the parts indicated.

(A) _____type

(B) _____type

(C) _____

(D) _____

(E) _____

(F) _____

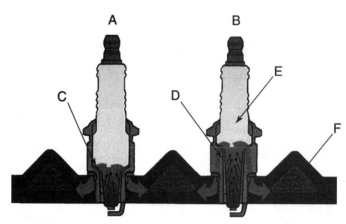

(Champion Spark Plug Co.)

Distributor Cap

63. After the high voltage leaves the ignition coil, it moves to the center terminal of the _____.
    (A) distributor cap
    (B) resistor assembly
    (C) internal gasket
    (D) metal connector

63. _____

64. Additional terminals, one per _____, are arranged around the center terminal of the distributor cap.

64. _____

65. Each of these outer (distributor cap) terminals will be connected to one of the _____ by high tension (voltage) wires.
    (A) metal connectors
    (B) spark plugs
    (C) carbon rods
    (D) None of the above.

65. _____

66. The distributor cap is made of _____ to reduce flashover tendency.
    (A) copper
    (B) aluminum
    (C) plastic
    (D) brass

66. _____

67. Identify the parts indicated on the distributor cap illustrated below.

(A) _____

(B) _____

(C) _____

(D) _____

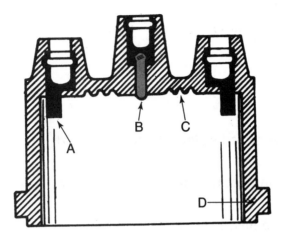

Rotor

68. The rotor carries the secondary voltage from the center terminal of the distributor cap to one of the _____ terminals.

68. _____

69. The rotor is connected to or mounted on the top of the _____.

(A) carbon post
(B) distributor shaft
(C) resistor
(D) internal gasket

69. _____

70. Why must resistor type wires always be used in late model vehicles? _____

_____

_____

71. The _____ of rotor rotation dictates whether a clockwise or counterclockwise firing order is required.

71. _____

72. The distributor cap, rotor, and _____ distribute the spark to the plug at the proper time.

72. _____

Ignition Timing and Advance

73. For correct ignition timing, the cylinders must receive a spark at the plug as the piston nears _____.
    (A) the correct temperature
    (B) BDC (bottom dead center)
    (C) camshaft
    (D) TDC (top dead center)

73. _____

74. The distributor shaft may be turned by _____ gearing with the camshaft.
    (A) one-to-one
    (B) one-to-two
    (C) one-to-three
    (D) two-to-three

74. _____

75. If a plug fires later than specified setting, the timing is said to be _____.

75. _____

76. If a plug fires earlier than specified, timing is said to be _____.

76. _____

77. Many engines have timing marks on the rim of the _____ damper.

77. _____

78. When the mark is located under the _____, the engine is ready to fire the number one cylinder.

78. _____

79. The following diagram illustrates a typical setup of ignition timing marks. Identify the parts indicated.

    (A) _____

    (B) _____

    (C) _____

    (D) _____

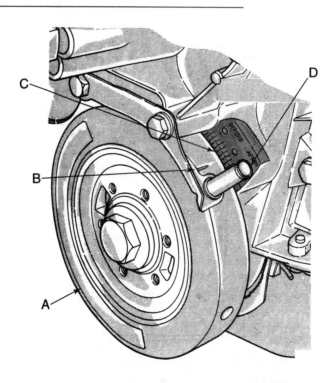

(Chrysler)

Setting Ignition Timing

80. Technician A says that a timing light illuminates every time that the coil fires. Technician B says that many modern vehicles do not have a provision for setting the timing. Who is right?
    (A) A only.
    (B) B only.
    (C) Both A and B.
    (D) Neither A nor B.

80. _____

81. To adjust the ignition timing, the distributor clamp is loosened and the _____ is turned by hand to align the timing mark.

81. _____

82. When the two timing marks are aligned, lock the timing in place by tightening the _____.
    (A) clamp
    (B) pointer
    (C) Both A and B.
    (D) Neither A nor B.

82. _____

Timing Advance Mechanisms

83. As engine speed increases, it is necessary to _____ the fuel mixture sooner.

83. _____

84. _____ is a method of advancing the ignition timing.
    (A) Centrifugal advance
    (B) Vacuum advance
    (C) Electronic advance
    (D) All of the above.

84. _____

85. When the engine is idling, _____ pressure keeps the two weights drawn together and the timing remains unchanged from its initial setting.

85. _____

86. As the engine speeds up, the weights are drawn out by _____ force.
    (A) vacuum
    (B) centrifugal
    (C) electronic
    (D) All of the above.

86. _____

87. The faster the engine runs, the _____ the weights swing out with a resulting increase in the timing advance.

87. _____

88. By calculating the pull of the springs and the size of the weights, it is possible to properly advance the timing over a long _____ range.

88. _____

89. The following diagram illustrates two different types of *distributor centrifugal advance mechanisms.*
Identify the parts indicated.

(A) _____

(B) _____

(C) _____

(D) _____

(E) _____

(F) _____

(G) _____

(H) _____

(Automotive Electric Assoc.)

90. At the partial throttle open position, all of the following state-
ments are true of the centrifugal advance timing method,
EXCEPT:
(A) the air-fuel mixture is compressed more and burns
faster.
(B) the vacuum draws in less air and fuel.
(C) there is high vacuum in the intake manifold.
(D) additional advance is desirable.

90. _____

91. To maximize fuel economy at part throttle, a _____ type
distributor advance is used.

91. _____

92. No vacuum advance is provided during periods of _____ or
full power.

92. _____

93. The electronic pickup or breaker points are mounted on a
movable _____.
(A) shaft
(B) panel
(C) plate
(D) bearing

93. _____

94. Advance in timing may be obtained by turning the plate
against distributor _____ rotation.

94. _____

95. The plate is rotated by means of a vacuum advance _____.

95. _____

96. When the vacuum advance is not operating, it can affect the engine performance and fuel _____.

96. _____

97. The following diagram illustrates *vacuum advance mechanism operation*. Identify the position of the distributor and the parts indicated.

   (A) The distributor is in the _____ position.

   (B) _____

   (C) _____

   (D) _____

   (E) _____

   (F) _____

   (G) _____

   (H) _____

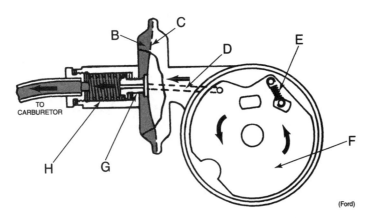

(Ford)

Computer Controlled Ignition Systems

98. Since the spark on modern computers is produced electronically, it follows that the spark _____ can be modified electronically.

98. _____

99. The computer monitors engine and other _____, such as RPM and temperature.

99. _____

100. Technician A says that the amount of advance in an electronic system is set by the computer, and cannot be adjusted. Technician B says that the in some systems, the computer contains the ignition module. Who is right?
   (A) A only.
   (B) B only.
   (C) Both A and B.
   (D) Neither A nor B.

100. _____

Name _____

Date _____ Period _____

Instructor _____

Score_____ Text Pages 141–164

9

Fuel Injection Systems

Objectives: After studying Chapter 9 in the textbook, and completing this section of the workbook, you will be able to:

- Describe the major parts of a gasoline fuel injection system.
- Describe the major parts of a diesel injection system.
- Identify the parts of gasoline and diesel injection systems.
- Summarize the operating principles of gasoline and diesel injection systems.
- Compare the different types of gasoline and diesel injection systems.
- Identify the parts of superchargers and turbochargers.
- Compare supercharger and turbocharger operation.

Tech Talk: All diesel engines and a few gasoline fuel injection systems are mechanical types. The majority of gasoline fuel injection systems are electronically controlled types, either with continuously open or injectors which are pulsed on and off. Injector nozzles spray a controlled amount of fuel into the engine intake manifold. Since all new vehicles have fuel injection systems, it is important that you learn their operating principles.

Instructions: Read the general instructions on pages 5–6 for answering the workbook questions. Then, as you study Chapter 9 of the text, answer the following questions in the spaces provided.

Fuel Injection

1. Define *direct fuel injection*. _____

_____

_____

2. Define *indirect fuel injection.*_____

_____

_____

3. Originally, most fuel injection systems were _____. They used an engine driven pump.

3. _____

4. Electronic fuel injection was made possible by the introduction of practical _____ components and _____.

4. _____

5. Electronic fuel injection systems use an electric fuel _____ to provide pressure for system operation.

5. _____

6. The ideal air-fuel mixture is _____ parts of air to one part of fuel by weight.
   (A) 12.7
   (B) 14.7
   (C) 900
   (D) 9000

6. _____

7. The following illustration depicts an electronic fuel injector. Identify the parts indicated.

   (A) _____
   (B) _____
   (C) _____
   (D) _____
   (E) _____
   (F) _____
   (G) _____
   (H) _____
   (I) _____

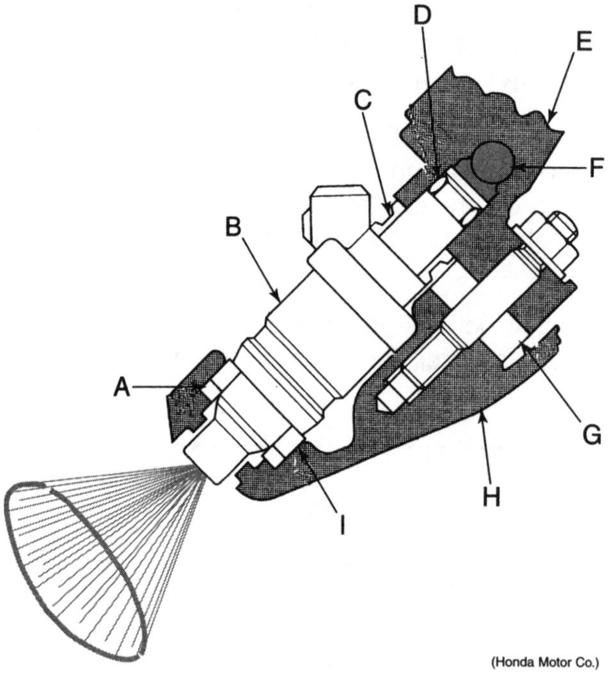

(Honda Motor Co.)

Types of Fuel Injection Systems

8. In the pulsed injection system the amount of fuel flow through the injector is _____. The total amount of fuel injected is determined by the length of time that the injector is held _____.

8. _____

_____

9. A non-timed injector system will spray fuel into the entrance
    to the _____ _____.

    9. _____

10. The throttle body injection system contains _____ fuel
    injector(s).
    (A) one
    (B) two
    (C) four
    (D) Either A or B.

    10. _____

11. Fuel pressure in a throttle body injection system is approxi-
    mately _____ psi.

    11. _____

12. A multiport injector has one injector for each _____.

    12. _____

13. The air induction system of a pulsed injection system con-
    sists of all of the following components, EXCEPT:
    (A) air cleaner.
    (B) fuel rail.
    (C) intake manifold.
    (D) throttle body.

    13. _____

14. On throttle body fuel injection systems, the _____ contains
    the throttle valve.
    (A) air cleaner
    (B) fuel rail
    (C) intake manifold
    (D) throttle body

    14. _____

15. The _____ fuel delivery system uses a water trap to remove
    water from the fuel.
    (A) multiport
    (B) throttle body
    (C) pulsed
    (D) diesel

    15. _____

16. Technician A says that pressure regulators used on throttle
    body pressure regulators are operated by spring pressure
    and vacuum. Technician B says that multiport injection sys-
    tems have pressure regulators that are operated by spring
    pressure alone. Who is right?
    (A) A only.
    (B) B only.
    (C) Both A and B.
    (D) Neither A nor B.

    16. _____

17. The fuel rail feeds fuel to the _____.
    (A) pressure regulator
    (B) injectors
    (C) intake manifold
    (D) Both B and C.

    17. _____

18. The length of time that an injector opens is usually measured in _____.
    (A) minutes
    (B) seconds
    (C) thousandths of a second
    (D) None of the above.

18. _____

19. A cold start valve adds extra _____ to the intake manifold when the engine is cold.
    (A) fuel
    (B) air
    (C) carbon monoxide
    (D) oxygen

19. _____

20. The following cutaway illustration depicts an electronic fuel injector with an internal integral fuel filter. Identify the parts as indicated.

    (A) _____

    (B) _____

    (C) _____

    (D) _____

    (E) _____

    (F) _____

    (G) _____

    (H) _____

    (I) _____

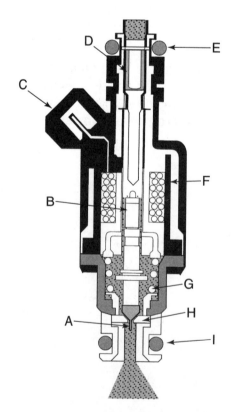

Engine Control Computer

21. The engine control computer is located in a protected area and is connected to the rest of the fuel injection system by a _____ _____ plug.

21. _____

22. The engine computer receives inputs from _____ when the engine is running.

22. _____

23. The oxygen sensor is usually installed in the exhaust _____.

23. _____

24. The throttle position sensor is installed on the _____.
    (A) intake manifold
    (B) exhaust manifold
    (C) distributor
    (D) throttle body

24. _____

25. Barometric pressure is the pressure of the _____.
    (A) exhaust
    (B) outside air
    (C) inside air
    (D) None of the above.

25. _____

26. The two types of airflow sensors are: _____
    _____.

27. The speed density method is used to calculate the _____ _____ from the input of other sensors.

27. _____
    _____

Continuous Fuel Injection System

28. On the continuous injection system, the injectors are always open and fuel pressure is varied to match the fuel flow with the _____ flow.

28. _____

29. During engine operation, the system feeds atomized fuel from the injectors _____.
    (A) as needed
    (B) at all times
    (C) in drops
    (D) None of the above.

29. _____

30. The _____ opens the injectors on a continuous injection system.
    (A) electric solenoid
    (B) manifold vacuum
    (C) fuel pump pressure
    (D) compression pressure

30. _____

31. The following illustrations depict airflow sensor plate actions. First identify the action (*idle, part throttle, or full throttle*), the measure of fuel flow, and then identify the parts as indicated.

(A) Figure A is at _____ and it has a _____ fuel flow.

(B) Figure B is at _____ and it has a _____ fuel flow.

(C) Figure C is at _____ and it has a _____ fuel flow.

(D) _____

(E) _____

(F) _____

(G) _____

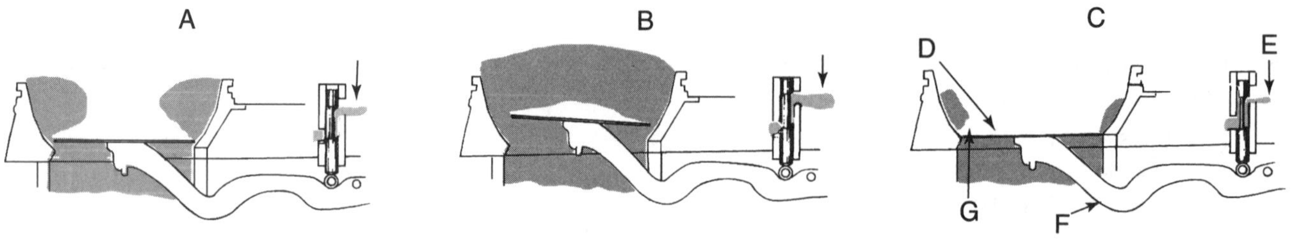

Diesel Fuel Injection

32. Compression stroke temperatures in a diesel engine can reach _____.
(A) 10,000°F (5380.2°C)
(B) 2000°F (1076.4°C)
(C) 1000°F (538.2°C)
(D) None of the above.

32. _____

33. As the piston completes the compression stroke, diesel fuel is sprayed into the _____.

33. _____

34. The intense heat of the _____ in the diesel engine ignites the fuel and the power stroke follows.
(A) pistons
(B) spark plugs
(C) compressed air
(D) None of the above.

34. _____

35. Explain the uses of 1-D and 2-D diesel fuel. _____

_____

_____

36. Technician A says that cetane number is the octane rating of diesel fuel. Technician B says that cetane is a test fuel for measuring diesel fuel burning characteristics. Who is right?
(A) A only.
(B) B only.
(C) Both A and B.
(D) Neither A nor B.

36. _____

37. Define *water in fuel sensor.* _____

    _____

    _____

38. Due to the high compression used in diesel engines, the   38. _____
    diesel _____ pump must be capable of producing pressures
    as high as 15,000 psi (103,425 kPa).

39. By using a plunger operating in a _____, the pump traps   39. _____
    fuel ahead of the plunger.

40. The inline injection pump uses a separate cylinder _____ for   40. _____
    each cylinder.

41. The following cutaway illustration depicts a distributor type injection pump. Identify the parts as
    indicated.

    (A) _____

    (B) _____

    (C) _____

    (D) _____

    (E) _____

    (F) _____

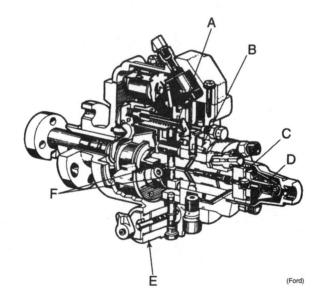

(Ford)

42. The two basic types of diesel injectors are: _____

    _____

43. To aid in igniting the compressed air-fuel mix during cold
starting, diesel engines use _____.
   (A) glow plugs
   (B) intake air heaters
   (C) Both A and B.
   (D) None of the above.

43. _____

44. The following illustration depicts a typical diesel engine. Identify the parts as indicated.

   (A) _____

   (B) _____

   (C) _____

   (D) _____

   (E) _____

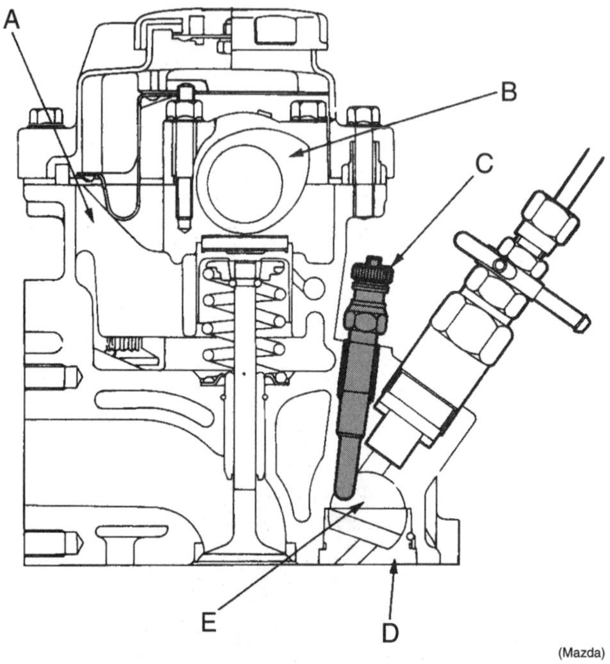

(Mazda)

Superchargers and Turbochargers

45. Indicate whether the following descriptions fit the *(A) Supercharger* or *(B) Turbocharger.*

   (A) Belt driven _____

   (B) Exhaust driven _____

   (C) Uses waste gate _____

   (D) Most are positive displacement _____

   (E) Has turbine wheel _____

   (F) Shaft speed of 150,000 RPM _____

   (G) Driven through gears _____

Name _____

46. If turbocharger boost pressure becomes too high, it may cause _____ and engine damage.

46. _____

47. The waste gate allows exhaust gases to _____ the turbine.

47. _____

48. The waste gate is operated mechanically or by a vacuum _____.

48. _____

49. Modern vehicles have electronic controls which retard the ignition _____ to prevent detonation.

49. _____

50. Identify the parts of the exhaust gas driven turbocharger as indicated in the illustration below.

(A) _____

(B) _____

(C) _____

(D) _____

(E) _____

(F) _____

(G) _____

(H) _____

(I) _____

(J) _____

(K) _____

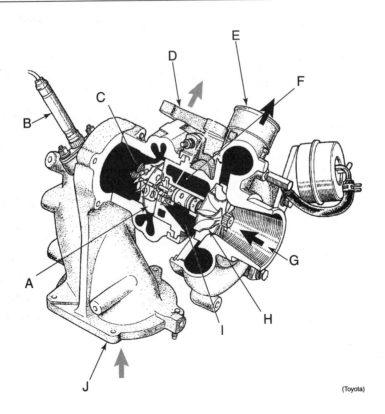

(Toyota)

Name _____

Date _____ Period _____

Instructor _____

Score_____ Text Pages 165–192

10

Fuel Supply and Carburetors

Objectives: After studying Chapter 10 in the textbook, and completing this section of the workbook, you will be able to:

- Describe the components of the fuel supply system.
- Explain the basic function of the fuel pump.
- Describe the major parts of the fuel pump.
- Identify the basic parts of a carburetor.
- Summarize carburetor operating principles.
- List the seven basic carburetor circuits.

Tech Talk: Although carburetors were phased out in the 1993 model year, millions of older cars and trucks are operating on carburetors. The technician will eventually encounter a carburetor. Therefore, this chapter should be studied carefully to obtain needed carburetor service information.

Instructions: Read the general instructions on pages 5–6 for answering the workbook questions. Then, as you study Chapter 10 of the text, answer the following questions in the spaces provided.

Fuel Tank

1. Technician A says that fuel tanks are usually made of thin sheet steel. Technician B says that plastic tanks are coated with a lead tin alloy for protection. Who is right?
   (A) A only.
   (B) B only.
   (C) Both A and B.
   (D) Neither A nor B.

1. _____

2. Internal tank _____ are installed to prevent the fuel from sloshing or splashing.

2. _____

3. A charcoal canister is used to trap gasoline _____.

3. _____

4. The pickup tube end is usually located about _____ from the tank bottom.
   (A) 1/4″
   (B) 1/2″
   (C) 1″
   (D) 3″

4. _____

5. Which of the following is heaviest?   5. _____
   (A) Water.
   (B) Gasoline.
   (C) Gasoline vapors.
   (D) Diesel fuel.

6. Water in the fuel tank can cause all of the following   6. _____
   problems, EXCEPT:
   (A) tank rusting.
   (B) tank bulging.
   (C) freezing in cold weather.
   (D) water drawn into other parts of the fuel system.

7. Identify the parts as indicated on the typical fuel tank illustrated below.

   (A) _____

   (B) _____

   (C) _____

   (D) _____

   (E) _____

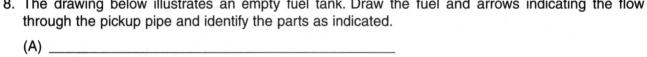

8. The drawing below illustrates an empty fuel tank. Draw the fuel and arrows indicating the flow
   through the pickup pipe and identify the parts as indicated.

   (A) _____

   (B) _____

   (C) _____

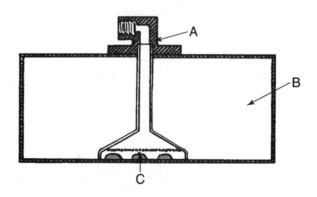

Name _____

9. The drawing below is a cutaway of the interior of a fuel tank. Draw and identify both the fuel and condensation as they would appear in the tank.

(A) _____

(B) _____

(C) _____

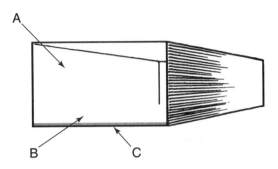

Mechanical Fuel Pumps

10. Since the fuel tank is lower than the rest of the fuel system, _____ must be overcome to deliver the fuel to the engine.

10. _____

11. A fuel pump mounted on the engine and operated by an eccentric on the camshaft is termed a _____ type fuel pump.

11. _____

12. The fuel pump consists of an air chamber divided in the center by a flexible _____.
(A) diaphragm
(B) winding
(C) check valve
(D) hose

12. _____

13. The parts inside a fuel pump which only allow flow in one direction are called _____.
(A) diaphragms
(B) windings
(C) check valves
(D) None of the above.

13. _____

14. A pull rod is fastened to the center of the diaphragm and a strong _____ pushes the diaphragm in an upward direction.
(A) winding
(B) return spring
(C) check valve
(D) None of the above.

14. _____

15. To pull the diaphragm down in a mechanical fuel pump, it is necessary to install a _____.

15. _____

16. The seal around the pull rod prevents _____.
    (A) engine oil from entering the lower chamber
    (B) gasoline from leaking into the engine
    (C) fumes from entering the lower chamber
    (D) All of the above.

16. _____

17. A pulsation damper or diaphragm is used to _____

_____

_____.

18. Identify the parts as indicated on the illustration below.

    (A) _____

    (B) _____

    (C) _____

    (D) _____

    (E) _____

    (F) _____

    (G) _____

    (H) _____

    (I) _____

    (J) _____

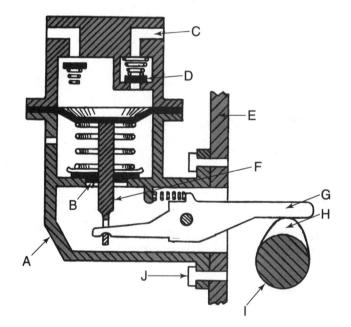

19. The following diagram illustrates a typical serviceable fuel pump construction. Identify the parts as indicated.

(A) _____

(B) _____

(C) _____

(D) _____

(E) _____

(F) _____

(G) _____

(H) _____

(I) _____

(J) _____

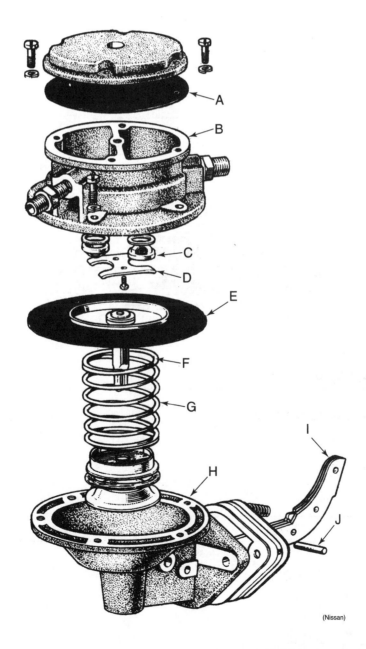

(Nissan)

Electric Fuel Pumps

20. Technician A says that electric fuel pumps are used on fuel injected engines. Technician B says that electric fuel pumps are used on some carbureted engines. Who is right?
    (A) A only.
    (B) B only.
    (C) Both A and B.
    (D) Neither A nor B.

20. _____

21. The electric fuel pump will fill the fuel lines when the _____.
    (A) key is turned on
    (B) engine is started
    (C) fuel system pressure drops
    (D) None of the above.

21. _____

22. Draw arrows showing the fuel flow through the pump below and identify the parts indicated.

    (A) _____
    (B) _____
    (C) _____
    (D) _____
    (E) _____
    (F) _____

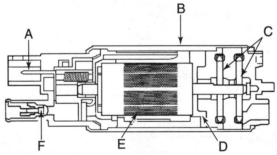

Fuel Filters and Fuel Lines

23. Fuel filters elements can be made of _____.
    (A) ceramic
    (B) treated paper
    (C) sintered bronze
    (D) All of the above.

23. _____

24. Define *vapor lock.* _____

_____

25. Some fuel systems can use _____ to prevent a vapor lock.
    (A) metal plates
    (B) a vapor return
    (C) heat shields
    (D) All of the above.

25. _____

26. The illustration below depicts a cutaway view of a paper or throwaway fuel filter. Label the components as indicated.

    (A) _____

    (B) _____

    (C) _____

    (D) _____

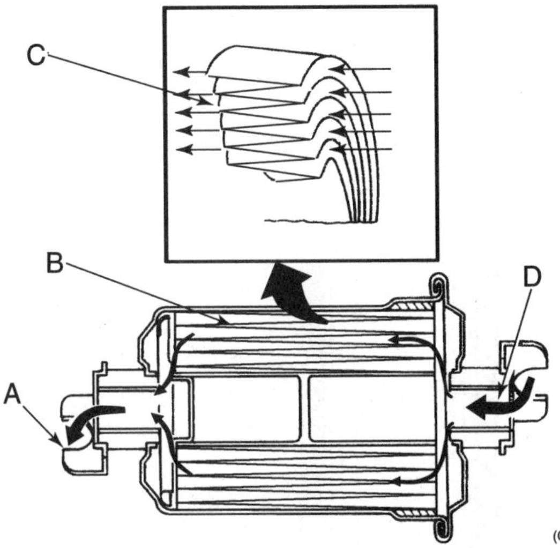

(Chevrolet)

Carburetors

27. The job of the fuel system is to constantly deliver a(n) _____ of the proper proportions to the engine.

27. _____

28. The proportions of gasoline and air can vary depending on _____.
    (A) engine load
    (B) engine speed
    (C) engine temperature and design
    (D) All of the above.

28. _____

29. Define *air horn*. _____

    _____

    _____

30. Define *fuel bowl*. _____

    _____

    _____

31. To control the amount of fuel entering the fuel bowl, a _____ is normally hinged inside the bowl.
    (A) tube
    (B) needle
    (C) float
    (D) None of the above.

31. _____

32. The main discharge tube allows gasoline to be _____
    _____.
    _____

33. In order to get the fuel to flow through the nozzle and into the air horn, a strong _____ is needed.

33. _____

34. The cutaway illustration below shows an air horn. Draw arrows indicating the airflow and identify the parts as indicated.

    (A) _____
    (B) _____
    (C) _____

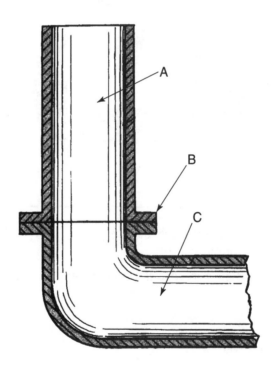

35. The illustration below shows the fuel bowl vent part of a carburetor. Identify the components as indicated.

(A) _____

(B) _____

(C) _____

(D) _____

(E) _____

(F) _____

(G) _____

(H) _____

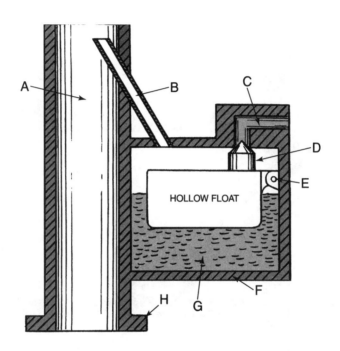

HOLLOW FLOAT

Creating Venturi Vacuum

36. By building a _____ or venturi in the air horn, the air will be forced to speed up.

36. _____

37. Define *secondary venturi.* _____

_____

_____

_____

38. Air bleeding is the adding of a small stream of air into the fuel as it travels through the nozzle. This will make the fuel drops _____.

38. _____

39. Jets are used in a carburetor to control _____ that can travel
    through a passageway.
    (A) air
    (B) gasoline
    (C) Both A and B.
    (D) None of the above.

39. _____

40. Normally, a jet is placed in the lower end of the _____ to
    control the amount of gasoline at high engine speeds.
    (A) main discharge tube
    (B) primary venturi
    (C) secondary venturi
    (D) None of the above.

40. _____

41. What does the *main discharge jet* illustrated below control? _____

_____

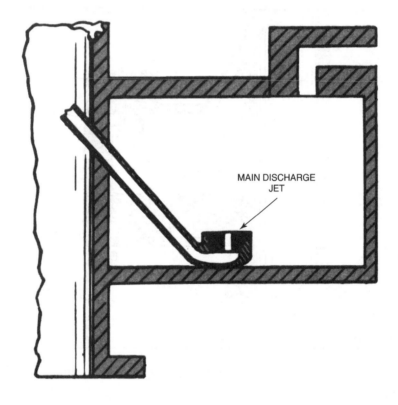

MAIN DISCHARGE
JET

42. Draw the fuel and air as they mix in the air horn illustrated below and identify the components as indicated.

   (A) _____

   (B) _____

   (C) _____

   (D) _____

   (E) _____

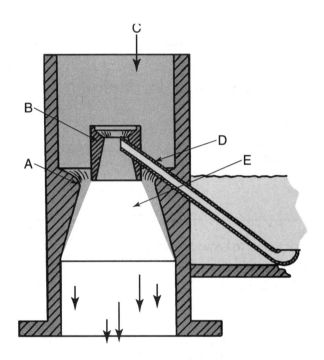

Choke and Throttle Valves

43. If an engine was started with no means of controlling the flow of air and resulting fuel flow, the engine would run _____.
   (A) wild
   (B) wide open
   (C) rough
   (D) Both A and B.

   43. _____

44. Define *throttle valve.* _____

   _____

   _____

   _____

45. A throttle valve is a circular metal plate placed between the bottom of the primary _____ and the mounting flange.

   45. _____

46. The throttle valve is controlled by _____ connected to the accelerator pedal.

   46. _____

Carburetor Circuits

47. Define *carburetor circuits.* _____

_____

_____

48. List the air-fuel ratios for the following conditions:

(A) Cold start _____

(B) Heavy load _____

(C) Highway cruising _____

(D) Ideal ratio _____

49. Basic circuits or systems on a carburetor include all of the following, EXCEPT:
(A) idle and low speed circuit.
(B) choke and acceleration circuit.
(C) high speed full power circuit.
(D) discharge circuit.

49. _____

Idle Circuit

50. When the throttle valve is closed to slow the engine to idle speed, the main _____ stops supplying fuel.
(A) idle port
(B) discharge nozzle
(C) main jet
(D) None of the above.

50. _____

51. All of the following statements about the idle circuit are true, EXCEPT:
(A) there is a vacuum above the throttle valve.
(B) there is a strong vacuum below the throttle.
(C) the vacuum will draw fuel from the bowl.
(D) the vacuum will draw air through the idle air bleed openings.

51. _____

52. All of the following statements are true about the idle mixture adjustment screw, EXCEPT:
(A) when turned in, it reduces the entering amount of fuel.
(B) they are sealed on modern carburetors to prevent adjustment.
(C) when turned out, it increases the amount of fuel.
(D) mixture adjustment procedures are flexible.

52. _____

53. The idle speed screw is installed at the base of the carburetor and touches a piece of _____ attached to the throttle shaft.

53. _____

Low Speed Circuit

54. When the throttle valve is opened beyond idle, more _____
is needed to keep the engine running.
    (A) vacuum
    (B) speed
    (C) fuel mixture
    (D) All of the above.

54. _____

55. All of the following statements about low speed circuit
operation are true, EXCEPT:
    (A) the idle screw port feeds fuel into the air horn.
    (B) the choke is part of the low speed circuit.
    (C) it furnishes extra fuel until the main discharge nozzle
        begins working.
    (D) can use a series of holes to feed fuel.

55. _____

High Speed Circuit

56. All of the following statements about high speed circuit
operation are true, EXCEPT:
    (A) air speed increases enough to build a vacuum in the
        venturi.
    (B) venturi action causes the main discharge nozzle to
        supply fuel.
    (C) the vacuum is lowered at the idle screw port.
    (D) idle and low speed circuits continue to supply fuel.

56. _____

57. As the throttle valve continues to open, the idle and low
speed circuits will not furnish enough _____ and the engine
would not gain speed.

57. _____

58. The amount of fuel flowing through the high speed circuit is
controlled by the _____.
    (A) needle valve
    (B) main passage size
    (C) main jet size
    (D) bowl size

58. _____

59. The two main types of enrichment systems are the _____.
    (A) discharge tube and the choke plate
    (B) power valve and step-up rod
    (C) metering rod and cable
    (D) None of the above.

59. _____

60. All of the following statements about momentary flat spots
are true, EXCEPT:
    (A) they cause engine hesitation.
    (B) they cause sudden acceleration.
    (C) they cause backfiring through the intake manifold.
    (D) they occur commonly at speeds below 30 mph (48 kmh).

60. _____

61. Identify the carburetor parts as indicated in the illustration below.

    (A) _____

    (B) _____

    (C) _____

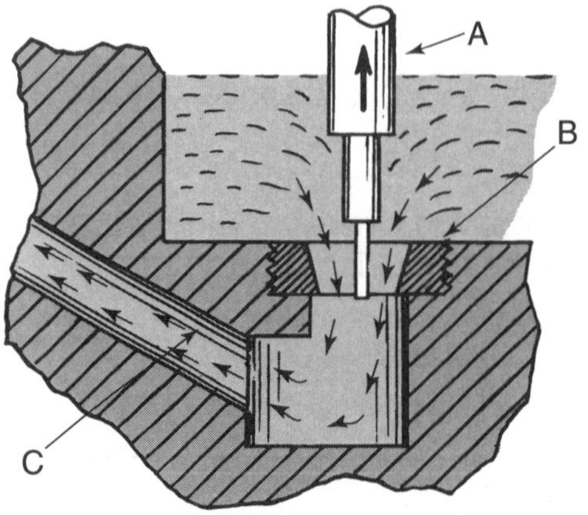

Accelerator Pump Circuit

62. To prevent an engine hesitation problem, a(n) _____, using either a piston or diaphragm, is used in the carburetor.

62. _____

63. In the diaphragm type pump, fuel can be discharged into the air horn through one or more _____.
    (A) discharge nozzles
    (B) check valves
    (C) engine nozzles
    (D) All of the above.

63. _____

64. In the piston type pump, the _____ pushes the piston downward when the throttle opens.

64. _____

65. For cold starting only, the fuel mixture must be _____.

65. _____

66. When the engine is cold, some gasoline will _____ in the intake manifold.

66. _____

67. Liquid gasoline will not _____ so the carburetor must provide a rich mixture to allow enough gasoline to stay in the vapor state.

67. _____

68. A cold engine must have a _____ fuel mixture to start. As the engine warms, the mixture must _____.
    (A) rich, liquefy
    (B) lean, become richer
    (C) rich, lean out
    (D) None of the above.

68. _____

    _____

69. A _____ is installed at the top of the air horn to aid cold engine starting.
   (A) discharge tube
   (B) cable
   (C) choke plate
   (D) None of the above.

69. _____

70. The choke plate is located at the _____ of the air horn.

70. _____

71. When the choke is closed, the supply of _____ entering the carburetor is greatly reduced.

71. _____

72. The closed choke forms an extremely high vacuum in the air horn which pulls a large quantity of _____ from the other carburetor systems.
   (A) air
   (B) fuel
   (C) oil
   (D) None of the above.

72. _____

73. To prime an engine with extra fuel for cold starts, older carburetors had a manual or hand _____.

73. _____

74. The figure below illustrates a mechanically operated accelerator fuel pump. Identify the parts as indicated.

   (A) _____

   (B) _____

   (C) _____

   (D) _____

   (E) _____

   (F) _____

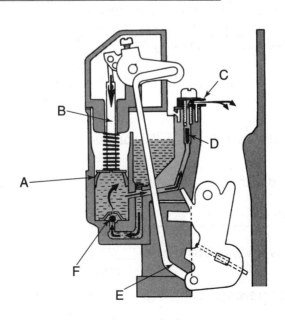

Choke Circuit

75. All of the following statements are true about the thermo-static coil spring, EXCEPT:
    (A) it is affected by temperature change.
    (B) it is attached to the housing cover.
    (C) it gains tension when hot.
    (D) it can be installed in the exhaust manifold.

75. _____

76. When does the choke vacuum break start operating? _____

_____

77. All of the following methods are used to supply heat to open the choke, EXCEPT:
    (A) exhaust heat.
    (B) engine coolant.
    (C) electric current.
    (D) air friction.

77. _____

78. Define *flooding*. _____

_____

79. While the engine is warming, it is necessary to idle the engine faster to prevent _____.

79. _____

80. The fast idle cam performs all of the following functions, EXCEPT:
    (A) closes the throttle valve to speed up the engine.
    (B) swings out in front of the idle speed adjustment screw.
    (C) holds the throttle valve partially open to speed up the engine.
    (D) swings down as the choke opens.

80. _____

81. Technician A says that small carburetor throats increase smoothness at low speeds. Technician B says that large throats increase high speed power. Who is right?
    (A) A only.
    (B) B only.
    (C) Both A and B.
    (D) Neither A nor B.

81. _____

82. Secondary throats are equipped with _____ that open only when needed.

82. _____

83. The choke valve is installed in the _____ throat.

83. _____

Other Carburetor Features

84. The hot idle compensator is a way of letting more _____ into a hot engine.

84. _____

85. The throttle return dashpot prevents _____.

85. _____

86. Technician A says that the idle speedup solenoid is used to prevent dieseling. Technician B says that the idle speedup solenoid is energized when the air conditioner is on. Who is right?
    (A) A only.
    (B) B only.
    (C) Both A and B.
    (D) Neither A nor B.

86. _____

87. The mixture control solenoid _____.
    (A) is a type of electromagnet
    (B) uses electrical current
    (C) is used to move the rod
    (D) All of the above.

87. _____

88. Throttle position sensors can be either resistance types or _____.

88. _____

89. All of the following statements apply to carburetor icing, EXCEPT:
    (A) happens when outside temperature is just above freezing and humidity is high.
    (B) ice forms on the throttle valves.
    (C) occurs during the cool-down period.
    (D) stops after the engine is fully warmed up.

89. _____

90. The altitude _____ adjusts the amount of fuel or the amount of air in the mixture for different elevations.

90. _____

91. On older engines, the adjustment (for different elevations) of fuel and air in the mixture was made by using a(n) _____.

91. _____

Air Cleaners

92. Air cleaner elements are made of treated _____.

92. _____

93. Air cleaners allow air to flow, but trap _____.

93. _____

94. Air cleaners can be _____.
    (A) round or flat
    (B) square or triangular
    (C) permanent
    (D) All of the above.

94. _____

Carburetor Classifications

95. The three main sections of a carburetor are _____.

96. Which of the following carburetor type(s) have not been used on automobiles for many years?
    (A) Updraft.
    (B) Sidedraft.
    (C) Downdraft.
    (D) Both A and B.

96. _____

97. Carburetor throats are often called _____.

97. _____

98. Single-barrel carburetors are used on _____ engines.
    (A) four
    (B) three
    (C) two
    (D) Both A and B.

98. _____

99. Each barrel on a two-barrel carburetor has its own _____.
    (A) throttle valve
    (B) discharge nozzle
    (C) idle port
    (D) All of the above.

99. _____

100. Which of the following carburetors can have secondary systems?
    (A) Single throat.
    (B) Two throat.
    (C) Four throat.
    (D) Both A and B.

100. _____

Name _____

Date _____ Period _____

Instructor _____

Score _____ Text Pages 193-210

11

Cooling Systems

Objectives: After studying Chapter 11 in the textbook, and completing this section of the workbook, you will be able to:

- List the functions of an engine cooling system.
- Identify the two major kinds of cooling systems.
- Identify the major components of a liquid cooling system.
- Trace the flow of coolant through the liquid cooling system.
- Identify the basic parts of an air cooling system.

Tech Talk: This chapter will cover the principles of cooling systems, why they are needed, and why the engine must operate within a certain temperature range. Without a properly operating cooling system, an engine can self-destruct in a matter of minutes. Combustion heat can transfer into the engine parts making cylinder heads crack or warp, pistons melt, piston rings and cylinder walls score or other parts fail. It is important for you to learn the operating principles of cooling systems and how they affect the service life and efficiency of an engine.

Instructions: Read the general instructions on pages 5–6 for answering the workbook questions. Then, as you study Chapter 11 of the text, answer the following questions in the spaces provided.

The Need for a Cooling System

1. About _____ of the engine heat is used to power the engine. The remaining heat must be carried off by the exhaust and cooling systems.
   (A) 1/2
   (B) 1/3
   (C) 1/4
   (D) 3/4

1. _____

2. Three jobs of the cooling system are _____

_____

_____.

3. Most car and light trucks have a _____ type cooling system.

3. _____

Liquid-Cooled Engines

4. Cooling passages are cast into the _____.
   (A) block
   (B) head
   (C) radiator
   (D) Both A and B.

   4. _____

5. The cooling passages through the inside of the engine are often termed _____.

   5. _____

6. Technician A says that freeze plugs will usually prevent block damage if the coolant freezes. Technician B says that freeze plugs seal holes left in the block during the casting process. Who is right?
   (A) A only.
   (B) B only.
   (C) Both A and B.
   (D) Neither A nor B.

   6. _____

7. The heat of the burning fuel is absorbed by the _____ before transferring into the coolant.

   7. _____

8. The engine coolant is the medium of heat _____.

   8. _____

9. If the coolant absorbs too much heat it will _____.

   9. _____

10. Using the figure below, draw arrows showing how the use of coolant will carry heat away from the bar. Also indicate the temperature on the gauge and identify the components as indicated.

    (A) _____

    (B) _____

    (C) _____

    (D) _____

    (E) _____

Coolant Pump

11. The coolant pump is used to _____

    _____.

12. The most common type of coolant pump is the centrifugal type which uses a(n) _____.

12. _____

13. When the impeller turns, coolant is thrown outward by _____.

13. _____

14. The coolant pump housing is cast of _____.
    (A) stainless steel
    (B) cast iron
    (C) aluminum
    (D) Both B and C.

14. _____

15. The impeller shaft is supported by _____.
    (A) a spring
    (B) ball bearings
    (C) plugs
    (D) None of the above.

15. _____

16. Identify the parts indicated in the illustration below.

    (A) _____

    (B) _____

    (C) _____

(Chrysler Corp.)

Belt Drive

17. A(n) _____ can be used to drive the water pump and is driven by a pulley on the front of the crankshaft.

17. _____

18. Excessive belt tightness will cause premature _____ in the alternator and water pump.

18. _____

19. A loose belt will permit slippage, which will reduce pump and fan speed thus causing _____.

19. _____

20. Identify the parts indicated on the engine illustrated below.

(A) _____

(B) _____

(C) _____

(D) _____

(E) _____

(F) _____

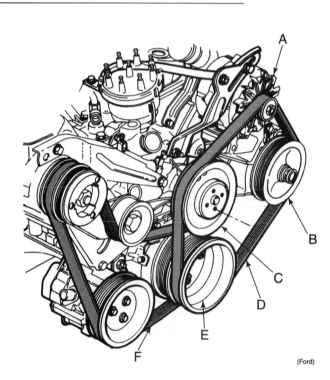

(Ford)

Radiator

21. Before the coolant can be reused in the engine, _____ must be removed.

21. _____

22. All of the following are used to make radiators, EXCEPT:
    (A) aluminum.
    (B) copper.
    (C) steel.
    (D) plastic.

22. _____

23. The radiator is placed in the front of the vehicle to take advantage of _____ flow when the car is moving.

23. _____

24. Coolant circulating through the radiator is cooled by _____ passing through the radiator fins.

24. _____

25. From the inlet tank of the radiator, water flows through a set   25. _____
of tubes known as the _____.
(A) radiator core
(B) copper
(C) steel
(D) plastic

26. By the time the water reaches the _____ of the radiator, it is   26. _____
cool enough to reuse.

27. The transmission oil cooler can be a separate unit or placed   27. _____
in _____.

28. Identify the parts indicated on the downflow radiator illustrated below.

(A) _____

(B) _____

(C) _____

(D) _____

(E) _____

(F) _____

(G) _____

(H) _____

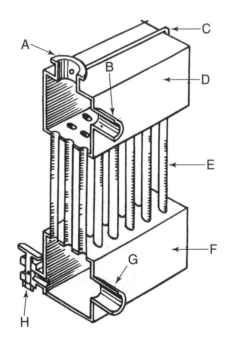

Forced Air

29. To speed up the action of the radiator, one or more fans are   29. _____
used to draw air through the radiator _____.

30. Engine driven fans are usually part of the _____ assembly.   30. _____

31. Engine driven fans use a shroud to _____.
    (A) keep the fan dry
    (B) avoid loss of fan efficiency
    (C) recirculate air
    (D) None of the above.

31. _____

32. A fan clutch is designed to do all of the following, EXCEPT:
    (A) save horsepower.
    (B) cause fan to freewheel.
    (C) prevent recirculation of air.
    (D) cut down on noise.

32. _____

33. Most electric fans are controlled by a _____ switch.

33. _____

Hoses and Clamps

34. The radiator is connected to the engine and pump by means of _____ hoses.

34. _____

35. All of the following statements are true about heater hoses, EXCEPT:
    (A) they bring hot coolant to the heater core.
    (B) they are larger than radiator hoses.
    (C) they carry a smaller amount of coolant.
    (D) they can have a shut-off valve installed inside.

35. _____

36. Hose clamps are used to _____ hoses to their fittings.

36. _____

37. A steel spring is sometimes placed inside a radiator hose to keep the hose from _____.

37. _____

38. Identify the types of hoses illustrated below.

    (A) _____

    (B) _____

    (C) _____

A

FABRIC
RUBBER

B

C

The Thermostat

39. The thermostat provides a way to _____ engine temperature.

39. _____

40. When the engine temperature is low, the thermostat is _____.

40. _____

41. All of the following statements are true about thermostat operation, EXCEPT:
   (A) it can open at any temperature.
   (B) it shuts off the flow of coolant from the cold engine to the radiator.
   (C) it may not open completely in extremely cold weather.
   (D) most modern thermostats contain a wax pellet.

41. _____

42. All of the following statements about pellet thermostat operation are true EXCEPT:
   (A) pressure from the wax expansion opens the valve.
   (B) the wax expands as the coolant warms.
   (C) it works well in a fully pressurized cooling system.
   (D) it is pressure sensitive.

42. _____

43. High range thermostats help with _____ control.

43. _____

44. Thermostat heat range is the point at which the thermostat

   _____.
   (A) is fully closed
   (B) begins to open
   (C) is fully open
   (D) is stuck

44. _____

45. A bypass is used to prevent _____ overheating.

45. _____

46. Most cooling systems have a _____ bypass.

46. _____

47. Identify the parts indicated in the illustration below.

   (A) _____

   (B) _____

   (C) _____

   (D) _____

   (E) _____

   (F) _____

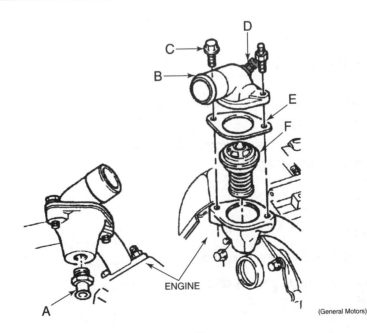

ENGINE

(General Motors)

48. Identify the parts indicated in the illustration below.

(A) _____

(B) _____

(C) _____

(D) _____

(E) _____

(F) _____

(G) _____

(H) _____

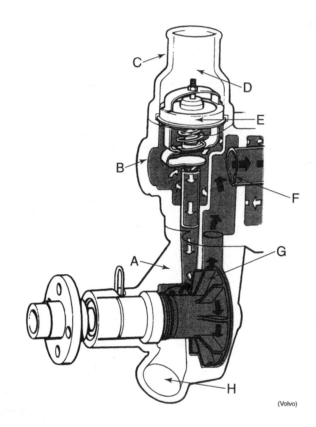

(Volvo)

Pressurized Cooling System

49. If the cooling system is pressurized, the boiling temperature of the water will be _____.

49. _____

50. Each pound of pressure on the cooling system will raise the boiling point of the water around _____.
    (A) 212°F (100°C)
    (B) 45°F (25°C)
    (C) 3°F (1.66°C)
    (D) None of the above.

50. _____

51. Pressurization increases cooling efficiency by reducing _____.

51. _____

52. Pressurizing of a cooling system is done by placing a _____ on the radiator _____.

52. _____

_____

53. Technician A says that a coolant recovery system consists of a coolant reservoir and no other modifications. Technician B says that a closed cooling system is a system equipped with a coolant recovery system. Who is right?
    (A) A only.
    (B) B only.
    (C) Both A and B.
    (D) Neither A nor B.

53. _____

54. Name two measures that coolant temperature can be monitored by_____

_____.

Using Antifreeze

55. Antifreeze contains _____.
    (A) ethylene glycol
    (B) soluble oils
    (C) corrosion inhibitors
    (D) All of the above.

55. _____

56. A mixture of antifreeze and water freezes at a(n) _____ temperature than either liquid by itself.

56. _____

57. A 50/50 mixture of water and antifreeze will boil at _____.
    (A) 212°F (100°C)
    (B) 223°F (106°C)
    (C) 275°F (135°C)
    (D) None of the above.

57. _____

58. All of the following statements are true about antifreeze, EXCEPT:
    (A) protects the cooling system from rust and corrosion.
    (B) should be flushed if dirty.
    (C) occasionally should be replaced with water.
    (D) should be mixed with water.

58. _____

Air-Cooled Engines

59. Technician A says that air must move over the fins of an air cooled engine to prevent overheating. Technician B says that an air cooled engine can have a thermostat. Who is right?
    (A) A only.
    (B) B only.
    (C) Both A and B.
    (D) Neither A nor B.

59. _____

60. All of the following statements are true about air-cooled engines, EXCEPT:
    (A) the fins are cast into the engine parts.
    (B) they are efficient and dependable.
    (C) they have no effective way to heat the passenger compartment.
    (D) they need very few cooling fins.

60. _____

61. In addition to adding fins, a fan or _____ is essential to produce a moving stream of air.

61. _____

62. Some air shrouds are designed to form a _____ on which the air pressure is higher than the surrounding atmospheric pressure.
    (A) plenum chamber
    (B) finned surface
    (C) Both A and B.
    (D) None of the above.

62. _____

63. The air-cooled engine can use a bellows _____ to accurately measure engine temperature.

63. _____

64. The bellows is filled with liquid under a _____.

64. _____

65. The _____ in a bellows thermostat will return open to full position if the bellows leaks or becomes inoperative.

65. _____

Name _____

Date _____ Period _____

Instructor _____

Score _____ Text Pages 211–228

12

Lubrication Systems

Objectives: After studying Chapter 12 in the textbook, and completing this section of the workbook, you will be able to:

- Explain the need for a lubrication system.
- Identify the major parts of a lubrication system.
- Explain engine oil classifications.
- Summarize the operation of an engine lubrication system.
- Identify the components of an engine lubrication system.
- List the different types of oil pumps.
- List the different types of oil filters.

Tech Talk: A lubrication system forces oil to the high friction points inside an engine. The oil allows the moving parts to move freely, with less friction and wear. If an engine's lubrication system fails, major engine damage will result in a very short period of time. Friction and heat could score, melt, gouge, and ruin cylinder walls, pistons, bearings, and other engine parts.

Instructions: Read the general instructions on pages 5–6 for answering the workbook questions. Then, as you study Chapter 12 of the text, answer the following questions in the spaces provided.

Friction

1. Lack of lubrication causes parts to overheat, tearing bits of
   _____ from each other.

   1. _____

2. What does friction cause in the engine? _____

   _____

3. Define *friction.* _____

   _____

   _____

4. The engine must operate under conditions of _____ friction.

   4. _____

5. Friction bearing is _____

   _____.

6. The antifriction bearing uses _____ between the two moving surfaces or parts.
   (A) balls
   (B) rollers
   (C) baffles
   (D) Both A and B.

6. _____

7. List the four jobs of motor oil. _____

_____

8. Identify the parts as indicated in the drawing below.

   (A) _____

   (B) _____

   (C) _____

   (D) _____

Engine Oil

9. Define *oil viscosity*. _____

_____

_____

10. The _____ is a measure of an oil's ability to resist changes in viscosity with changing temperatures.
    (A) additive index (AI)
    (B) viscosity index (VI)
    (C) polymer index (PI)
    (D) None of the above.

10. _____

11. Technician A says that, under normal conditions, engine oil in turbocharged engines should be changed every 7500 miles or 12,000 km. Technician B says that an engine in poor condition or one that is operated in dusty conditions should have its oil changed every 3000 miles or 1800 km. Who is right?
    (A) A only.
    (B) B only.
    (C) Both A and B.
    (D) Neither A nor B.

11. _____

12. The latest oil grade designation is _____.
    (A) SE
    (B) SH
    (C) SL
    (D) SB

12. _____

13. The job of the engine lubrication system is to get oil to the _____ parts.

13. _____

14. It is important that all bearings have the proper _____ between surfaces. They should be loose enough to allow oil entry but tight enough to prevent _____.

14. _____
      _____

15. List the three types of engine lubrication systems. _____
_____

_____

16. The full pressure lubrication system uses _____ to force oil to the crankshaft and other parts.
    (A) bearings
    (B) dippers
    (C) an oil pump
    (D) All of the above.

16. _____

17. Identify the parts as indicated in the illustration below.

    (A) _____

    (B) _____

    (C) _____

    (D) _____

    (E) _____

    (F) _____

    (G) _____

    (H) _____

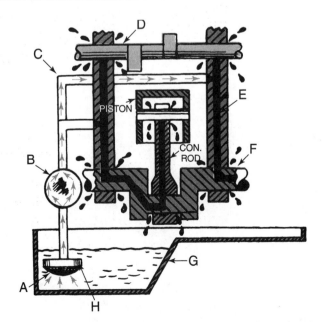

Oil Pumps

18. The oil pan reservoir is called the _____.

18. _____

19. All of the following statements about oil pickups are true, EXCEPT:
    (A) they always contain a screen.
    (B) they do *not* touch the bottom.
    (C) they sit on the bottom.
    (D) the screen is bypassed sometimes.

19. _____

20. The two most widely used engine oil pumps are _____.
    (A) the gear and rotary
    (B) the vane and gear
    (C) the vane and rotary
    (D) the splash and vane

20. _____

21. The gear pump uses _____ gears as the moving force to pump oil.

21. _____

22. The vane pump contains at least _____ vanes.

22. _____

23. A good oil pump will produce more _____ than necessary.

23. _____

24. The pressure relief valve opens to allow oil to return to the _____.

24. _____

25. The pressure relief valve will allow the pressure reaching the bearings to remain at a(n) _____ level.

25. _____

26. Oil galleries are passages between the pump and pressure relief valve and the _____.
    (A) sump
    (B) bearings
    (C) oil pan
    (D) All of the above.

26. _____

27. Camshaft lobes are lubricated by oil _____.

27. _____

28. All oil eventually flows back into the _____.

28. _____

Engine Oil Flow

29. Using a pen or pencil, darken the oil passages in the engine illustrated below. Draw arrows showing the direction of flow and identify the parts as indicated.

(A) _____

(B) _____

(C) _____

(D) _____

(E) _____

(F) _____

(G) _____

(H) _____

(I) _____

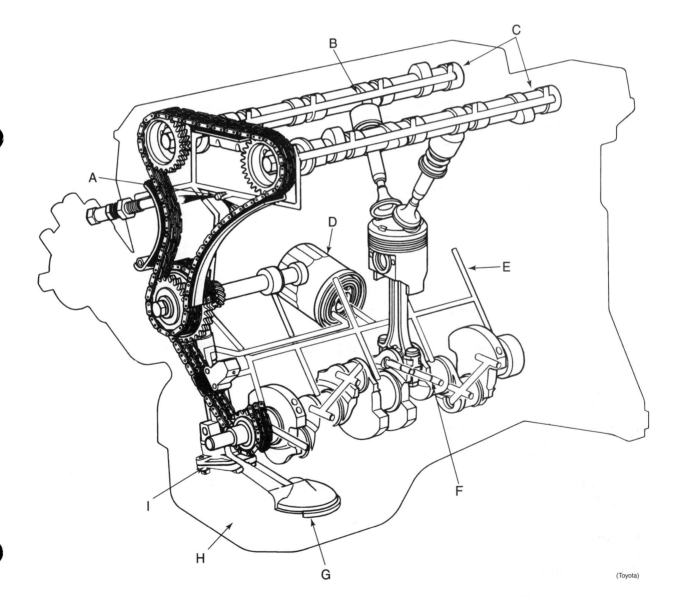

(Toyota)

30. Modern detergent oils keep contaminants _____ instead of allowing them to build up on the inside of the engine.
    (A) in the lower chamber
    (B) in suspension
    (C) under pressure
    (D) None of the above.

30. _____

Oil Filters

31. Technician A says that depth filters are made of various treated papers. Technician B says that most modern filters are replaced by discarding the entire assembly. Who is right?
    (A) A only.
    (B) B only.
    (C) Both A and B.
    (D) Neither A nor B.

31. _____

32. On a full flow filter system, _____ of the pump output is filtered.
    (A) 50%
    (B) 75%
    (C) 80%
    (D) 100%

32. _____

33. In a full-flow filter system, if the filter becomes clogged, a _____ valve opens to allow oil to reach the bearings.

33. _____

34. The better a job the filter does of removing contaminants, the sooner it will become _____.

34. _____

35. Most manufacturers recommend changing the oil filter at every _____.
    (A) oil change
    (B) other oil change
    (C) every third oil change
    (D) Either A or B.

35. _____

Positive Crankcase Ventilation

36. Blowby is what gets past the _____ when the engine is running.

36. _____

37. Blowby is composed of _____.
    (A) exhaust gas and fluid
    (B) unburned fuel and exhaust gas
    (C) water and gas
    (D) Both A and B.

37. _____

38. If not vented, blowby could cause all of the following, EXCEPT:
    (A) moisture to form.
    (B) build up of acids.
    (C) rough idle.
    (D) engine damage.

38. _____

39. When the PCV system takes clean air from the breather cap, this is called a(n) _____ system.

39. _____

40. The closed PCV system keeps toxic fumes from entering the atmosphere when the engine is _____.
   (A) under a load
   (B) decelerating
   (C) stopped
   (D) Both A and C.

40. _____

41. A PCV system causes blowby to be drawn into the _____ where it is burned in the cylinders.
   (A) intake manifold
   (B) combustion chamber
   (C) crankcase
   (D) Either A or B.

41. _____

42. Draw arrows showing circulation in the illustration below and identify the parts as indicated.

   (A) _____

   (B) _____

   (C) _____

   (D) _____

   (E) _____

   (F) _____

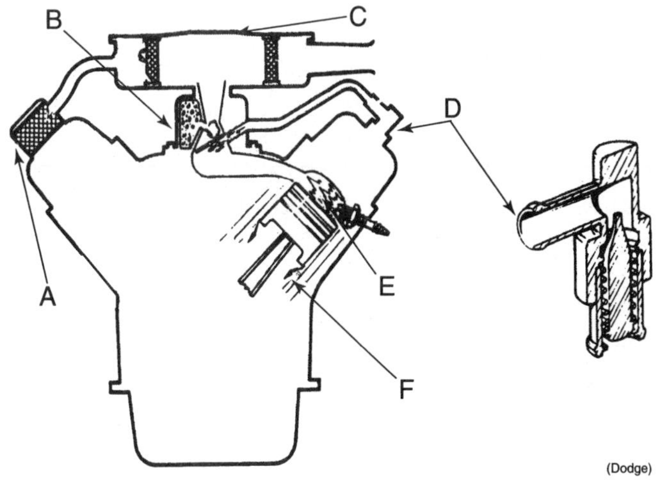

(Dodge)

Other Lubrication System Parts

43. Oil is retained in the engine by _____.
   (A) sealants
   (B) oil seals
   (C) gaskets
   (D) All of the above.

43. _____

44. What does an oil slinger do? _____

_____

_____

45. Technician A says that a balancing coil type of oil pressure gauge depends on a heating coil in the pressure sender to register pressure. Technician B says that a balancing coil pressure gauge depends on resistance changes in the sender to register pressure. Who is right?
    (A) A only.
    (B) B only.
    (C) Both A and B.
    (D) Neither A nor B.

45. _____

46. Oil pressure can be determined by _____.
    (A) a monitor
    (B) a warning light
    (C) a gauge
    (D) Both B and C.

46. _____

47. Define *dipstick*. _____

_____

_____

_____

48. In the average engine, the main way in which the oil is cooled is by air passing over the _____.
    (A) valve covers
    (B) engine block
    (C) oil filter
    (D) oil pan

48. _____

49. When would an auxiliary engine oil cooler be needed? _____

_____

_____

50. An auxiliary oil cooler can use _____ or _____ to cool the oil.

50. _____

_____

Name _____

Date _____ Period _____

Instructor _____

Score _____ Text Pages 229–238

13

Exhaust Systems

Objectives: After studying Chapter 13 in the textbook, and completing this section of the workbook, you will be able to:

- Explain the purpose of the exhaust system.
- Describe the operation of the exhaust system.
- Identify exhaust system components.

Tech Talk: While exhaust systems are relatively simple, they should be carefully studied. They are vitally important to the efficient and safe operation of a vehicle's engine. Careless installation can cause leaks allowing exhaust gases to enter the passenger compartment. Inhalation of exhaust gases can cause breathing difficulties and carbon monoxide poisoning. This will lead to reduced alertness or even to death by asphyxiation. Always do exhaust system work carefully.

Instructions: Read the general instructions on pages 5–6 for answering the workbook questions. Then, as you study Chapter 13 of the text, answer the following questions in the spaces provided.

Purpose of the Exhaust System

1. Technician A says that the exhaust system is designed to reduce exhaust noise. Technician B says that the exhaust system is designed to keep exhaust gases out of the engine compartment. Who is right?
   (A) A only.
   (B) B only.
   (C) Both A and B.
   (D) Neither A nor B.

   1. _____

2. Back pressure occurs when the flow of exhaust gases is _____.

   2. _____

3. Excessive back pressure makes it harder to remove the exhaust gases from the _____.
   (A) manifold
   (B) converter
   (C) cylinders
   (D) All of the above.

   3. _____

4. All of the following are a result of excessive back pressure, EXCEPT:
   (A) loss of engine power.
   (B) lower emissions.
   (C) lower mileage.
   (D) burned exhaust valves.

4. _____

Exhaust System Designs

5. Burned gases first leave the engine through the open exhaust valve and then enter the _____ and from there, they travel through the exhaust pipe.

5. _____

6. After going through the exhaust pipe, the burned gases travel through the _____, the muffler, and then leave the car via a tailpipe.

6. _____

7. Dual exhaust systems are used primarily on _____ engines.
   (A) G-type
   (B) V-type
   (C) L-type
   (D) None of the above.

7. _____

8. Self canceling is a method of _____ reduction.

8. _____

Exhaust System Components

9. Exhaust manifolds are constructed of _____.
   (A) stainless steel
   (B) cast iron
   (C) copper
   (D) Either A or B.

9. _____

10. Explain *scavenging* in the exhaust manifold. _____

_____

_____

11. The exhaust manifold is bolted to the _____.

11. _____

12. Any pipe other than the tail pipe is called an _____ pipe.

12. _____

13. A double-walled pipe is used to reduce _____.
    (A) noise
    (B) vibration
    (C) corrosion
    (D) All of the above.

13. _____

14. Describe the two basic types of muffler design. _____

_____

_____

15. Resonators are small extra _____ designed to further reduce exhaust noise.

15. _____

16. Exhaust hangers provide _____ while allowing the system to flex.

16. _____

17. Technician A says that heat shields cool the exhaust system by transferring heat to other parts of the vehicle. Technician B says that heat shields keep converter heat from igniting anything that the vehicle drives over. Who is right?
(A) A only.
(B) B only.
(C) Both A and B.
(D) Neither A nor B.

17. _____

18. Exhaust components are subjected to _____.
(A) intense heat
(B) dirt, salt, and water
(C) corrosive gases
(D) All of the above.

18. _____

19. _____ is widely used for exhaust pipes, tailpipes, and mufflers.
(A) Stainless steel
(B) Aluminized copper
(C) Aluminized steel
(D) None of the above.

19. _____

20. Identify the parts as indicated on the left-hand exhaust manifold illustrated below.

(A) _____

(B) _____

(C) _____

(D) _____

(E) _____

(F) _____

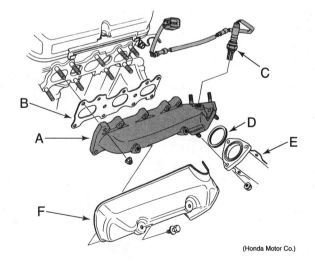

(Honda Motor Co.)

Sealing the Exhaust System

21. A semi-ball exhaust connector requires no _____.

21. _____

22. Muffler clamps are used to seal pipes to _____.
    (A) each other
    (B) the muffler
    (C) the exhaust manifold
    (D) Both A and B.

22. _____

23. All of the following statements about catalytic converters are true, EXCEPT:
    (A) they are connected with semi-ball connections.
    (B) air tubes are usually welded on.
    (C) they are connected with full-ball connections.
    (D) connections are sometimes welded together.

23. _____

24. Name three vehicle devices which may be connected to the exhaust system on modern vehicles.

    _____

    _____

25. Identify the parts as indicated on the exhaust system illustrated below.

    (A) _____

    (B) _____

    (C) _____

    (D) _____

    (E) _____

    (F) _____

    (G) _____

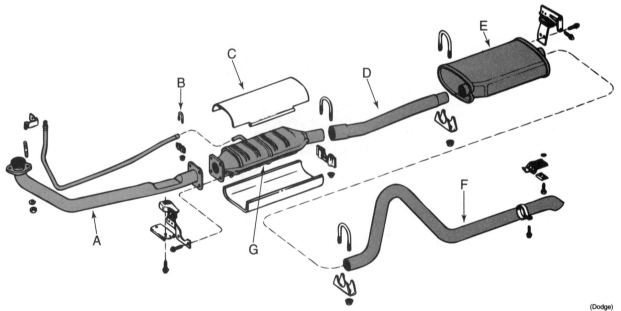

(Dodge)

Name _____

Date _____ Period _____

Instructor _____

Score _____ Text Pages 239–258

14

Emission Controls

Objectives: After studying Chapter 14 in the textbook, and completing this section of the workbook, you will be able to:

- Define automotive emissions.
- List the three most harmful automotive emissions.
- List the three major classes of emission controls.
- Explain the operating principles of common emission control systems.
- Identify the major parts of common emission control systems.

Tech Talk: Many emission control devices have been developed over the last 30 years. Modern emission controls are an integral part of the engine and drivetrain, and they must be serviced, not disabled or removed. These modern systems are fully integrated into the overall engine system and are usually monitored and controlled by the engine control computer. A well-maintained system will keep emissions as low as possible and help keep the air we breathe clean.

Instructions: Read the general instructions on pages 5–6 for answering the workbook questions. Then, as you study Chapter 14 of the text, answer the following questions in the spaces provided.

The Need for Emission Controls

1. All of the following exhaust emissions can pose health and environmental problems, EXCEPT:
   (A) oxides of nitrogen.
   (B) carbon dioxide.
   (C) carbon monoxide.
   (D) hydrocarbons.

1. _____

2. Hydrocarbon emissions, when they react with sunlight, tend to produce _____.

2. _____

3. List and define the three general types of emission controls:

   (A) _____

   _____

   (B) _____

   _____

   (C) _____

   _____

Engine Modifications and Controls

4. Modern combustion chambers are designed to reduce fuel _____.

4. _____

5. Technician A says that lower compression ratios allow the engine to operate on leaded gas. Technician B says that lower compression ratios reduce the amount of NO_x formed. Who is right?
   (A) A only.
   (B) B only.
   (C) Both A and B.
   (D) Neither A nor B.

5. _____

6. Thermostats that open at higher cooling system temperature help reduce the formation of _____.

6. _____

7. An air fuel ratio of 14.7:1 is ideal for _____ and emissions.
   (A) mileage
   (B) power
   (C) drivability
   (D) Both A and C.

7. _____

8. When the engine tries to keep running after the ignition is turned off, the engine is said to be _____.

8. _____

9. Technician A says that heating the incoming air on a cold engine reduces HC formation. Technician B says that heating the incoming air reduces carburetor icing. Who is right?
   (A) A only.
   (B) B only.
   (C) Both A and B.
   (D) Neither A nor B.

9. _____

10. A thermostatic air cleaner is used to heat incoming air and employs a _____ in the air inlet section of the air cleaner housing.

10. _____

11. All of the following statements about thermostatic air cleaners are true, EXCEPT:
    (A) air control door is actuated by a vacuum valve or motor.
    (B) ambient temperature air is drawn in when the valve is closed.
    (C) the air bleed closes when the thermal sensor warms.
    (D) uses both a diaphragm and spring pressure.

11. _____

12. An early fuel evaporation system prevents fuel condensation by use of _____ heat.

12. _____

13. When coolant temperature in an EFE system is below a certain point, the _____ applies vacuum to the EFE valve.

13. _____

14. The vacuum advance restrictor is installed between the vacuum advance unit and the _____ .

14. _____

15. Identify the parts as indicated on the drawing below.

(A) _____

(B) _____

(C) _____

(D) _____

(E) _____

(F) _____

(G) _____

(H) _____

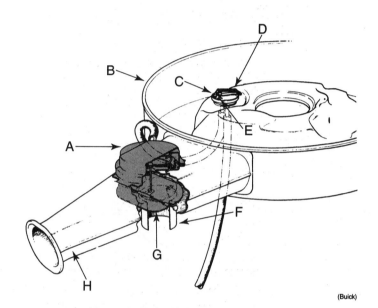

(Buick)

Exhaust Gas Recirculation

16. When peak combustion temperature exceeds _____, the   16. _____
    nitrogen in the air mixes with the oxygen to produce toxic
    oxides of nitrogen.
    (A) 2500°F (1372°C)
    (B) 5000°F (2744°C)
    (C) 1250°F (686°C)
    (D) None of the above.

17. List the four types of EGR valves. _____

    _____

    _____

18. A ported vacuum connection ensures that no vacuum   18. _____
    reaches the advance unit at _____ speeds.

19. The EGR valve should remain closed when the engine is cold because a cold engine will run _____ if the EGR valve is opened.

19. _____

20. The electronic EGR valve is cycled on and off many times per _____.

20. _____

21. Label the parts and draw arrows showing air and exhaust gas flow in the EGR system illustrated below.

(A) _____

(B) _____

(C) _____

(D) _____

(E) _____

(F) _____

(G) _____

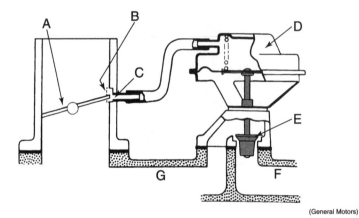

(General Motors)

External Cleaning Systems

22. External cleaning systems clean up the exhaust gases after they leave the _____ .
    (A) engine
    (B) exhaust manifold
    (C) catalytic converter
    (D) tailpipe

22. _____

23. Hydrocarbon and carbon monoxide emission from the exhaust can be reduced by more complete _____.

23. _____

24. A relief valve limits the amount of _____ an air pump can develop.

24. _____

25. The _____ will seat and prevent back feeding of hot exhaust into the hoses or pump.
    (A) air switching valve
    (B) check valve
    (C) diverter valve
    (D) needle bearing

25. _____

26. The _____ is designed to momentarily divert the airstream away from the injection nozzles and prevent backfiring.
    (A) check valve
    (B) needle bearing
    (C) air switching valve
    (D) diverter valve

26. _____

27. The switching valve does all of the following, EXCEPT:
    (A) reduces emissions.
    (B) improves operation of the converter.
    (C) channels air to the intake manifold.
    (D) diverts oil to the sump.

27. _____

28. Label the parts in the injection system illustrated below.

    (A) _____

    (B) _____

    (C) _____

    (D) _____

    (E) _____

    (F) _____

    (G) _____

    (H) _____

    (I) _____

    (J) _____

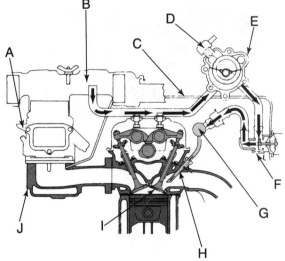

(Chevrolet)

29. Label the parts indicated on the air injection pump illustrated below.

(A) _____

(B) _____

(C) _____

(D) _____

(E) _____

(F) _____

(G) _____

(H) _____

(I) _____

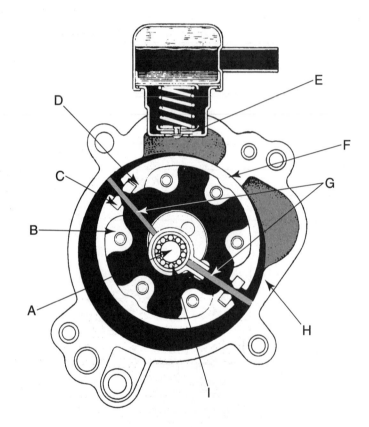

30. Identify the parts indicated on the pulse air injection system illustrated below.

(A) _____

(B) _____

(C) _____

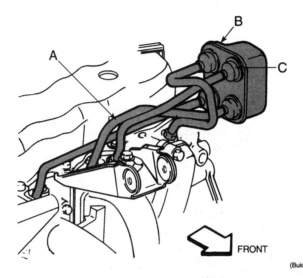

(Buick)

Catalytic Converter

31. Define *catalytic converter.* _____

_____

32. Inside a pellet converter, thousands of tiny beads of porous
_____, covered with a thin coating of platinum and palla-
dium are placed inside a perforated container.
(A) honeycomb
(B) coal
(C) aluminum oxide
(D) None of the above.

32. _____

33. All of the following statements are true about the monolith
converter, EXCEPT:
(A) exhaust gases flow through the porous beads.
(B) treated with a thin coating of platinum and palladium.
(C) block is coated with alumina.
(D) uses a ceramic honeycomb-like block.

33. _____

34. All of the following happens to the catalyst during normal
converter operation, EXCEPT:
(A) changes carbon monoxide and hydrocarbons into H_2O
and CO_2.
(B) it is altered and consumed.
(C) cause rapid increase in the exhaust temperature.
(D) it is not altered or consumed.

34. _____

35. All of the following are true of a reducing catalyst, EXCEPT: 35. _____
    (A) it makes use of the element rhodium.
    (B) it is used in three way converters.
    (C) it is placed after the oxidizing catalyst.
    (D) it reduces NO_X levels.

36. Identify the parts indicated on the converter illustrated below.

    (A) _____

    (B) _____

    (C) _____

    (D) _____

    (E) _____

    (F) _____

    (G) _____

    (H) _____

    (I) _____

    (J) _____

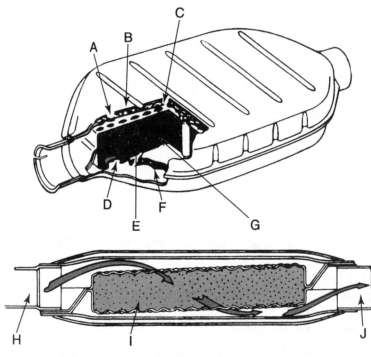

(Pontiac)

37. Identify the parts indicated on the converter system illustrated below.

(A) _____

(B) _____

(C) _____

(D) _____

(E) _____

(F) _____

(G) _____

(H) _____

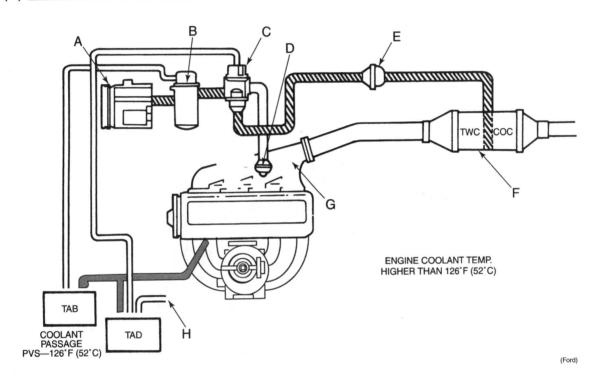

(Ford)

Fuel Vapor Controls

38. A major source of pollution is the release of HC in the form of _____.

38. _____

39. A PCV valve is a _____ control valve used to prevent up-setting fuel system operation.

39. _____

40. When the engine is stopped, the PCV valve is held _____.

40. _____

41. When the engine is at normal load, the PCV valve spring pushes the plunger _____ and increases air flow through the system.

41. _____

42. Label the parts indicated and draw arrows showing the flow through the engine.

(A) _____

(B) _____

(C) _____

(D) _____

(E) _____

(F) _____

(G) _____

(H) _____

(I) _____

(J) _____

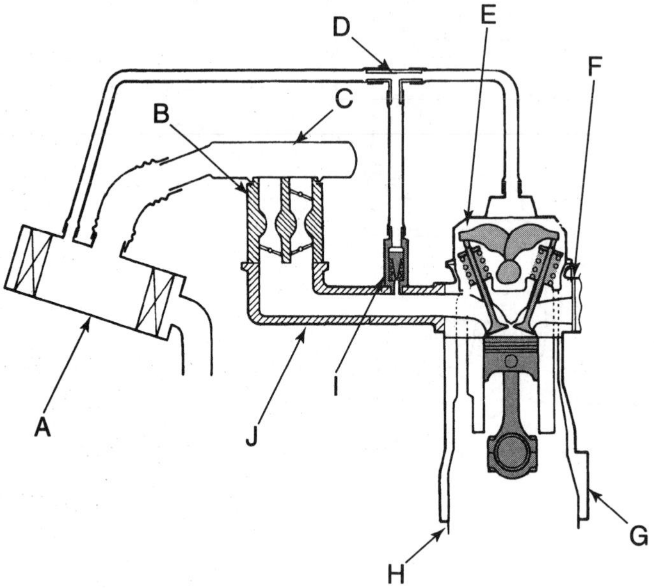

(Suzuki)

Evaporation Control System (ECS)

43. The evaporative control system is designed to prevent _____.

    (A) the release of gasoline into the atmosphere

    (B) leakage from the tank in the event of a rollover

    (C) the release of gasoline vapors into the atmosphere

    (D) All of the above.

43. _____

44. An evaporative control system is composed of _____

_____

_____

45. In an ECS system, the canister is filled with activated _____   45. _____
    granules.

46. The canister must never receive _____ fuel.   46. _____

47. Identify the parts indicated on the evaporation control system illustrated below.

    (A) _____

    (B) _____

    (C) _____

    (D) _____

    (E) _____

    (F) _____

    (G) _____

    (H) _____

    (I) _____

    (J) _____

    (K) _____

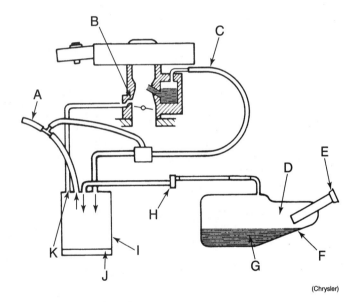

(Chrysler)

Computer Controlled Emission Systems

48. Technician A says that some emission controls are operated   48. _____
    by the engine computer. Technician B says that precise con-
    trol of the air-fuel ratio by the computer means that some
    emission controls can be eliminated. Who is right?
    (A) A only.
    (B) B only.
    (C) Both A and B.
    (D) Neither A nor B.

49. Adjustment or alteration of one emission system will often affect _____ _____ .

49. _____

50. When servicing vehicle emissions systems, always follow _____.
    (A) manufacturers recommendations
    (B) state emissions laws
    (C) federal emissions laws
    (D) All of the above.

50. _____

15

Computer Systems

Objectives: After studying Chapter 15 in the textbook, and completing this section of the workbook, you will be able to:

- Explain why computers are used in modern vehicles.
- Describe computer control system operation.
- Describe the major components of an on-board computer.
- Identify and describe computer input sensors.
- Identify and describe computer output devices.

Tech Talk: It is impossible to fix modern vehicles without some knowledge of computers. The computer controls almost every engine and drivetrain system, as well as other vehicle systems. If you do not understand computers, you are a parts changer, not a technician. Study this chapter carefully to understand computer operation.

Instructions: Read the general instructions on pages 5–6 for answering the workbook questions. Then, as you study Chapter 15 of the text, answer the following questions in the spaces provided.

Computers on Modern Vehicles

1. Technician A says only a few new cars are not equipped with computers. Technician B says that here may be as many as six computers in new cars. Who is right?
   (A) A only.
   (B) B only.
   (C) Both A and B.
   (D) Neither A nor B.

1. _____

2. The primary reason for using computers in modern vehicles is to meet _____ regulations.
   (A) fuel economy
   (B) emissions
   (C) drivability
   (D) Both A and B.

2. _____

3. The use of computers allows the engine _____ to be controlled precisely. The end result is an air-fuel ratio as close to 14.7 to 1 as possible.
   (A) fuel system
   (B) emission system
   (C) ignition system
   (D) All of the above.

3. _____

4. The _____ is *not* one of the three basic components of a computer system.
   (A) computer
   (B) output devices
   (C) combustion process
   (D) input sensors

4. _____

5. The system programming instructions are stored in the computer _____.
   (A) KAM
   (B) RAM
   (C) ROM
   (D) PAM

5. _____

6. The random access memory (RAM) is a _____ storage place for sensor inputs.

6. _____

7. Keep alive memory (KAM) can compensate for parts and _____ wear.

7. _____

Computer Control Operation

8. If the engine is below a certain temperature, the ECU operates in _____ mode.

8. _____

9. Voltage sent to sensors by the ECU is the _____ voltage.

9. _____

10. An on-off switch is operated by _____ linkage.
    (A) speed
    (B) pressure
    (C) mechanical
    (D) gear

10. _____

11. A(n) _____ is *not* a type of speed and position sensor.
    (A) magnetic pickup coil
    (B) transducer
    (C) hall-effect switch
    (D) optical sensor

11. _____

12. The _____ sensor uses a piezoelectric element.

12. _____

13. The two main types of temperature sensors are the _____ and _____ sensors.

13. _____
    _____

14. What is the difference between vacuum and manifold absolute pressure? _____

_____

_____

15. The airflow meter uses a spring-loaded _____ to measure the rate of air entering the engine.

15. _____

16. All of the following statements about the mass airflow sensor are true, EXCEPT:
    (A) uses a wire placed across the air path.
    (B) measures airflow with mechanical linkage.
    (C) some use a heated film.
    (D) can compensate for amount of humidity.

16. _____

17. Technician A says that the oxygen sensor can generate its own voltage signal. Technician B says that the ECU may send a reference voltage to the oxygen sensor. Who is right?
    (A) A only.
    (B) B only.
    (C) Both A and B.
    (D) Neither A nor B.

17. _____

18. Some V-type engines have an oxygen sensor in each _____.
    (A) muffler
    (B) exhaust manifold
    (C) tail pipe
    (D) None of the above.

18. _____

19. The throttle position sensor monitors the _____ change of the throttle valve.
    (A) temperature
    (B) opening
    (C) angle
    (D) None of the above.

19. _____

20. The EGR position sensor monitors the _____ of the EGR valve.
    (A) opening
    (B) temperature
    (C) angle
    (D) None of the above.

20. _____

21. If the ECU reads low system voltage, how can it compensate? _____

    _____

    _____

Output Devices

22. The idle speed solenoid is used on many _____ vehicles.

22. _____

23. The idle air control (IAC) performs all of the following, EXCEPT:
    (A) the valve moves the throttle blade to adjust idle speed.
    (B) bypasses airflow around the throttle blades.
    (C) regulates the amount of air entering the engine.
    (D) extends and retracts as necessary.

23. _____

24. The fuel injector is a _____ through which fuel is metered.

24. _____

25. The mixture control solenoid is used only on _____ engines.

25. _____

Ignition Devices

26. Many computer controlled ignitions have a _____ ignition module.

26. _____

27. Distributorless ignition systems do not use conventional _____.
   (A) distributors
   (B) rotors
   (C) coils
   (D) All of the above.

27. _____

28. Relays are used when an output device draws more _____ than the ECU can handle.

28. _____

29. All of the following statements are true about electric cooling fan operation, EXCEPT:
   (A) the ECU energizes the fan relay.
   (B) it will remain off until the sensor signals the ECU.
   (C) it will run whenever the ignition is on.
   (D) the fan relay turns the engine cooling fan on.

29. _____

30. The transmission control solenoid _____.
   (A) modifies transmission fluid flow
   (B) moves the flow control valves
   (C) operates the shift valves
   (D) All of the above.

30. _____

31. When OBD II is fully implemented, all new vehicles will have the same _____.
   (A) engines
   (B) electrical systems
   (C) service manuals
   (D) diagnostic trouble codes

31. _____

32. Identify the parts as indicated in the following illustration.

(A) _____

(B) _____

(C) _____

(D) _____

(E) _____

(F) _____

(G) _____

(H) _____

(I) _____

(J) _____

(K) _____

(L) _____

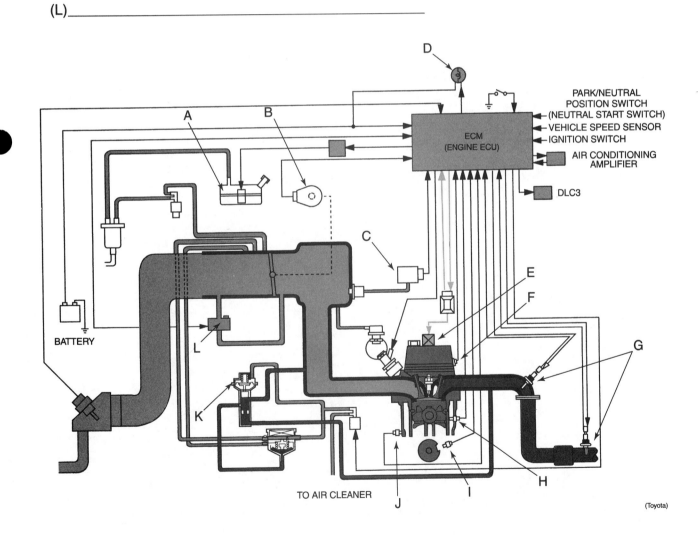

On-Board Diagnostic Systems

33. Early diagnostic systems are referred to as _____ systems.

33. _____

34. An OBD II system will set a trouble code if the vehicle is producing excess _____.

34. _____

35. List four operating conditions that are monitored by OBD II systems. _____

_____

_____

_____

Name _____

Date _____ Period _____

Instructor _____

Score _____ Text Pages 277–302

16

Charging and Starting Systems

Objectives: After studying Chapter 16 in the textbook, and completing this section of the workbook, you will be able to:

- Describe the construction and operation of an automotive battery.
- Explain the operating principles of a charging system.
- Identify the major parts of a charging system.
- Explain the operating principles of a starting system.
- Identify the major parts of a starting system.

Tech Talk: Today's automotive technician must have a solid understanding of the fundamentals of electricity and electronics in order to service and repair automobiles. This chapter will cover the fundamentals of vehicle charging and starting systems. These systems are vital to the operation of almost every system on the vehicle. Without the electrical components discussed here, the ignition system, fuel injection, emission controls, electronic control unit, air conditioner, lights, and radio would not be functional. Studying this chapter will give you an understanding of the battery and charging and starting systems.

Instructions: Read the general instructions on pages 5–6 for answering the workbook questions. Then, as you study Chapter 16 of the text, answer the following questions in the spaces provided.

Battery and Battery Cells

1. A battery stores energy in _____ form.

1. _____

2. The battery is made of separate elements called _____, each with an open circuit voltage of _____ volts.

2. _____

_____

3. Define *positive plate*. _____

_____

4. Define *negative plate*. _____

_____

5. Separators are made of a _____ material such as plastic, rubber, glass, or cellulose fiber.

5. _____

6. Define *electrolyte*. _____

_____

179

7. The modern automobile and light truck battery is a _____ volt unit.
    (A) 6
    (B) 8
    (C) 12
    (D) 24

7. _____

8. When battery electrolyte is low, _____ should be added to bring the level to normal.
    (A) sulfuric acid
    (B) hydrochloric acid
    (C) distilled water
    (D) a mixture of water and acid

8. _____

9. Identify the parts indicated on the following sectioned view of a 12 volt battery.

    (A) _____

    (B) _____

    (C) _____

    (D) _____

    (E) _____

    (F) _____

    (G) _____

    (H) _____

    (I) _____

    (J) _____

    (K) _____

    (L) _____

    (M) _____

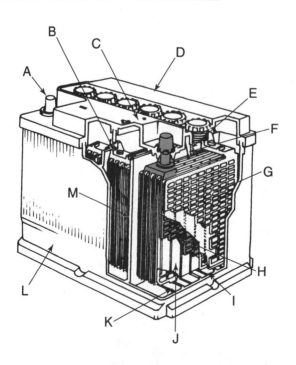

10. Identify the parts of the battery container illustrated below.

(A) _____

(B) _____

(C) _____

(D) _____

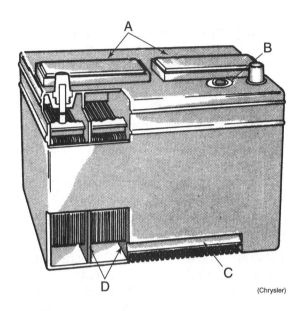

(Chrysler)

Battery Chemical Reaction

11. As the battery discharges, chemical energy is converted into _____.

11. _____

12. If lead peroxide is forming on the positive battery plates, the battery must be _____.

12. _____

13. Specific gravity is the relative weight of a material, compared to the same amount of _____.

13. _____

14. When the battery is fully charged, the specific gravity of the battery is around _____.

14. _____

15. When the float of a hydrometer floats on top of the battery acid, the battery state of charge is _____. If the float sinks, then the battery state of charge is _____.
    (A) low, high
    (B) high, low
    (C) weak, high
    (D) None of the above.

15. _____

16. The lower the hydrometer float sinks, the _____ the state of the battery charge.

16. _____

17. All of the following statements are true about the effect of temperature on a battery, EXCEPT:
    (A) electrolyte temperature does not affect the specific gravity.
    (B) the battery can burst if the electrolyte freezes.
    (C) electrolyte temperature affects the specific gravity.
    (D) if the battery is discharged too much, the electrolyte can freeze.

17. _____

18. Technician A says that a discharged battery will freeze more easily than a fully charged one. Technician B says that specific gravity is not affected by temperature. Who is right?
    (A) A only.
    (B) B only.
    (C) Both A and B.
    (D) Neither A nor B.

18. _____

Battery Ratings

19. Electrical size has almost no relation to battery _____ size.

19. _____

Match the terms on the right with the descriptions on the left.

20. Measure of the number of minutes that a battery can produce 25 amps at 10.2 volts.

(A) Cold cranking amps (CCA)
(B) Cranking amps (CC)
(C) Reserve capacity (RC)

20. _____

21. Standard measurement for modern batteries.

21. _____

22. Measure of maximum current flow at 0°F (–18°C) and 7.2 volts.

22. _____

23. Measure of maximum current flow at 32°F (0°C) and 7.2 volts.

23. _____

24. Indicates how long the battery can operate the electrical system if the charging system fails.

24. _____

25. Sometimes called hot cranking amps (HCA) or marine cranking amps (MCA).

25. _____

Parasitic Battery Loads

26. Define *parasitic battery load.* _____

27. Parasitic battery loads _____.
    (A) draw a large current flow
    (B) often cause the battery to go dead
    (C) draw a small current flow
    (D) None of the above.

27. _____

28. When testing parasitic battery loads, a(n) _____ must be used to determine whether current flow is excessive.

28. _____

Identifying Battery Terminals

29. The positive battery terminal is usually marked _____ or _____.

29. _____

_____

30. The positive terminal can be colored _____.
    (A) green
    (B) black
    (C) red
    (D) blue

30. _____

31. The positive and negative posts can vary in _____.
    (A) shape
    (B) size
    (C) color
    (D) All of the above.

31. _____

32. A dry-charged battery is shipped without _____.

32. _____

Alternator

33. The alternator is driven by a _____ from the engine.

33. _____

34. The alternator changes _____ energy into _____.

34. _____

_____

35. What are the two factors upon which the amount of current induced in a wire passed through a magnetic field depend?

_____

_____

36. The AC generator spins the field coil inside a set of _____.
    (A) housings
    (B) slip rings
    (C) stationary stator windings
    (D) All of the above.

36. _____

37. Direct current from the battery is fed to the alternator field coil by using _____ rubbing against slip rings.

37. _____

38. Identify the parts indicated on the rotor assembly illustrated below.

(A) _____

(B) _____

(C) _____

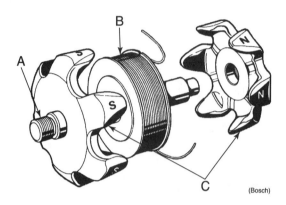

(Bosch)

39. Identify the parts as indicated in the illustration below.

(A) _____

(B) _____

(C) _____

(D) _____

(E) _____

(F) _____

(G) _____

(H) _____

(I) _____

(J) _____

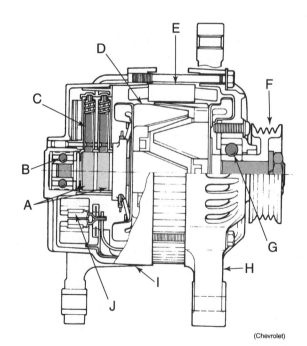

(Chevrolet)

Alternator Output

40. The alternator stator is made of _____ separate windings.

40. _____

41. The stator windings produce _____ alternating current.

41. _____

42. The electrical system of a car is designed to use DC current, so the AC flow out of the alternator must be _____.

42. _____

43. All of the following statements are true about the operation of diodes, EXCEPT:
    (A) they have the ability to allow current flow in two directions.
    (B) they have the ability to change AC current to DC.
    (C) they allow current flow readily in one direction.
    (D) they are located in one end plate or shield.

43. _____

44. The arrangement of the rectifiers allow current to leave the _____ in the proper direction.

44. _____

45. Identify the parts as indicated on the drawing below.

    (A) _____

    (B) _____

    (C) _____

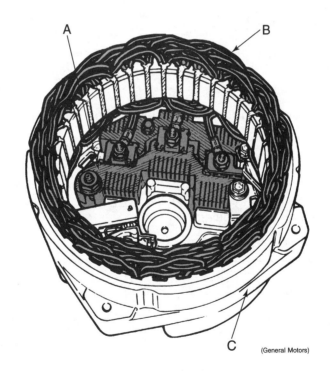

(General Motors)

Alternator Control

46. The alternator can produce much more current than is needed _____.
    (A) at extremely high speeds
    (B) at idle
    (C) at normal speeds
    (D) None of the above.

46. _____

47. At high speeds, potential alternator _____ must be reduced.
    (A) winding
    (B) flow
    (C) input
    (D) output

47. _____

48. Rotor field strength can be controlled through the use of a _____ regulator.

48. _____

49. An electromechanical regulator uses _____ to regulate alternator output.
    (A) contact points
    (B) electromagnets
    (C) springs
    (D) All of the above.

49. _____

50. Technician A says that a single unit electromechanical regulator is used with a dashboard warning light. Technician B says that a two unit regulator is used with a dashboard ammeter. Who is right?
    (A) A only.
    (B) B only.
    (C) Both A and B.
    (D) Neither A nor B.

50. _____

51. Electronic voltage regulators have no _____.
    (A) transistors
    (B) resistors
    (C) contact points
    (D) All of the above.

51. _____

52. Modern regulators are small enough to be installed in the _____.

52. _____

53. The most important part of the electronic regulator is the _____ diode.

53. _____

54. Some alternators are now controlled through the _____, eliminating the need for a separate regulator.

54. _____

Starter System

55. Define *engine cranking*. _____

_____

56. Define *armature loop*. _____

_____

_____

57. A small gear on the starting motor meshes with a _____ on the flywheel.

57. _____

58. To pass electric current into the revolving loop in the starter, the loop ends must be fastened to the _____ segments.

58. _____

59. To pass current out of the loop ends and segments, _____ ride on the segments.

59. _____

60. When current is fed into the starter brushes, current flows through the loop and creates a _____ in and around the loops.

60. _____

61. In starter electrical circuits, the heavy field windings are made of _____.
(A) copper
(B) steel
(C) Both A and B.
(D) Neither A nor B.

61. _____

62. Identify the parts as indicated on the drawing below.

(A) _____

(B) _____

Starter Drive System

63. All of the following statements are true about the ring gear in a starter drive system, EXCEPT:
(A) it is expanded by heat and fitted on the flywheel while hot.
(B) it is attached to the flywheel.
(C) it has 300 to 350 teeth.
(D) it has 150 to 200 teeth.

63. _____

64. A small gear, called a(n) _____, is attached to the end of the starter armature shaft.
(A) action gear
(B) ring gear
(C) two-point gear
(D) pinion gear

64. _____

65. The pinion gear turns _____ times to crank the flywheel one revolution.
(A) 5–10
(B) 15–30
(C) 35–45
(D) 45–65

65. _____

66. The two types of pinion engagement devices are the _____

_____.

67. The overrunning clutch drive is engaged by a(n) _____.
    (A) mechanical solenoid
    (B) electric solenoid
    (C) solenoid plunger
    (D) None of the above.

67. _____

68. The overrunning clutch engages the pinion only when _____

    _____.

69. If an iron core is placed in a coil of wire and current is passed through the coil, the moveable iron core will _____.

69. _____

70. A movable iron core inside an electric coil is used where a _____ motion is desired.
    (A) pull
    (B) push
    (C) Either A or B.
    (D) None of the above.

70. _____

71. In some starters, planetary gears _____.
    (A) are used to obtain desired gear reduction
    (B) use permanent magnets
    (C) mesh with the teeth of the internal or ring gear
    (D) All of the above.

71. _____

72. Identify the parts indicated on the starter motor (*with a Bendix drive*) illustrated below.

    (A) _____

    (B) _____

    (C) _____

    (D) _____

    (E) _____

    (F) _____

    (G) _____

    (H) _____

    (I) _____

    (J) _____

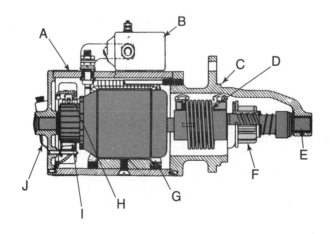

73. Identify the parts indicated on the starter motor illustrated below.

(A) _____

(B) _____

(C) _____

(D) _____

(E) _____

(F) _____

(G) _____

(H) _____

(I) _____

(J) _____

(K) _____

(L) _____

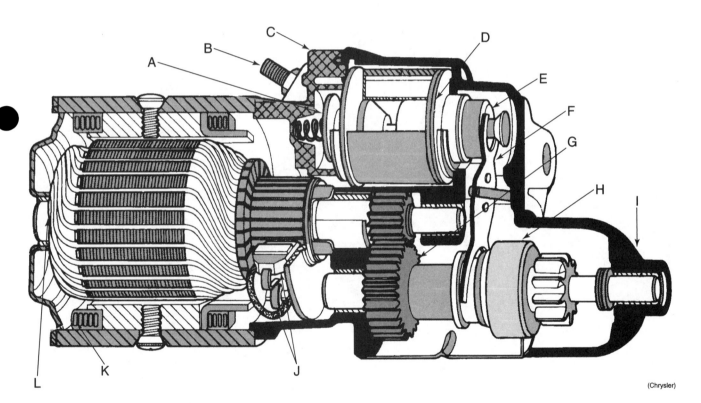

(Chrysler)

Starter Actuating Switches

74. On most cars, turning the key fully clockwise closes the switch to the _____ and the starter begins to operate.

74. _____

75. Technician A says that the neutral safety switch prevents starting a manual transmission vehicle until the clutch is depressed. Technician B says that the neutral safety switch prevents starting an automatic transmission vehicle until selector is in neutral or park. Who is right?
    (A) A only.
    (B) B only.
    (C) Both A and B.
    (D) Neither A nor B.

75. _____

Name _____

Date _____ Period _____

Instructor _____

Score _____ Text Pages 303-322

17

Chassis Electrical

Objectives: After studying Chapter 17 in the textbook, and completing this section of the workbook, you will be able to:

- Identify and define chassis wiring and related electronic components.
- Identify and define circuit protection devices.
- Identify and define common vehicle chassis lights.
- Identify common chassis electrical equipment.

Tech Talk: At one time chassis electrical systems consisted only of the headlights, taillights, horn, and maybe a dome light. Today, however, chassis electrical equipment includes a vast number of lights, solenoids, relays, motors, and electronic devices. To successfully work on modern vehicles, you must know what types of electrical devices are used. This chapter covers chassis electrical equipment and should be studied thoroughly.

Instructions: Read the general instructions on pages 5–6 for answering the workbook questions. Then, as you study Chapter 17 of the text, answer the following questions in the spaces provided.

Chassis Wiring

1. Wiring that will not be used except when the vehicle is being operated is wired through the _____.

1. _____

2. Technician A says that 18 gage wire would be thick enough for a starter cable. Technician B says that 16 gage wire would be thick enough for a single bulb. Who is correct?
    (A) A only.
    (B) B only.
    (C) Both A and B.
    (D) Neither A nor B.

2. _____

3. Wiring harnesses are groups of wires that are _____ together.

3. _____

4. Describe a *printed circuit*. _____

_____

5. A junction block has no _____.
    (A) wires
    (B) plug-in connections
    (C) terminal screws
    (D) bus bar

5. _____

6. Identify the following electrical symbols used on vehicle wiring diagrams.

(A) _____

(B) _____

(C) _____

(D) _____

(E) _____

(F) _____

(G) _____

(H) _____

(I) _____

(J)_____

(K) _____

(L)_____

A   D   G   J

B   E   H   K

C   F   I   L

Circuit Protection Devices

7. Excess current will cause the conductor in a fuse to _____ and break the circuit.

7. _____

8. Most vehicle fuses are installed in the _____.

8. _____

9. The advantage of the circuit breaker is that it does not require _____ after an overload.

9. _____

10. A fusible link is a kind of special _____.

10. _____

11. An overloaded circuit can be detected when the _____ around the fusible link begins to blister and smoke.

11. _____

Vehicle Lights and Light Switches

12. A bulb filament is a _____ element which glows when current passes through it.

12. _____

13. The bulb filament in a bulb is under a _____ to increase filament life.

13. _____

Name _____

14. The outer sealed beam of a four headlight system contains
_____ filaments.

14. _____

15. A composite headlight assembly is a type of _____
headlight.
(A) halogen
(B) sealed beam
(C) light emitting diode
(D) liquid crystal

15. _____

16. The job of the headlight switch rheostat is to _____

_____.

17. Technician A says that a dimmer switch will direct current to
the high and low beams at the same time. Technician B says
that the dimmer switch is usually on the turn signal lever.
Who is correct?
(A) A only.
(B) B only.
(C) Both A and B.
(D) Neither A nor B.

17. _____

18. The stoplight switch is operated by the _____.

18. _____

19. What is the purpose of the canceling cam in the steering column? _____

_____

20. The backup lights are _____ filament lights connected to
the transmission linkage or part of the neutral safety switch.

20. _____

21. _____ lights light up the dashboard gauges and controls.

21. _____

22. _____ lights warn of engine problems, such as charging
system problems, overheating, low oil pressure, etc.

22. _____

23. Lights intended only for illumination of the passenger
sections of the vehicle are called _____ lights.

23. _____

Chassis Mounted Solenoids and Relays

24. Power door lock solenoids are _____ position solenoids.
(A) one
(B) two
(C) three
(D) Varies with manufacturer.

24. _____

25. The horn consists of a _____ which is flexed by the making
and breaking of a set of contact points.

25. _____

26. A motor control relay is used when it is not desired to pass
heavy _____ through the dashboard switches or ECU.

26. _____

27. Most horn circuits make use of a _____ to avoid voltage
drop.

27. _____

Chassis Mounted Motors

28. Switches to control most motors are spring loaded to return to the off position with the exception of the switch that controls the _____ motor.

28. _____

29. Some windshield wiper motors operate the _____.
    (A) sunroof
    (B) windshield washer pump
    (C) power windows
    (D) None of the above.

29. _____

30. Most convertible top motors are used to operate a _____.

30. _____

31. Most power antennas are operated by an _____ relay.

31. _____

Air Bag Systems

32. When an air bag inflates, it is said to _____.

32. _____

33. The diagnostic control module _____.
    (A) contains a safing sensor
    (B) serves as a monitoring system
    (C) can serve as an alternative source of power
    (D) All of the above.

33. _____

34. The inflator module contains all of the following, EXCEPT:
    (A) fabric air bag.
    (B) safing sensor.
    (C) initiator squib.
    (D) inflator.

34. _____

35. Air bag operation involves all of the following, EXCEPT:
    (A) a squib that generates a thermal reaction.
    (B) a gas generating material in the inflator.
    (C) impactor sensors that open upon impact.
    (D) a diagnostic module that sends a signal to the squib.

35. _____

18

Engine Clutches

Objectives: After studying Chapter 18 in the textbook, and completing this section of the workbook, you will be able to:

- Explain clutch operation.
- Name the different types of clutches.
- List the various clutch release mechanisms.
- Define the basic parts of a clutch.
- Identify the parts of a clutch.

Tech Talk: The clutch is used with manual transmissions to connect or disconnect the engine and the drive wheels. Depressing the clutch pedal disengages the engine and transmission. The engine crankshaft will then spin without spinning the transmission gears. When the clutch pedal is released, the clutch locks up to engage the transmission and propel the car. Besides the many design variations, all clutches work on the same basic principles.

Instructions: Read the general instructions on pages 5–6 for answering the workbook questions. Then, as you study Chapter 18 of the text, answer the following questions in the spaces provided.

Clutch Purpose

1. A clutch is a mechanism designed to connect and disconnect the transmission of power from _____ to another.

1. _____

2. The following parts are all components of the clutch, EXCEPT:
   (A) flywheel and clutch linkage.
   (B) pressure plate assembly.
   (C) clutch disc.
   (D) safing sensor.

2. _____

3. The flywheel is thick to enable it to absorb _____.

3. _____

4. The bearing in the center of the flywheel is a support for the transmission _____.
   (A) input shaft
   (B) output shaft
   (C) shock absorber
   (D) None of the above.

4. _____

5. A dual mass flywheel is sometimes used on _____ engines.

5. _____

Clutch Disc

6. The clutch disc splines engage splines on the transmission _____.

6. _____

7. The clutch disc contains friction materials on the _____ side.
   (A) flywheel
   (B) transmission
   (C) Both A and B.
   (D) Neither A nor B.

7. _____

8. Warning: The clutch friction materials can contain _____, a known carcinogen.

8. _____

9. For smooth engagement, the metal disc outer edges are _____.
   (A) split
   (B) cupped
   (C) warped
   (D) Both A and B.

9. _____

Pressure Plate Assembly

10. On a coil spring type of pressure plate, there are usually _____ release levers.

10. _____

11. The coil spring pressure plate uses _____ to release the clutch.
    (A) weight
    (B) pressure
    (C) fingers
    (D) None of the above.

11. _____

12. On the diaphragm pressure plate, the diaphragm fingers take the place of the _____.

12. _____

13. Technician A says that the ball bearing throw-out bearing does not need service during its normal life. Technician B says that the graphite throw-out bearing does not use ball bearings. Who is right?
    (A) A only.
    (B) B only.
    (C) Both A and B.
    (D) Neither A nor B.

13. _____

14. The release fork usually pivots on a _____ head stud.

14. _____

15. Identify the parts indicated on the coil spring clutch assembly shown below.

   (A) _____

   (B) _____

   (C) _____

   (D) _____

   (E) _____

   (F) _____

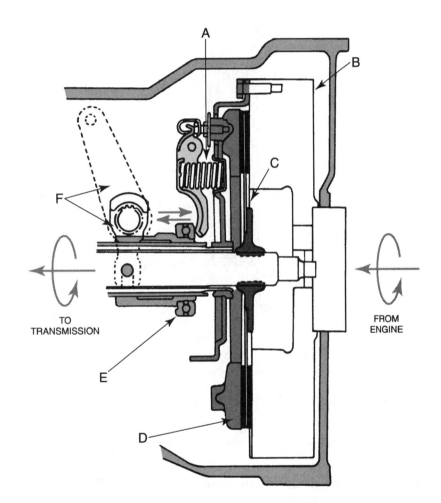

16. Identify the parts indicated on the illustration below.

(A) _____

(B) _____

(C) _____

(D) _____

(E) _____

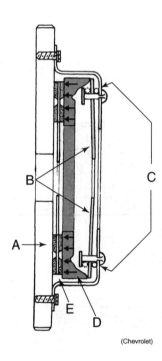

(Chevrolet)

Clutch Operation

17. The mechanical clutch linkage makes use of levers and rods, or _____.

17. _____

18. Hydraulic clutch linkage makes use of a master cylinder operated by depressing the _____.

18. _____

19. Pressure created in the master cylinder is transmitted to the _____ cylinder that operates the fork.

19. _____

20. Some _____ operated clutches are self-adjusting.

20. _____

21. If the throw-out bearing touches the pressure plate with the clutch engaged, what two things could happen? _____

_____

Name _____

22. Define *clutch pedal free travel.* _____

_____

_____

23. Why should riding the clutch be avoided? _____

_____

_____

24. Identify the parts indicated on the clutch system illustrated below.

(A) _____

(B) _____

(C) _____

(D) _____

(E) _____

(F) _____

(G) _____

(H) _____

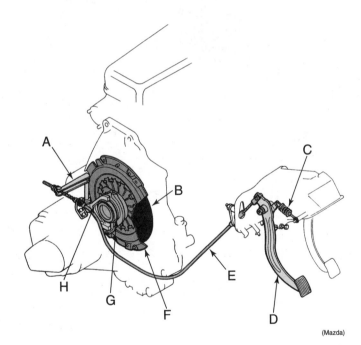

(Mazda)

25. Identify the parts indicated on the hydraulic clutch system illustrated below.

(A) _____

(B) _____

(C) _____

(D) _____

(E) _____

(F) _____

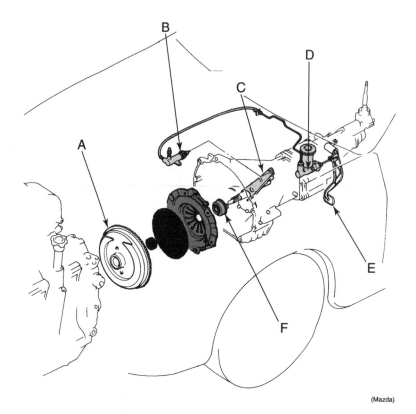

(Mazda)

Name _____

Date _____ Period _____

Instructor _____

Score _____ Text Pages 335–354

19

Manual Transmissions and Transaxles

Objectives: After studying Chapter 19 in the textbook, and completing this section of the workbook, you will be able to:

- Explain how a manual transmission operates.
- Identify the basic parts of a manual transmission.
- Trace power flow through transmission gears.
- Identify the differences between a manual transmission and manual transaxle.
- Identify the similarities between a manual transmission and manual transaxle.
- Identify the basic parts of a manual transaxle.
- Trace power flow through transaxle gears.

Tech Talk: Generally, a manual or standard transmission provides higher fuel economy than an automatic transmission. Since the manual transmission uses a friction clutch, there is no slippage between the engine and transmission. For a manual transmission to provide high fuel economy, however, it must be shifted at the correct shift points. Tachometers or shift lights tell the driver when to shift a manual transmission.

Instructions: Read the general instructions on pages 5–6 for answering the workbook questions. Then, as you study Chapter 19 of the text, answer the following questions in the spaces provided.

Manual Transmissions and Transaxles

1. Transmissions are used on vehicles with _____.
   (A) front engines and front-wheel drive
   (B) front engines and rear-wheel drive
   (C) rear engines and rear-wheel drive
   (D) All of the above.

1. _____

2. Transaxles are used on vehicles with _____.
   (A) front engines and rear-wheel drive
   (B) rear engines and rear-wheel drive
   (C) front engines and front-wheel drive
   (D) Both B and C.

2. _____

3. The simplest engine torque multiplier is a _____.

3. _____

4. By using a torque multiplier, it is possible to adapt the available power of the engine to meet _____.
   (A) changing load conditions
   (B) changing road conditions
   (C) Both A and B.
   (D) None of the above.

4. _____

5. As the engine's strength increases, the speed with which the car is moved becomes _____.

5. _____

6. If the speed of an engine remains constant and its torque is multiplied, the engine will lift

_____.

7. Identify the parts and actions in the drawing below.

   (A) _____

   (B) _____

   (C) _____

   (D) _____

(Honda)

Torque Multiplication Through Gears

8. As engine torque multiplication increases, the car road speed will _____. Car road speed will _____ as multiplication of torque decreases.
   (A) decrease, increase
   (B) increase, decrease
   (C) decrease, remain constant
   (D) remain constant, increase

8. _____

9. Define *gear ratios*. _____

_____

10. The reduction gears provide gear ratios of approximately _____ to about 1.5:1.
    (A) 1:1
    (B) 3.5:1
    (C) .7:1
    (D) 6.0:1

10. _____

11. The direct drive gear has a _____ gear ratio.
    (A) 1:1
    (B) 3.5:1
    (C) .7:1
    (D) 6.0:1

11. _____

12. The overdrive gears have a gear ratio of approximately
    _____.
    (A) 1:1
    (B) 3.5:1
    (C) .7:1
    (D) 6.0:1

12. _____

13. All of the following statements apply to transmission gear
    construction, EXCEPT:
    (A) they are made of aluminized steel.
    (B) they have tough interiors.
    (C) they are made of heat-treated, quality steel.
    (D) they are drop forged while red hot.

13. _____

14. Helical gears _____.
    (A) have teeth cut at an angle to the centerline of the gear
    (B) run quietly
    (C) are stronger than spur gears
    (D) All of the above.

14. _____

15. Helical gears can _____ apart during use.

15. _____

16. Gear end play is controlled by the use of bronze and steel
    _____ washers.

16. _____

17. Define backlash. _____

    _____

18. The transmission case holds all of the following, EXCEPT:
    (A) transmission washers and bearings.
    (B) clutch housing.
    (C) transmission gears.
    (D) transmission shafts.

18. _____

19. The extension housing supports the _____ shaft.

19. _____

20. Sliding gears are moved in and out of _____ by shift linkage.

20. _____

21. Identify the parts and actions indicated on the illustration below.

(A) _____

(B) _____

(C) _____

(D) _____

(E) _____

(F) _____

(G) _____

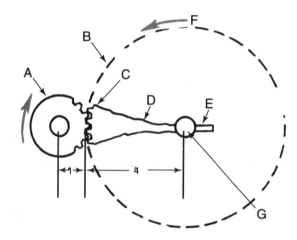

22. Identify the gear tooth shapes illustrated below and the direction in which their teeth are cut in relation to the gear centerline.

(A) _____

(B) _____

(C) _____

(D) _____

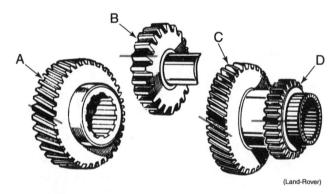

(Land-Rover)

Synchronizing Mechanism

23. Synchronizers are used to reduce gear _____.

23. _____

24. The synchronizer unit brings the _____ speed of two meshing gears together.

24. _____

25. All synchronizers in use today use a _____ or _____ that engages a tapered surface on the part to be synchronized.

25. _____

_____

Transmission Operation

26. When two gears are always engaged, no matter what the gear ratio, they are called _____ gears.

26. _____

27. Identify the parts and actions of the transmission illustrated below in neutral. Also, draw a line with arrows showing power flow through the gears and shafts in each transmission.

(A) _____

(B) _____

(C) _____

(D) _____

(E) _____

(F) _____

(G) _____

(H) _____

(I) _____

(J) _____

(K) _____

(L) _____

(M) _____

(N) _____

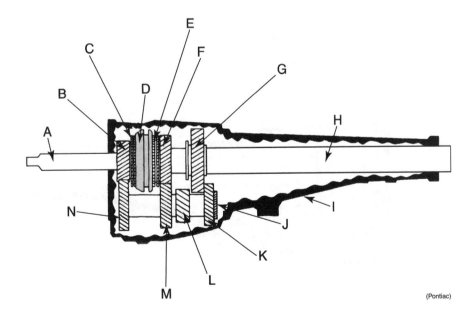

(Pontiac)

28. Identify the parts and actions of the transmission illustrated below in first gear. Also, draw a line with arrows showing power flow through the gears and shafts in each transmission.

(A) _____

(B) _____

(C) _____

(D) _____

(E) _____

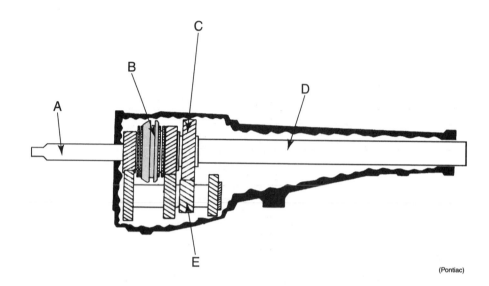

(Pontiac)

29. Identify the parts and actions of the transmission illustrated below in second gear. Also, draw a line with arrows showing power flow through the gears and shafts in each transmission.

(A) _____

(B) _____

(C) _____

(D) _____

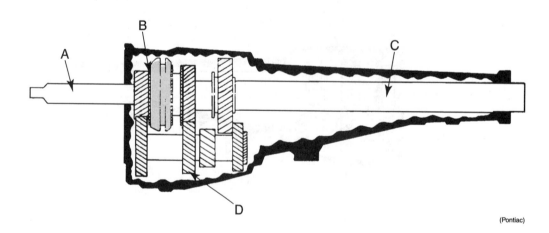

(Pontiac)

Name _____

30. Identify the parts and actions of the transmission illustrated below in direct drive. Also, draw a line with arrows showing power flow through the gears and shafts in each transmission.

(A) _____

(B) _____

(C) _____

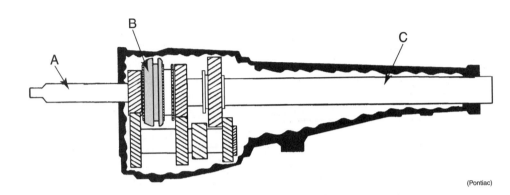

(Pontiac)

31. Identify the parts and actions of the transmission illustrated below in reverse gear. Also, draw a line with arrows showing power flow through the gears and shafts in each transmission.

(A) _____

(B) _____

(C) _____

(D) _____

(E) _____

(F) _____

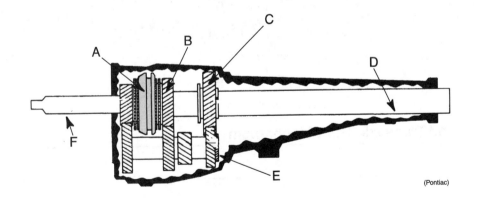

(Pontiac)

Manual Transaxles

32. The transaxle consists of a transmission and _____ unit in a single housing.

32. _____

33. The two types of transaxle designs are based on placement of the vehicle _____.

33. _____

34. Identify the parts indicated on the transaxle illustrated below.

(A) _____

(B) _____

(C) _____

(D) _____

(E) _____

(F) _____

(G) _____

(H) _____

(I) _____

(J) _____

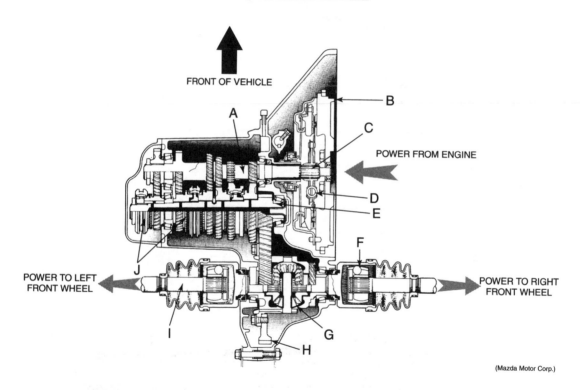

(Mazda Motor Corp.)

Transmission and Transaxle Shift Mechanism

35. Define *shifter fork*. _____

_____

36. To hold the shift mechanism into the gear selected, _____ steel balls pop into notches cut into the cam assembly.

36. _____

37. The shift levers can be operated by linkage attached to a _____ lever.

37. _____

38. Manual transmissions and transaxle are lubricated with
    _____.
    (A) 90 weight gear oil
    (B) 140 weight gear oil
    (C) automatic transmission fluid
    (D) All of the above, depending on the manufacturer.

38. _____

39. Technician A says that speed shifting can damage the synchronizers. Technician B says that speed shifting can damage the gears. Who is right?
    (A) A only.
    (B) B only.
    (C) Both A and B.
    (D) Neither A nor B.

39. _____

40. Identify the parts indicated on the five-speed transaxle illustrated below.

    (A) _____

    (B) _____

    (C) _____

    (D) _____

    (E) _____

    (F) _____

    (G) _____

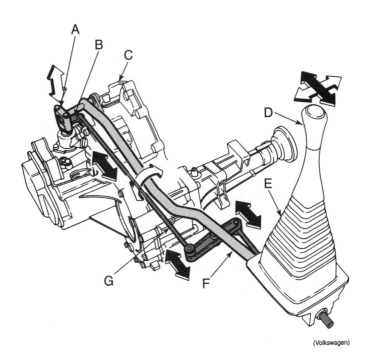

(Volkswagen)

Name _____

Date _____ Period _____

Instructor _____

Score _____ Text Pages 355-366

20
Four-Wheel Drive

Objectives: After studying Chapter 20 in the textbook, and completing this section of the workbook, you will be able to:

- Explain the purpose of four-wheel drive.
- Explain the operation of four-wheel drive transfer cases.
- Identify the components of four-wheel drive transfer cases.

Tech Talk: Four-wheel drive systems are very popular in trucks, off-road vehicles, and even in some passenger cars. Four-wheel drive is also useful for driving on wet or ice-covered roads. Many systems offer the option of part-time operation. Sooner or later you will encounter a four-wheel drive system in need of service. Study this chapter carefully.

Instructions: Read the general instructions on pages 5–6 for answering the workbook questions. Then, as you study Chapter 20 of the text, answer the following questions in the spaces provided.

Four-Wheel Drive

1. The main four-wheel drive components are _____

_____.

2. The transfer case is installed behind the vehicle _____ and   2. _____
   the drive shafts.

3. Both drive shafts are attached to the _____.   3. _____

4. A full-time transfer case drives the _____ axle at all times.   4. _____
   (A) front
   (B) rear
   (C) Both A and B.
   (D) Neither A nor B.

5. A full-time transfer case contains a device to compensate   5. _____
   for the difference in front and rear axle _____.

6. The viscous coupling is filled with _____ fluid.   6. _____

7. Identify the parts indicated on the full-time transfer case illustrated below.

(A) _____

(B) _____

(C) _____

(D) _____

(E) _____

(F) _____

(G) _____

(H) _____

(I) _____

(J) _____

(K) _____

(L) _____

(M) _____

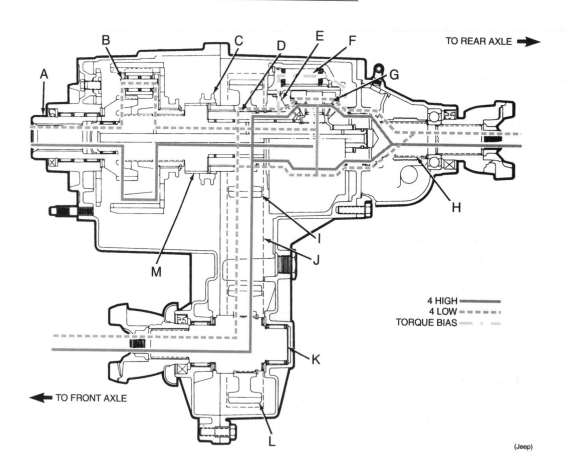

Part-Time Transfer Case

8. Part-time transfer cases should *not* be operated in four-wheel drive when on _____.

8. _____

9. In a part-time transfer case, the gearing ratio for high is typically _____ and _____ for low range.
   (A) 1:2, 2.6:1
   (B) 1:1, 2.6:1
   (C) 2:2, 3.3:1
   (D) 2:2, 3.5:1

9. _____

10. Drive ranges for part-time transfer cases include all of the following, EXCEPT:
    (A) two-wheel high.
    (B) two-wheel low.
    (C) four-wheel high.
    (D) four-wheel low.

10. _____

11. What is windup and its cause? _____

   _____

12. All of the following apply to transfer case lubrication and construction, EXCEPT:
    (A) they have serviceable viscous couplings.
    (B) the housing is partially filled with lubricant.
    (C) it is lubricated by gear oil or transmission fluid.
    (D) leakage is controlled by sealant, seals, and gaskets.

12. _____

13. Identify the parts indicated on the illustration below.

   (A) _____

   (B) _____

   (C) _____

   (D) _____

   (E) _____

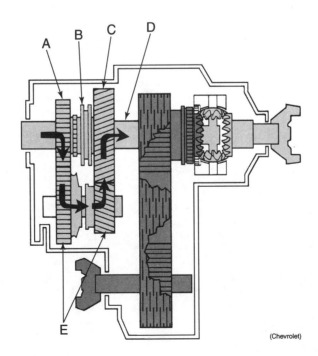

(Chevrolet)

Locking Hubs

14. Technician A says that locking hubs are not controlled by the transfer case. Technician B says that locking hubs are engaged by one-way clutches in the front drive axles. Who is right?
    (A) A only.
    (B) B only.
    (C) Both A and B.
    (D) Neither A nor B.

14. _____

15. Some locking hubs can be automatically released by moving the transfer case to the _____ position and backing up the vehicle a short distance.
    (A) two-wheel
    (B) four-wheel
    (C) front-wheel
    (D) rear-wheel

15. _____

Name _____

Date _____ Period _____

Instructor _____

Score _____ Text Pages 367–394

21

Automatic Transmissions and Transaxles

Objectives: After studying Chapter 21 in the textbook, and completing this section of the workbook, you will be able to:

- Describe the parts of an automatic transmission.
- Describe the parts of an automatic transaxle.
- Explain how both automatic transmissions and transaxles function.
- Identify the major components of an automatic transmission or transaxle.
- Compare the different types of automatic transmissions and transaxles.

Tech Talk: Automatic transmissions and transaxles use a system of hydraulic and electrical controls that operate the mechanical parts. Instead of a friction clutch, a torque converter connects the engine and transmission. Planetary gears replace the sliding gears of the manual transmission. Hydraulic controls operate the holding members to place the planetaries in various gears as vehicle speed and throttle opening dictate. On the latest vehicles, the hydraulic system is controlled by electrical solenoids operated by the vehicle computer. Since the vast majority of vehicles have automatic transmissions or transaxles, the modern technician must learn something about how they operate. Study this chapter carefully to learn the basics of automatic transmissions.

Instructions: Read the general instructions on pages 5–6 for answering the workbook questions. Then, as you study Chapter 21 of the text, answer the following questions in the spaces provided.

Automatic Transmission and Transaxle Components

1. In an automatic transmission or transaxle, the torque converter is used to _____

   _____ .

2. An automatic transmission or transaxle contains _____.
   (A) hydraulic servos and pistons
   (B) one or more oil pumps
   (C) one or more planetary gearsets and shafts
   (D) All of the above.

   2. _____

3. Valves in an automatic transmission or transaxle control and direct _____.

   3. _____

4. The automatic transmission or transaxle must have a means of _____ the fluid.

   4. _____

5. The automatic transmission or transaxle contains a manual control system used by the _____.

   5. _____

6. All of the following statements apply to the transaxle, EXCEPT: 6. _____
   (A) integral differential assembly.
   (B) valve body is on side of case.
   (C) torque converter is part of unit.
   (D) separate differential bolted to transmission case.

7. Identify the parts of the automatic transmission illustrated below.

   (A) _____

   (B) _____

   (C) _____

   (D) _____

   (E) _____

   (F) _____

   (G) _____

   (H) _____

   (I) _____

   (J) _____

   (K) _____

   (L) _____

   (M) _____

   (N) _____

   (O) _____

   (P) _____

   (Q) _____

   (R) _____

   (S) _____

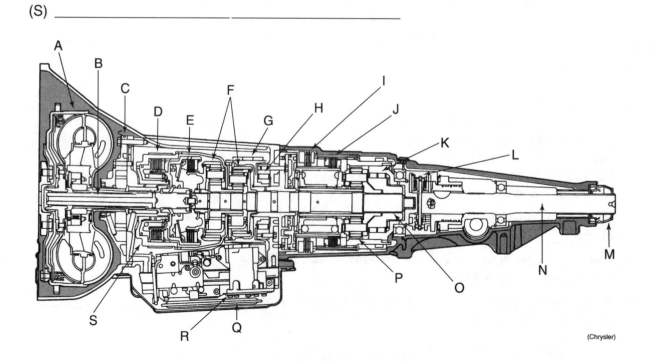

(Chrysler)

8. Identify the parts of the automatic transaxle illustrated below.

(A) _____

(B) _____

(C) _____

(D) _____

(E) _____

(F) _____

(G) _____

(H) _____

(I) _____

(J) _____

(K) _____

(L) _____

(M) _____

(N) _____

(O) _____

(P) _____

(Q) _____

(R) _____

(S) _____

(T) _____

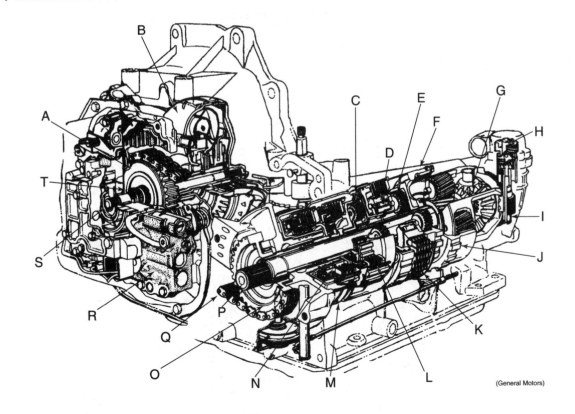

(General Motors)

Torque Converter

9. The part of the torque converter attached to the flywheel is called the _____.

9. _____

10. The part of the torque converter that is attached to the transmission input shaft is called the _____.

10. _____

11. If two fans were facing each other at close range and one was operating, the air blast would cause the other fan to _____.

11. _____

12. Technician A says that the circular motion of fluid in the impeller is called rotary flow. Technician B says that power transfer is from turbine to fluid to impeller. Who is right?
    (A) A only.
    (B) B only.
    (C) Both A and B.
    (D) Neither A nor B.

12. _____

13. The hydraulic coupling is most efficient at _____.
    (A) low speeds
    (B) heavy acceleration
    (C) normal vehicle speeds
    (D) None of the above.

13. _____

Stator

14. What is the job of the torque converter stator? _____

_____

_____

15. When the stator unlocks, the torque converter becomes a _____

_____.

16. Identify the parts indicated in the illustration below.

    (A) _____

    (B) _____

    (C) _____

    (D) _____

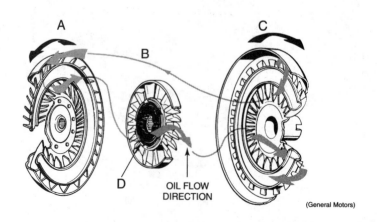

A   B   C

D   OIL FLOW
     DIRECTION

(General Motors)

Planetary Gearsets

17. The lockup converter eliminates _____ and this improves fuel economy.

17. _____

18. The planetary gearset can be used to obtain _____ gears.
    (A) reverse
    (B) reduction
    (C) overdrive
    (D) All of the above.

18. _____

19. Technician A says that planetary gearsets take up more room than sliding gears. Technician B says that planetary gears do not go in and out of engagement. Who is right?
    (A) A only.
    (B) B only.
    (C) Both A and B.
    (D) Neither A nor B.

19. _____

20. The Simpson geartrain is composed of two planetary gearsets with a _____ sun gear.

20. _____

21. The compound planetary gearset contains all of the following, EXCEPT:
    (A) short pinions.
    (B) long pinions.
    (C) compound sun gear.
    (D) ring gear.

21. _____

22. Identify the parts indicated in the illustration below.

    (A) _____

    (B) _____

    (C) _____

    (D) _____

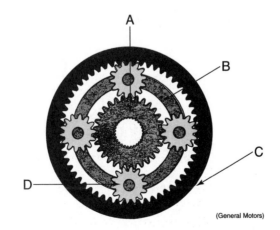

(General Motors)

Holding Members

23. All of the following statements apply to the use of bands and
    their construction, EXCEPT:
    (A) it promotes rotation.
    (B) one end is fastened to a hydraulic piston.
    (C) one end is fastened to the case.
    (D) it is a flexible steel device.

23. _____

24. The band face is covered with a _____ lining.

24. _____

25. A band stops the rotation of a part by locking it to the _____.

25. _____

26. Technician A says that hydraulic pressure is used to release
    servos. Technician B says that hydraulic pressure is used to
    apply servos. Who is right?
    (A) A only.
    (B) B only.
    (C) Both A and B.
    (D) Neither A nor B.

26. _____

27. A clutch pack is composed of clutch discs having _____
    splines.
    (A) internal
    (B) external
    (C) no
    (D) Both A and B.

27. _____

28. In a clutch apply piston, when the hydraulic or fluid pressure
    is removed, the piston is released by _____.
    (A) bolts
    (B) springs
    (C) bands
    (D) All of the above.

28. _____

29. Pressing the clutch discs together causes the _____ and
    hub to be locked together.

29. _____

30. Roller and sprag clutches are the two types of _____ or
    _____ clutches.

30. _____

    _____

31. Identify the parts indicated on the "single-wrap" band illustrated below.

    (A) _____

    (B) _____

    (C) _____

    (D) _____

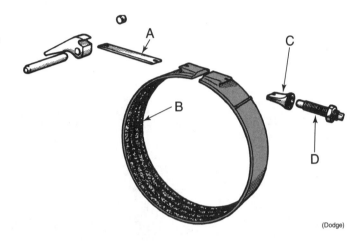

(Dodge)

32. Identify the parts indicated on the "double-wrap" band illustrated below.

    (A) _____

    (B) _____

    (C) _____

    (D) _____

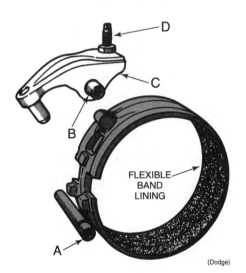

(Dodge)

33. Identify the parts indicated in the illustration below.

(A) _____

(B) _____

(C) _____

(D) _____

(E) _____

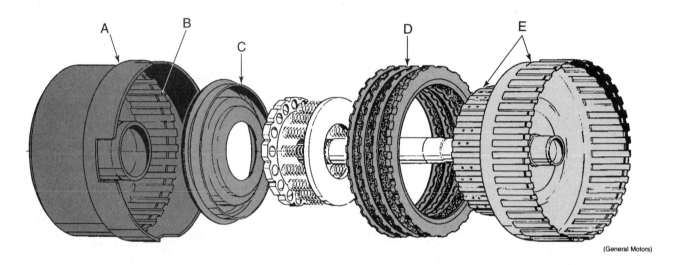

(General Motors)

Hydraulic Control System

34. Liquids cannot be _____.

34. _____

35. List the three types of automatic transmission oil pumps. _____

_____

36. The main pressure regulator controls _____ output.

36. _____

37. To engage the transmission/transaxle in gear, the manual valve is operated by the _____.

37. _____

38. The transmission changes gears when the _____ valve moves.

38. _____

39. Technician A says that the throttle valve tries to move the shift valve to the upshifted position. Technician B says that the governor valve tries to move the shift valve to the downshifted position. Who is right?
(A) A only.
(B) B only.
(C) Both A and B.
(D) Neither A nor B.

39. _____

40. The governor valve is always driven by the _____ shaft.   40. _____

41. Passing gear is obtained by use of a _____ valve.   41. _____

Transmission and Transaxle Shifting

42. The vacuum modulator is used on some older transmissions to operate the _____ valve.   42. _____

43. A three speed automatic transmission or transaxle has _____ shift valves. A four speed automatic has _____ shift valves.   43. _____
    (A) one, two
    (B) two, three
    (C) three, four
    (D) four, five

44. Computer-controlled shifting uses all of the following, EXCEPT: 44. _____
    (A) solenoids controlled by the ECU.
    (B) an electronic control for shifting.
    (C) TV linkage and governor valve.
    (D) shift valves.

45. All of the following statements about transmission fluid are true, EXCEPT: 45. _____
    (A) Dexron III replaces Dexron II.
    (B) Synthetic fluid is used in some automatic transmissions.
    (C) Type A, Suffix A fluid is obsolete.
    (D) Dexron II can be substituted for Dexron III.

46. Identify the parts indicated in the illustration below.

(A) _____

(B) _____

(C) _____

(D) _____

(E) _____

(F) _____

(G) _____

(H) _____

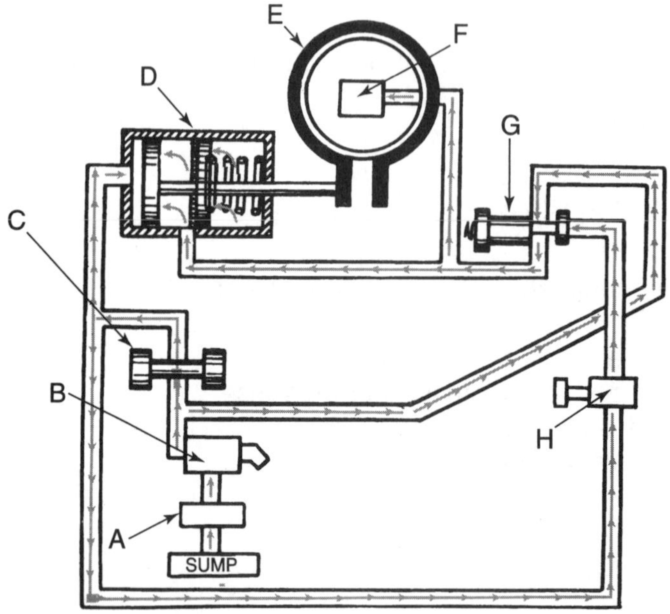

Transmission Lubrication and Fluid Cooling

47. Technician A says that filter shapes can vary. Technician B says that filter locations can vary. Who is right?
(A) A only.
(B) B only.
(C) Both A and B.
(D) Neither A nor B.

47. _____

48. Most transmission fluid is cooled by pumping it into a cooler in the _____.

48. _____

49. The fluid is pumped to the cooler from the _____, which is the hottest part of the transmission.
(A) solenoid
(B) accumulator
(C) torque converter
(D) retainer

49. _____

50. Extra or add-on coolers are installed in front of the _____. They cool by direct contact with the _____.

50. _____

_____

22

Axles and Drives

Objectives: After studying Chapter 22 in the textbook, and completing this section of the workbook, you will be able to:

• List the basic parts of a rear-wheel driveline.
• Explain the function of each rear-wheel drive shaft part.
• List the basic parts of a front-wheel driveline.
• Explain the function of each front-wheel drive axle part.
• Describe various types of front- and rear-wheel drivelines.
• Explain the construction of the solid rear-wheel drive axle assemblies.
• Explain the construction of the independent rear-wheel drive axle assemblies.
• Describe the front drive axles used on four-wheel drives.
• Explain the operation of the ring and pinion.
• Explain the operation of the differential unit.
• Explain the operation of limited-slip differentials.
• Compare rear-wheel and front-wheel drive differential assemblies.

Tech Talk: In the past, the drivelines of all cars and light trucks were much the same. The drive shaft extended from the rear of the transmission to the rear axle and differential assembly and contained two U-joints. All rear axles were similar if not identical. Today, however, the driveline and drive axles include solid and independent rear axles, one and two piece drive shafts, several types of front wheel drives, and a variety of flexible joints including U-joints, CV joints, and tripod joints. The modern technician must be familiar with all of these to service modern vehicles.

Instructions: Read the general instructions on pages 5–6 for answering the workbook questions. Then, as you study Chapter 22 of the text, answer the following questions in the spaces provided.

Rear-Wheel Drive Shafts

1. On a rear-wheel drive vehicle, the drive shaft can be made
   of _____.
   (A) aluminum
   (B) steel
   (C) graphite
   (D) All of the above.

   1. _____

2. Using universal joints allows driveline _____ to change as the vehicle is driven.
   (A) angle
   (B) length
   (C) fluctuation
   (D) Both A and B.

2. _____

3. The type of universal joint in common use is the _____ joint.

3. _____

4. Explain why the drive shaft length changes as the vehicle is driven. _____

   _____

   _____

5. A slip yoke can be described as a _____ sleeve.

5. _____

6. Most modern drive lines are the _____ drive type.

6. _____

7. To reduce excessive drive shaft length, a _____ drive shaft is sometimes used.

7. _____

8. A constant velocity universal joint used on a rear-wheel drive vehicle consists of two conventional _____.

8. _____

9. Identify the parts indicated in the illustration below.

   (A) _____

   (B) _____

   (C) _____

   (D) _____

   (E) _____

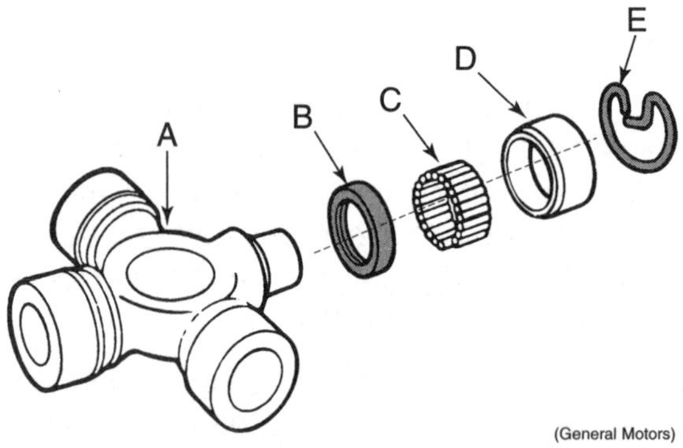

(General Motors)

Constant Velocity (CV) Axles

10. All of the following statements about CV axles are true, EXCEPT:
    (A) CV axles are used on front-wheel drive vehicles.
    (B) CV axles cannot change length as the suspension moves.
    (C) CV axles allow the front wheels to be turned while still delivering power.
    (D) CV axles are smaller in diameter than rear-wheel drive shafts.

10. _____

11. Technician A says that the typical front-wheel drive system   11. _____
    has at least 4 CV joints. Technician B says that some front-
    wheel drive systems use a series of balls in a slotted cross
    and housing assembly. Who is right?
    (A) A only.
    (B) B only.
    (C) Both A and B.
    (D) Neither A nor B.

12. CV joints will usually last the life of the vehicle if the _____   12. _____
    are not damaged.

13. Identify the parts indicated in the tripod constant velocity joint illustrated below.

    (A) _____

    (B) _____

    (C) _____

    (D) _____

    (E) _____

    (F) _____

    (G) _____

    (H) _____

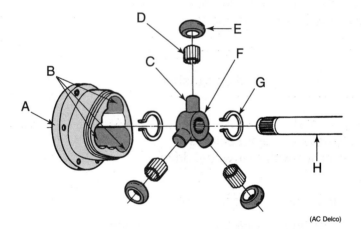

(AC Delco)

14. Identify the parts indicated on the Rzeppa constant velocity joint illustrated below.

(A) _____

(B) _____

(C) _____

(D) _____

Rear-Wheel Drive Axle Assemblies

15. The rear-wheel drive axle must _____.
    (A) allow one wheel to turn faster than the other
    (B) propel the vehicle forward or backward
    (C) hold the wheels on
    (D) All of the above.

15. _____

16. The rear axle provides a(n) _____ for the rear springs.

16. _____

17. Rear axle assemblies _____.
    (A) can be lightly constructed
    (B) may be broken into several major sections
    (C) is used on some vehicles with rear-wheel drive
    (D) Both A and B.

17. _____

18. The rear axle contains the rear _____ assemblies.

18. _____

19. The two basic types of axle housing are the _____ axle and the _____ axle.

19. _____

    _____

20. All of the following statements about axle housings are true, EXCEPT:
    (A) the removable carrier contains the differential assembly.
    (B) the integral carrier contains the ring and pinion.
    (C) the removable carrier contains the ring and pinion.
    (D) the integral carrier is installed in the housing.

20. _____

21. The inner ends of the axles are _____ and are supported by the differential assembly.

21. _____

22. The two methods that are employed to secure the wheel hubs to solid axles are _____ and _____.

22. _____

    _____

23. On independent rear suspensions, the axles resemble _____

_____ .

24. The full-floating axle transmits _____ but does not carry any vehicle weight.

24. _____

25. Most cars use the _____ floating axle.

25. _____

26. Identify the parts indicated on the rear axle shaft illustrated below.

(A) _____

(B) _____

(C) _____

(D) _____

(E) _____

(F) _____

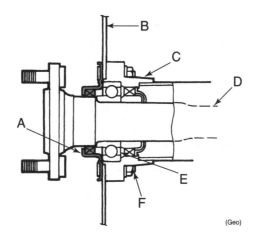

(Geo)

Differential Construction

27. The differential allows both axles to be _____, while allowing them to turn at different _____ when necessary.

27. _____

_____

28. The ring and pinion allow the engine power to make a _____ turn.
    (A) 45°
    (B) 60°
    (C) 90°
    (D) 180°

28. _____

29. The pinion is the smaller _____ gear. The ring is the larger _____ gear.
    (A) driving, driven
    (B) driven, driving
    (C) shifting, driven
    (D) driving, shifting

29. _____

30. When the vehicle is moving straight ahead, the differential side and pinion gears are turning _____.
    (A) in opposite directions at different speeds
    (B) in the same direction, but at different speeds
    (C) in the opposite directions, but at the same speeds
    (D) as a unit

30. _____

31. When the vehicle makes a turn, the pinion gears begin to turn on the _____ shaft.
    (A) axle
    (B) pinion
    (C) drive
    (D) Any of the above, depending on the turning radius.

31. _____

32. The carrier bearings support the _____ case.

32. _____

33. Identify the parts indicated on the rear axle differential unit illustrated below.

    (A) _____

    (B) _____

    (C) _____

    (D) _____

    (E) _____

    (F) _____

    (G) _____

    (H) _____

    (I) _____

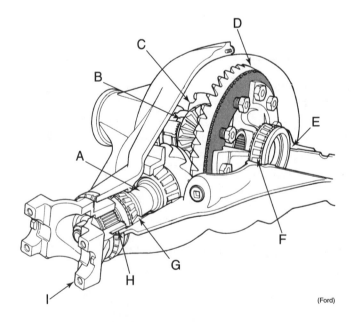

(Ford)

Limited-Slip Differentials

34. When the rear wheel begins slipping, the differential will send power to the wheel that is not _____.

    34. _____

35. Limited slip differentials use clutch _____ or _____ clutches.
    (A) axle
    (B) plates
    (C) cone
    (D) Both B and C.

    35. _____

    _____

36. When the drive shaft drives the pinion gear, the _____ thrust is transmitted to the ring gear.

    36. _____

37. The ramps on the pinion shafts apply pressure to the clutches on both axles when the vehicle is _____.
    (A) driving straight ahead
    (B) making a right turn
    (C) making a left turn
    (D) slipping at one wheel

    37. _____

38. In a cone clutch differential, the cones are under _____ tension.

    38. _____

39. On a Torsen® differential, the _____ have a hard time turning the _____ gears.

    39. _____

    _____

40. Many differential pinion gears enter and drive the ring gear below the _____ of the axles. This gearing setup uses a modified spiral bevel gear which is called a _____ gear.

    40. _____

    _____

Ring and Pinion Adjustments

41. The ring and pinion adjustment in relation to _____ is very important.
    (A) the drive shaft
    (B) the axles
    (C) each other
    (D) All of the above.

    41. _____

42. List the three main ring and pinion adjustments. _____

    _____

43. Ring and pinion gears are always matched and must be installed as a(n) _____.

    43. _____

44. The difference between the number of teeth on the ring gear and pinion gear is the _____.

    44. _____

Axle Lubrication

45. Most rear axles are lubricated by _____.
    (A) SAE 80 to SAE 120
    (B) SAE 10-W40
    (C) automatic transmission fluid
    (D) All of the above.

45. _____

46. Special oil additives are required for use with _____ differentials.

46. _____

47. Oil is thrown all over the internal parts by the _____.

47. _____

Transaxle Differential Assembly

48. Technician A says that a front-wheel drive differential operates in the same manner as a rear-wheel drive differential. Technician B says that the light weight of the average front-wheel drive car means that a limited-slip differential must be used. Who is right?
    (A) A only.
    (B) B only.
    (C) Both A and B.
    (D) Neither A nor B.

48. _____

49. The major difference between a front- and rear-wheel drive axle is that on the front axle, some provision must be made for _____.

49. _____

50. Identify the parts indicated in the automatic transaxle illustrated below.

(A) _____

(B) _____

(C) _____

(D) _____

(E) _____

(F) _____

(G) _____

(H) _____

(I) _____

(J) _____

(K) _____

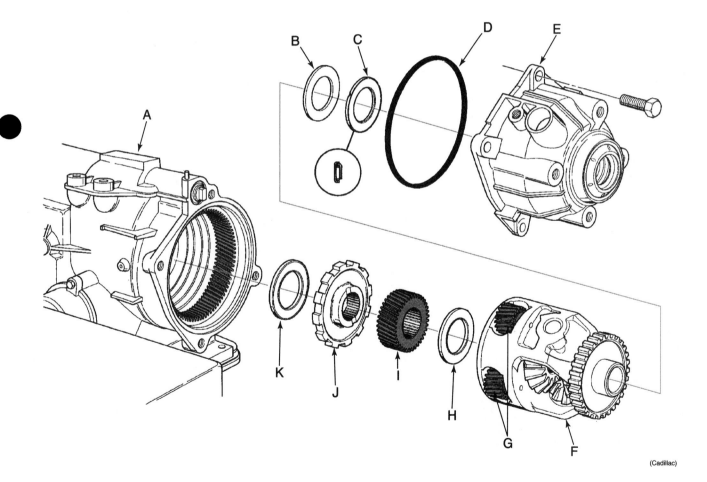

(Cadillac)

Name _____

Date _____ Period _____

Instructor _____

Score _____ Text Pages 419–452

23

Brakes

Objectives: After studying Chapter 23 in the textbook, and completing this section of the workbook, you will be able to:

- Identify the basic parts of the brake hydraulic system.
- Describe the principles used for brake hydraulic system operation
- Identify the basic parts of the brake friction system.
- Describe the principles used for brake friction system operation.
- Explain the differences between drum and disc brakes.
- Describe the principles and components of the vacuum power brake system.
- Describe the principles and components of the hydraulic power brake system.
- Describe the principles and components of anti-lock brake systems.
- List the safety hazards and precautions involved in brake system repairs.

Tech Talk: Modern brake systems have changed greatly over the last few years. In addition to increased use of rear disc brakes and the substitution of other friction materials for the traditional asbestos, more vehicles than ever contain anti-lock brake (ABS) systems. Since brake linings work in part by wearing, brake service is an inevitable part of automotive life. As an automotive technician, you will be involved in brake work sooner or later, and you should learn to service brakes as efficiently as possible. Study this chapter thoroughly.

Instructions: Read the general instructions on pages 5–6 for answering the workbook questions. Then, as you study Chapter 23 of the text, answer the following questions in the spaces provided.

Hydraulic Basics

1. The modern brake system is subdivided into the _____ system and the _____ system.

1. _____

_____

2. Hydraulics is the practical application of the principles of _____ in motion.

2. _____

3. When a liquid is confined and placed under pressure, it cannot be _____.

3. _____

4. Technician A says that liquids can be used to transmit force.
   Technician B says that liquids can be used to increase force.
   Who is right?
   (A) A only.
   (B) B only.
   (C) Both A and B.
   (D) Neither A nor B.

4. _____

5. Identify the parts indicated on the illustration below.

   (A) _____

   (B) _____

   (C) _____

   (D) _____

   (E) _____

   (F) _____

   (G) _____

   (H) _____

   (I) _____

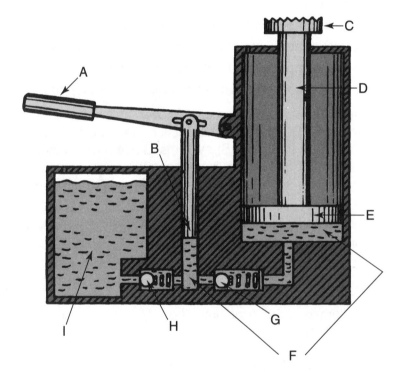

Brake Fluid

6. All of the following statements about brake fluid are true, EXCEPT:
   (A) brake fluid is purposely made to absorb water.
   (B) the fluid freezing point is much lower than during the coldest weather conditions.
   (C) brake fluid is made from various petroleum products.
   (D) brake fluids should not be mixed under normal conditions.

6. _____

7. List some liquids which should *never* be put into the brake system. _____

_____

_____

Master Cylinder

8. Brake system hydraulic pressure is developed in the _____.

8. _____

9. When the driver pushes the brake pedal and exerts a force on the master cylinder _____, this force is transmitted to each wheel cylinder.

9. _____

10. The reservoir provides additional fluid to compensate for _____.
    (A) small leaks
    (B) lining wear
    (C) heat expansion
    (D) Both A and C.

10. _____

11. Modern master cylinders have _____ aluminum pistons.

11. _____

12. A dual brake system provides a margin of _____.

12. _____

13. In the diagonal split brake system, each master cylinder piston operates _____.
    (A) the front or rear brakes
    (B) one front and one rear brake
    (C) one brake, front or rear
    (D) Either A or B.

13. _____

14. The need to pump the brakes under normal conditions indicates a _____.
    (A) faulty brake adjustment
    (B) worn brake linings
    (C) hydraulic system leak
    (D) Any of the above.

14. _____

15. Identify the parts indicated on the illustration below.

(A) _____

(B) _____

(C) _____

(D) _____

(E) _____

(F) _____

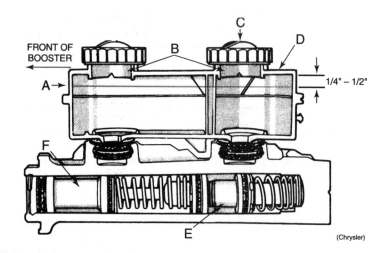

(Chrysler)

Brake System Hydraulic Control Valves

16. The _____ provides even braking and warns of problems.
    (A) pressure differential switch
    (B) metering valve
    (C) proportioning valve
    (D) All of the above.

16. _____

17. The metering valve _____ application of the front brakes.

17. _____

18. The pressure differential switch _____.
    (A) turns the dashboard light on by grounding a switch
    (B) uses a pressure drop to ground the switch for the warning light
    (C) has a small piston floating in a cylinder
    (D) All of the above.

18. _____

19. A combination valve contains _____ of the other system valves.
    (A) one or two
    (B) two or three
    (C) three or four
    (D) four or five

19. _____

20. All of the following statements about brake lines are true,   20. _____
    EXCEPT:
    (A) they are copper plated and lead coated.
    (B) they are made of copper or aluminum tubing.
    (C) they are made of high quality steel tubing.
    (D) they are made of double-walled tubing.

21. Flexible brake hoses are needed in some places since _____

    _____.

22. The _____ pulls the caliper piston back when the brakes are   22. _____
    released.

23. Floating calipers have _____ piston.   23. _____

24. Wheel cylinders are used with _____ brakes.   24. _____

25. What is the purpose of the bleeder screw? _____

    _____

26. If the brake fluid has a low boiling point, all of the following   26. _____
    could happen, EXCEPT:
    (A) the brakes could lock up at high temperatures.
    (B) the brake fluid will change to a gas at high
        temperatures.
    (C) proper braking force cannot be transmitted from the
        master cylinder to the wheels.
    (D) boiling brake fluid can be compressed.

27. Identify the parts indicated on the disc brake assembly illustrated on the right.

    (A) _____
    (B) _____
    (C) _____
    (D) _____
    (E) _____
    (F) _____
    (G) _____
    (H) _____
    (I) _____
    (J) _____
    (K) _____
    (L) _____
    (M) _____

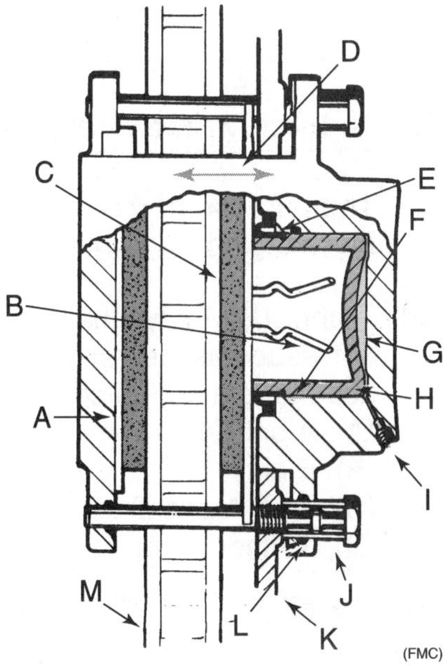

(FMC)

28. Identify the parts indicated on the double-piston wheel cylinder illustrated below.

(A) _____

(B) _____

(C) _____

(D) _____

(E) _____

(F) _____

(G) _____

(H) _____

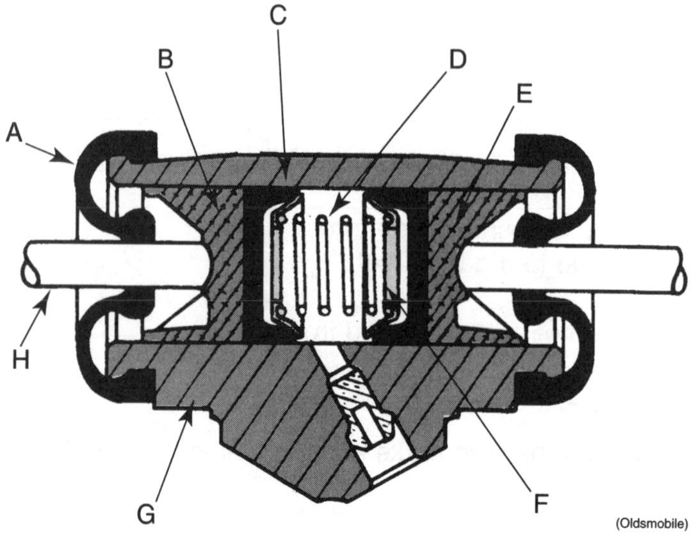

(Oldsmobile)

Brake Friction Members

29. The purpose of the friction members is to stop the vehicle by changing _____ into _____.

29. _____

_____

30. Technician A says that modern brake linings are made without asbestos. Technician B says that metallic linings are used to reduce the chance of brake fade. Who is right?
(A) A only.
(B) B only.
(C) Both A and B.
(D) Neither A nor B.

30. _____

31. Why are brake friction materials designed to melt at a certain temperature? _____

_____

_____

Disc Brake Assembly

32. Why do disc brakes resist brake fade? _____

_____

33. Some rotors have internal fins for _____ purposes.

33. _____

34. Technician A says that disc brakes are prone to grabbing. Technician B says that the hydraulic pressure needed to apply a disc brake is higher than that for a similar drum brake. Who is right?
    (A) A only.
    (B) B only.
    (C) Both A and B.
    (D) Neither A nor B.

34. _____

35. The lining of a disc brake is _____ to the metal plate.
    (A) nailed
    (B) riveted
    (C) bonded
    (D) Both B and C.

35. _____

36. The wear sensor will produce a _____ when the disc brake pads wear out.

36. _____

37. During braking, there is a transfer of weight to the _____ of the car.

37. _____

38. The average braking ratio for front brakes is _____.
    (A) 30% to 35%
    (B) 40% to 45%
    (C) 55% to 60%
    (D) 65% to 70%

38. _____

39. The average braking ratio for rear brakes is _____.
    (A) 30% to 35%
    (B) 40% to 45%
    (C) 55% to 60%
    (D) 65% to 70%

39. _____

40. The backing plate serves as a _____ for the caliper and rotor.

40. _____

Drum Brake Assembly

41. All drum brake assemblies use two brake _____.

41. _____

42. The primary shoe faces the _____ of the vehicle.

42. _____

43. The secondary shoe faces the _____ of the vehicle.

43. _____

44. Brake return or _____ springs are used to pull the shoes together when hydraulic pressure is released.

44. _____

45. The drum is very close to the _____ to keep out water and dust.

45. _____

46. Why is a brake drum designed to be heavy? _____

_____

47. Define *servo action*. _____

_____

48. Define *self-energizing*. _____

_____

49. Servo and self-energizing action reduces the amount of
_____ needed.
    (A) brake fluid
    (B) heat
    (C) friction
    (D) pedal pressure

49. _____

50. Identify the parts indicated on the illustration below.

    (A) _____

    (B) _____

    (C) _____

    (D) _____

    (E) _____

    (F) _____

    (G) _____

    (H) _____

    (I) _____

    (J) _____

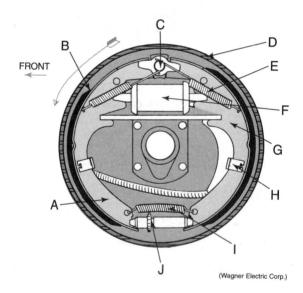

(Wagner Electric Corp.)

Self-Adjusting Brakes

51. Which shoe does more of the braking?
    (A) Primary.
    (B) Secondary.
    (C) Both do the same amount.

51. _____

52. All of the following are types of drum brake self-adjustment   52. _____
   mechanisms, EXCEPT:
   (A) lever.
   (B) link.
   (C) hydraulic.
   (D) cable.

53. Technician A says that some self-adjusters work only when   53. _____
   the vehicle is braked while moving in reverse. Technician B
   says that the self-adjuster will tighten the brakes every time
   that the brakes are applied. Who is right?
   (A) A only.
   (B) B only.
   (C) Both A and B.
   (D) Neither A nor B.

54. On most vehicles, the parking brake is installed on the   54. _____
   _____ wheels.

55. How is the average parking brake applied?   55. _____
   (A) Foot pedal.
   (B) A series of cables and levers.
   (C) Hand-operated lever.
   (D) All of the above.

Power Brake Systems

56. Power brakes are designed to reduce the amount of _____   56. _____
   pressure necessary to stop the vehicle.

57. Vacuum suspended power brake boosters have an internal   57. _____
   piston or diaphragm with _____ on both sides.

58. An atmospheric suspended power brake booster has   58. _____
   atmospheric pressure on _____ of the piston.

59. All of the following statements apply to vacuum power   59. _____
   booster operation, EXCEPT:
   (A) the vacuum power brake has four stages of operation.
   (B) pressing the brake pedal down closes off the atmos-
       pheric pressure to the brake cylinder.
   (C) the vacuum power has two stages of operation.
   (D) it uses both atmospheric pressure and a vacuum.

60. The _____ booster uses two diaphragm plates to increase   60. _____
   booster-to-master cylinder pressure.

61. To provide several brake applications without engine vacuum,   61. _____
   the booster is designed to maintain a vacuum _____.

62. If vacuum to the booster is lost, the _____ will allow some   62. _____
   vacuum to remain in the booster body.

63. If booster vacuum fails completely, the brakes may still be   63. _____
   applied by _____.

64. Identify the parts indicated on the vacuum power booster illustrated below.

(A) _____

(B) _____

(C) _____

(D) _____

(E) _____

(F) _____

(G) _____

(H) _____

(I) _____

(J) _____

(K) _____

(L) _____

(M) _____

(N) _____

(O) _____

(P) _____

(Q) _____

(R) _____

(S) _____

(T) _____

(U) _____

(V) _____

(W) _____

(X) _____

(Y) _____

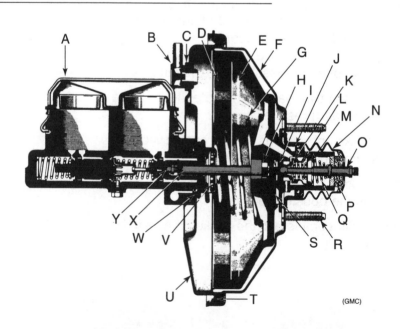

(GMC)

Hydraulic Pressure-Operated Power Booster

65. Technician A says that hydraulic brake boosters are often used with diesel engines. Technician B says that hydraulic pressure for the brake booster is often supplied by the power steering pump. Who is right?
(A) A only.
(B) B only.
(C) Both A and B.
(D) Neither A nor B.

65. _____

66. What is the purpose of the accumulator on the hydraulic power booster? _____

_____

_____

Anti-Lock Brake Systems (ABS)

67. The ABS system used on some trucks operates only on the _____ wheels.
(A) front
(B) rear

67. _____

68. Define *brake pulsing*. _____

_____

69. Wheel speed sensors are used to determine whether any wheels are _____.

69. _____

70. Technician A says that many ABS systems have self-diagnostics. Technician B says that the base brakes of an ABS system will not interchange with non-ABS systems. Who is right?
(A) A only.
(B) B only.
(C) Both A and B.
(D) Neither A nor B.

70. _____

71. When the ABS system detects a wheel locking up, it _____ hydraulic pressure to the brakes of that wheel.

71. _____

72. To increase traction, a traction control system can _____.
(A) reduce engine power
(B) operate the brake system
(C) change transmission gears
(D) Both A and B.

72. _____

73. Traction control systems provide higher levels of _____ performance.

73. _____

74. Identify the parts indicated on the anti-lock brake system illustrated below.

(A) _____

(B) _____

(C) _____

(D) _____

(E) _____

(F) _____

(G) _____

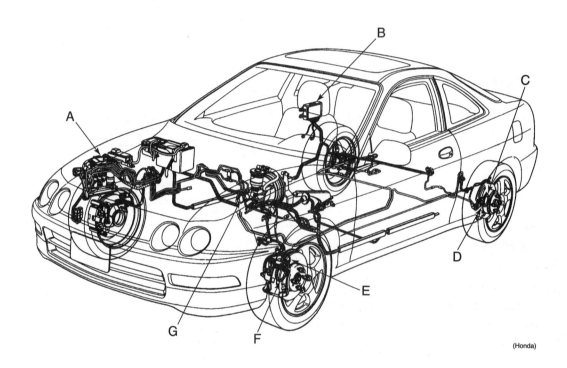

(Honda)

75. Identify the parts indicated on the rear-wheel anti-lock (RWAL) breaking system illustrated below.

(A) _____

(B) _____

(C) _____

(D) _____

(E) _____

(F) _____

(G) _____

(H) _____

(I) _____

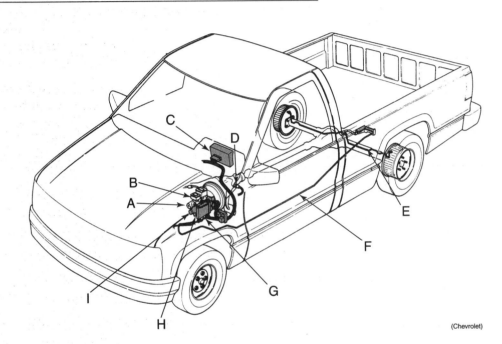

(Chevrolet)

Name _____

Date _____ Period _____

Instructor _____

Score _____ Text Pages 453–478

24

Suspension Systems

Objectives: After studying Chapter 24 in the textbook, and completing this section of the workbook, you will be able to:

- Identify the purpose of the suspension system.
- Explain the difference between sprung and unsprung weight.
- Name the different types of vehicle frames.
- Describe the function and operation of chassis springs.
- Describe the function of control arms and struts.
- Describe the function and operation of ball joints.
- Describe the function and operation of shock absorbers.
- Explain the differences between conventional and MacPherson strut suspensions.
- Explain the operation of front suspension components.
- Explain the operation of rear suspension components.
- Explain the operation of automatic level controls.

Tech Talk: To improve fuel economy and performance, today's vehicles are being built much lighter. Lighter vehicles require more sophisticated suspension systems to preserve ride quality. There are many variations in the design of modern suspension systems and between front and rear suspensions. However, they all operate on basic principles and have the same basic purpose—reducing road shock transferred to the passenger compartment and improving handling. The automotive technician must learn all he can to deal with these new systems.

Instructions: Read the general instructions on pages 5–6 for answering the workbook questions. Then, as you study Chapter 24 of the text, answer the following questions in the spaces provided.

The Need for a Suspension System

1. The modern suspension system allows the vehicle to _____ and _____ well.

1. _____

   _____

2. Sprung weight refers to the parts of the vehicle that are supported by the _____ system.

2. _____

3. All of the following are examples of unsprung weight,
   EXCEPT:
   (A) the rear axle.
   (B) the transmission.
   (C) the wheels.
   (D) the steering knuckles.

3. _____

4. The car frame provides a _____

   _____.

5. There are two common types of frames in use today: the
   _____ frame to which the body is bolted and the _____ in
   which the frame and body are welded together as a single
   unit.

5. _____

   _____

Springs

6. Every vehicle has some kind of spring between the frame or
   body and the _____.

6. _____

7. List the three types of springs in use today. _____

   _____

8. Where are leaf springs usually used? _____

   _____

9. The semielliptical leaf spring consists of a number of flat
   steel _____, bolted together to form a single unit.

9. _____

10. Rebound clips keep the spring leaves from _____ when the
    spring rebounds _____.

10. _____

    _____

11. A hinge type of shackle is used to allow the spring to change
    _____ as it flexes up and down.

11. _____

12. A rubber-bushed shackle uses rubber bushing between the
    spring eye and the spring _____.

12. _____

13. Technician A says that coil springs are used in many con-
    ventional front and rear suspensions. Technician B says that
    coil springs are used in MacPherson strut suspensions.
    Who is right?
    (A) A only.
    (B) B only.
    (C) Both A and B.
    (D) Neither A nor B.

13. _____

14. A torsion bar is designed to _____ to absorb shocks.

14. _____

15. Identify the parts indicated on the illustration below.

(A) _____

(B) _____

(C) _____

(D) _____

(E) _____

(F) _____

(G) _____

(H) _____

(I) _____

(J) _____

(K) _____

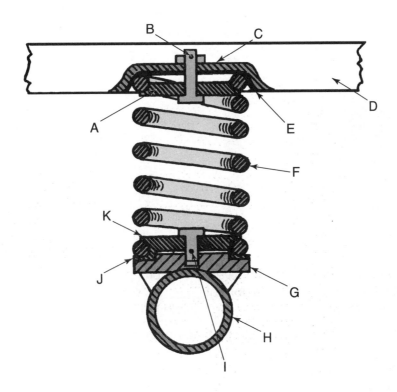

16. Identify the parts indicated on the illustration below.

(A) _____

(B) _____

(C) _____

(D) _____

(E) _____

(F) _____

(G) _____

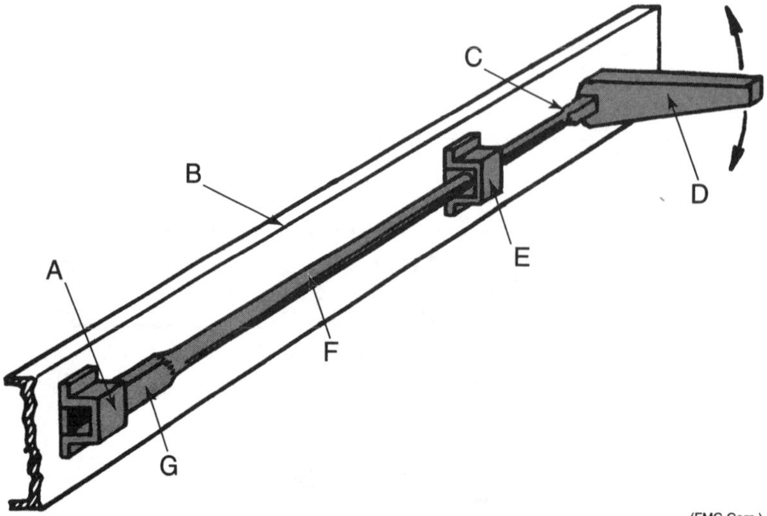

(FMC Corp.)

Shock Absorbers

17. After a suspension spring has been compressed by a bump in the road, it will attempt to return to its normal _____. In so doing, it will rebound, causing the body of the vehicle to lift.

17. _____

18. When a spring continues to rebound several times after its initial compression, it is called _____.
    (A) bar oscillation
    (B) shock oscillation
    (C) spring oscillation
    (D) None of the above.

18. _____

19. To overcome spring bounce, a dampening device, called a _____ is used.
    (A) torsion bar
    (B) shock absorber
    (C) retainer
    (D) crossmember

19. _____

20. The telescoping shock absorber contains _____.   20. _____
    (A) a series of valves
    (B) a piston and piston rod
    (C) an inner cylinder
    (D) All of the above.

21. Identify the parts indicated on the shock absorber illustrated below.

    (A) _____

    (B) _____

    (C) _____

    (D) _____

    (E) _____

    (F) _____

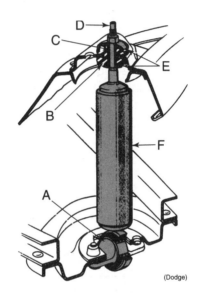

(Dodge)

Air Shock Absorbers

22. Technician A says that air shock absorbers have hydraulic   22. _____
    dampening systems. Technician B says that air shock
    absorbers have a sealed air chamber. Who is right?
    (A) A only.
    (B) B only.
    (C) Both A and B.
    (D) Neither A nor B.

23. All vehicles have _____ to keep the wheel in position.   23. _____
    (A) control arms
    (B) torsion bars
    (C) struts
    (D) Both A and C.

Ball Joints

24. What are the two functions of the ball joint? _____

_____

25. _____ loading means that forces are trying to pull the ball
    joint apart.
    (A) Bearing
    (B) Ball joint
    (C) Tension
    (D) None of the above.

25. _____

26. The bearing surfaces of a preloaded ball joint are in _____
    contact.

26. _____

Stabilizer Bars

27. The stabilizer bar is installed to prevent _____ on corners.

27. _____

28. Technician A says that stabilizer bars are used on the front
    of the vehicle only. Technician B says that twisting forces are
    applied to the stabilizer bar when the vehicle makes a turn.
    Who is right?
    (A) A only.
    (B) B only.
    (C) Both A and B.
    (D) Neither A nor B.

28. _____

Front Suspension Systems

29. Define *independent front suspension*. _____

_____

30. A few four-wheel drive vehicles and large trucks continue to
    use _____ axle front suspension systems.

30. _____

31. Identify the parts indicated on the front suspension system illustrated below.

   (A) _____ _____

   (B) _____

   (C) _____

   (D) _____

   (E) _____

   (F) _____

   (G) _____

   (H) _____

   (I) _____

   (J) _____

   (K) _____

   (L) _____

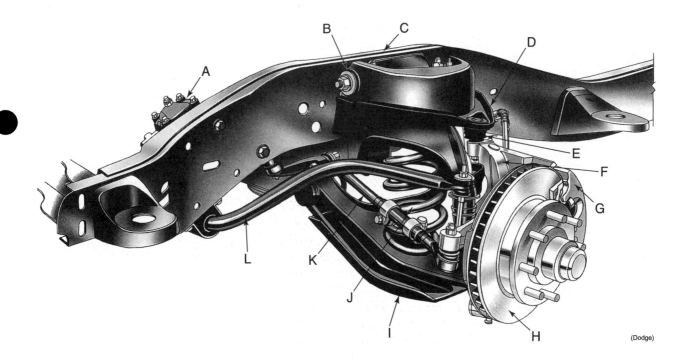

(Dodge)

MacPherson Strut Front Suspension

32. The MacPherson strut assembly contains a _____ spring.   32. _____
    (A) leaf
    (B) coil
    (C) torsion bar
    (D) All of the above, depending on the manufacturer.

33. The damper in the MacPherson strut takes the place of the   33. _____
    _____ in the conventional suspension system.

34. The major advantage of the MacPherson strut is _____.   34. _____
    (A) smoother ride
    (B) quicker rebound
    (C) compact design
    (D) extreme strength

35. Identify the parts indicated on the MacPherson strut assembly illustrated on the facing page.

    (A) _____

    (B) _____

    (C) _____

    (D) _____

    (E) _____

    (F) _____

    (G) _____

    (H) _____

    (I) _____

    (J) _____

    (K) _____

    (L) _____

    (M) _____

    (N) _____

    (O) _____

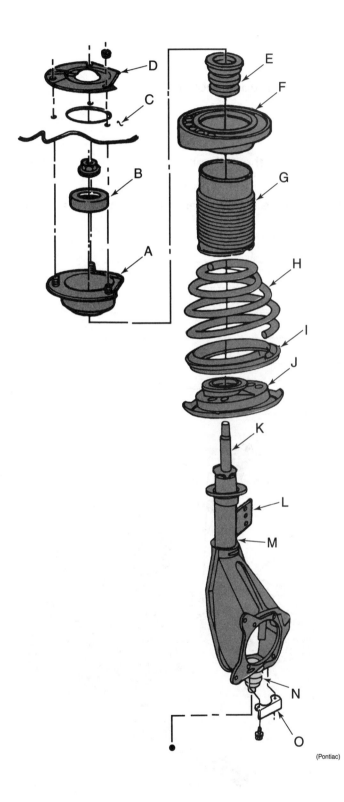

(Pontiac)

Rear Suspension Systems

36. Solid axle rear suspensions may use _____ springs.   36. _____
    (A) leaf
    (B) coil
    (C) Both A and B.
    (D) Neither A nor B.

37. Why are rear shock absorbers straddle mounted? _____
    _____
    _____

38. On an independent rear axle, the differential housing is   38. _____
    attached to the vehicle _____.

39. Identify the parts indicated on the rear suspension system illustrated below.

    (A) _____

    (B) _____

    (C) _____

    (D) _____

    (E) _____

    (F) _____

    (G) _____

    (H) _____

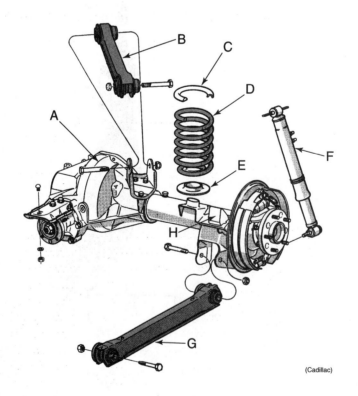

(Cadillac)

40. Identify the parts indicated on the rear suspension system illustrated below.

(A) _____

(B) _____

(C) _____

(D) _____

(E) _____

(F) _____

(G) _____

(H) _____

(I) _____

(J) _____

(K) _____

(L) _____

(M) _____

(N) _____

(O) _____

(P) _____

(Q) _____

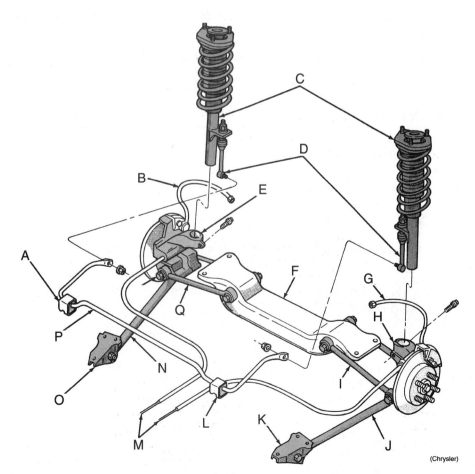

(Chrysler)

Suspension Lubrication

41. Chassis grease is compounded to _____.
    (A) lubricate well and adhere to moving parts
    (B) enter fittings regularly and resist water
    (C) stay flexible at low temperatures
    (D) All of the above.

41. _____

42. Where chassis grease is needed _____ are provided.

42. _____

43. If plugs are used, they must be replaced with _____.

43. _____

Automatic Level Control

44. A basic automatic level control will get its air supply from a(n) _____.
    (A) vacuum operated air pump
    (B) shop or other external air compressor
    (C) electrically operated air pump
    (D) Either A or C.

44. _____

45. When air pressure in the reservoir is equal to the pressure generated by the pump, what happens?
    (A) The pump starts.
    (B) The pump stops.
    (C) Excess air is bled off.
    (D) None of the above.

45. _____

46. The amount of air pressure delivered to the shock absorbers is controlled by a _____ control sensor.

46. _____

47. What prevents the sensor in question number 46 from being activated by bumps? _____

Computerized Ride Control Systems

48. Computerized ride control systems contain _____.
    (A) input sensors
    (B) a ride control computer
    (C) actuators
    (D) All of the above.

48. _____

49. On a computerized ride control system, the output actuators control the flow of _____ to the shock absorbers.

49. _____

50. The control module can override the driver ride settings under all of the following conditions, EXCEPT:
    (A) hard braking.
    (B) heavy acceleration.
    (C) slick roads.
    (D) sharp turns.

50. _____

Name _____

Date _____ Period _____

Instructor _____

Score _____ Text Pages 479–502

25

Steering Systems

Objectives: After studying Chapter 25 in the textbook, and completing this section of the workbook, you will be able to:

- Identify the major parts of a parallelogram steering system.
- Identify the major parts of a rack-and-pinion steering system.
- Compare the parallelogram and rack-and-pinion steering systems.
- Explain the operation of a parallelogram power steering gear.
- Explain the operation of a rack-and-pinion power steering gear.
- Describe the different types of power steering pumps.

Tech Talk: Vehicle steering is one of the most basic, and often overlooked, systems on the vehicle. Modern steering systems are either parallelogram systems or rack-and-pinion systems. Both are available in manual and power-assisted versions. Failure to properly service the steering assembly can cause poor handling and tire wear, or even loss of steering control. Study this chapter carefully to learn how to properly service the steering system.

Instructions: Read the general instructions on pages 5–6 for answering the workbook questions. Then, as you study Chapter 25 of the text, answer the following questions in the spaces provided.

Steering System

1. List the three main assemblies of the steering system. _____

   _____

2. The spindle assemblies swivel on _____.   2. _____

3. The wheel and brake drum or rotor _____ on the spindle.   3. _____

Steering Linkage

4. The parallelogram linkage was the most common arrange-   4. _____
   ment and is still used on _____.
   (A) large cars
   (B) large pickup trucks
   (C) small cars
   (D) Both A and B.

5. The pitman arm is attached to the output shaft of the _____.   5. _____

6. What purpose does the center link serve? _____

_____

7. What is the purpose of the idler arm? _____

_____

8. All of the following statements about tie rods are true,   8. _____
   EXCEPT:
   (A) the parallelogram system has two tie rods.
   (B) there is a ball joint socket on each tie rod.
   (C) connect the steering arms to the center link.
   (D) the parallelogram system has four tie rods.

9. The tie rod sleeve is used to adjust _____.   9. _____
   (A) the length of the assembly
   (B) vehicle toe
   (C) vehicle height
   (D) Both A and B.

10. The _____ is a steering linkage part used on a rack-and-   10. _____
    pinion steering system.
    (A) center link
    (B) idler arm
    (C) pitman arm
    (D) None of the above.

11. How are toe adjustments made on a rack-and-pinion steering system? _____

_____

12. Identify the parts indicated on the parallelogram linkage illustrated below.

    (A) _____

    (B) _____

    (C) _____

    (D) _____

    (E) _____

    (F) _____

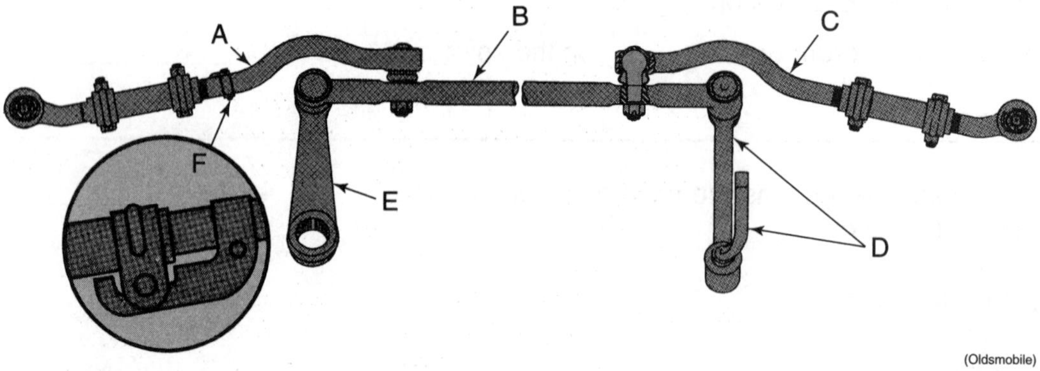

(Oldsmobile)

Steering Wheel, Steering Shaft, and Steering Gear

13. Technician A says that the smaller the steering wheel, the
    less turning effort is required. Technician B says that the
    upper steering shaft is often made in two sections for safety.
    Who is right?
    (A) A only.
    (B) B only.
    (C) Both A and B.
    (D) Neither A nor B.

    13. _____

14. Identify the parts indicated in the worm and roller manual steering gear illustrated below.

    (A) _____

    (B) _____

    (C) _____

    (D) _____

    (E) _____

    (F) _____

    (G) _____

    (H) _____

    (I) _____

    (J) _____

    (K) _____

    (L) _____

    (M) _____

    (N) _____

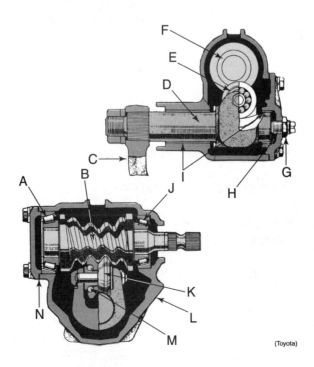

(Toyota)

15. Identify the parts indicated in the rack-and-pinion assembly illustrated below.

(A) _____

(B) _____

(C) _____

(D) _____

(E) _____

(F) _____

(G) _____

(H) _____

(I) _____

(J) _____

(K) _____

(L) _____

(M) _____

(N) _____

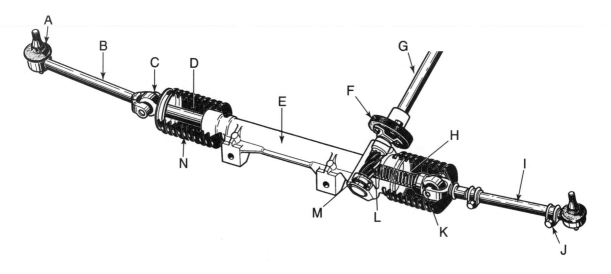

Power Steering

16. All of the following statements about power steering sys-   16. _____
    tems are true, EXCEPT:
    (A) all modern power steering systems are integral
        systems.
    (B) the control valve is activated by the driver.
    (C) the hydraulic piston is outside of the steering gear
        assembly.
    (D) the power steering gear contains all of the basic man-
        ual gear parts.

Name _____

17. In a self-contained power steering gear assembly, pressure is directed to the power chamber through a _____ valve.

17. _____

18. Technician A says, that in the neutral or straight-ahead position on some power steering gears, hydraulic pressure is directed to both sides of the power piston. Technician B says that in the neutral position, hydraulic pressure is directed to neither power chamber. Who is right?
(A) A only.
(B) B only.
(C) Both A and B.
(D) Neither A nor B.

18. _____

19. A steering unit that uses a spool valve that rotates a small amount inside the valve body is referred to as a(n) _____.
(A) rotary spool valve
(B) open-center
(C) three-way valve
(D) All of the above.

19. _____

20. The hydraulic pressure needed to operate the power steering system is supplied by a pump which is usually driven by the engine through a _____.

20. _____

21. Power steering gears and pumps are connected by _____ and _____.

21. _____
_____

22. When the hydraulic power fails, the vehicle can still be steered because there is a _____ connection through the gears.

22. _____

23. Most modern power steering systems use _____ as fluid.
(A) engine oil
(B) transmission fluid
(C) brake fluid
(D) special power steering fluid

23. _____

24. Identify the parts indicated on the power steering unit illustrated on the facing page.

(A) _____

(B) _____

(C) _____

(D) _____

(E) _____

(F) _____

(G) _____

(H) _____

(I) _____

(J) _____

(K) _____

(L) _____

(M) _____

(N) _____

(O) _____

(P) _____

(Q) _____

(R) _____

(S) _____

(T) _____

(U) _____

(V) _____

(W) _____

(X) _____

(Y) _____

(Z) _____

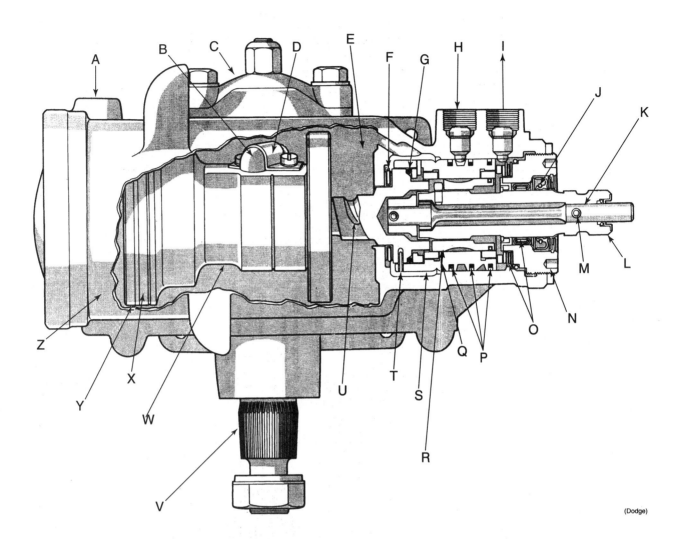

(Dodge)

25. Identify the parts indicated on the illustration below.

(A) _____

(B) _____

(C) _____

(D) _____

(E) _____

(F) _____

(G) _____

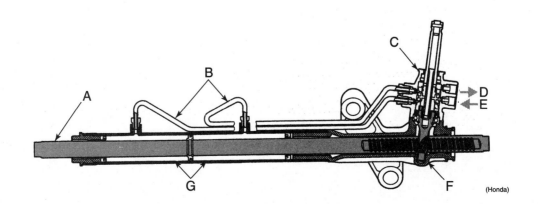

(Honda)

26

Wheels and Tires

Objectives: After studying Chapter 26 in the textbook, and completing this section of the workbook, you will be able to:

- Describe basic wheel rim design and construction.
- Describe various types of wheel hubs and bearings.
- Explain the methods of modern tire construction.
- Explain different tire construction and size designations.
- Identify tire and wheel size designations.
- Select appropriate tire inflation and rotation procedures.

Tech Talk: The basic principles of wheel rims, hubs and bearings, and tires have not changed much in the last half century. However, the increased use of custom wheels and front wheel drives, the adoption of metric measurements, and the increased use of radial tires, continue to change size, rating, and service information. Studying this chapter thoroughly will help you to identify the major types of wheel rims, identify the differences in wheel hubs and bearings used in both front- and rear-wheel drive vehicles, and use the most current tire rating system.

Instructions: Read the general instructions on pages 5–6 for answering the workbook questions. Then, as you study Chapter 26 of the text, answer the following questions in the spaces provided.

Wheels

1. In the past, all wheel rims were made of _____.

1. _____

2. Wheel rims can be made of _____ or other materials.
   (A) magnesium
   (B) graphite
   (C) aluminum
   (D) All of the above.

2. _____

3. The center section of a rim is "dropped" to allow the tire to be _____.

3. _____

4. To prevent the tire from coming off the rim during a blowout, some rims have _____.

4. _____

5. _____ is not a measurement of rim size.
   (A) Rim width
   (B) Bolt pattern
   (C) Rim diameter
   (D) Flange width

5. _____

6. Identify the parts indicated on the drop center wheel illustrated below.

   (A) _____

   (B) _____

   (C) _____

   (D) _____

   (E) _____

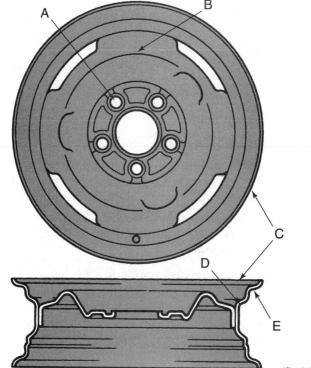

(Chrysler)

Wheel Lug Bolts and Nuts

7. Some vehicles use _____ that thread directly into the hub.

7. _____

8. The wheel is held to the hub with threaded studs called wheel _____.

8. _____

9. Tapered nuts that are sometimes used to hold the wheel to the hub are called _____.

9. _____

10. Torque sticks limit the output of a(n) _____. If a torque stick is not available, the wheel should be tightened with a(n) _____.
    (A) torque wrench, impact wrench
    (B) lug wrench, torque wrench
    (C) impact wrench, torque wrench
    (D) torque wrench, lug wrench

10. _____

Wheel Hubs and Bearings

11. The wheel hubs are the mounting surface for the _____ and tire.

11. _____

12. Wheel hubs revolve around the steering knuckle spindle on _____ bearings .
    (A) tapered roller
    (B) ball
    (C) Either A or B.
    (D) Neither A nor B.

12. _____

13. Technician A says that tapered roller bearings can be adjusted. Technician B says that tapered bearings can be cleaned and repacked. Who is right?
    (A) A only.
    (B) B only.
    (C) Both A and B.
    (D) Neither A nor B.

13. _____

14. A castellated nut is a nut with _____.

14. _____

15. The safety washer has a tab that rides in a _____ in the spindle.

15. _____

16. To hold the nut in place, a _____ is installed through the holes in the nut and spindle.

16. _____

17. Technician A says that a staked nut is dented into a groove in the spindle. Technician B says that most front-wheel drive bearings use a staked nut to hold the bearing in place. Who is right?
    (A) A only.
    (B) B only.
    (C) Both A and B.
    (D) Neither A nor B.

17. _____

Tires

18. Tires provide _____.
    (A) traction
    (B) cushioning
    (C) Both A and B.
    (D) Neither A nor B.

18. _____

19. Tires are constructed of various types of _____ and _____ rubber.

19. _____

_____

20. Tire cords are made of all of the following, EXCEPT:
   (A) aluminum.
   (B) fiberglass.
   (C) Kevlar.
   (D) rayon.

20. _____

21. Today, _____ tires are used for almost all applications.
   (A) bias
   (B) bias-belted
   (C) radial
   (D) cross-hatch

21. _____

Tire Rating Information

22. The DOT temperature resistance rating uses three _____ grades.

22. _____

23. A tire DOT graded A for traction has _____ traction than a tire rated C.

23. _____

24. The DOT grades for tread wear vary from _____.
   (A) 50–100
   (B) 100–500
   (C) 500–650
   (D) 500–700

24. _____

25. A typical tire marking is illustrated below. Identify the markings as indicated.

   (A) _____

   (B) _____

   (C) _____

   (D) _____

   (E) _____

   (F) _____

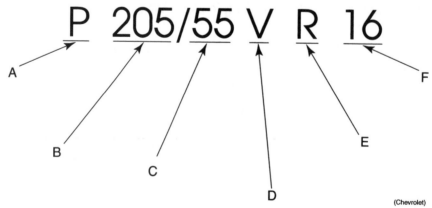

(Chevrolet)

Tire Valves, Pressure, Rotation, Runout, and Balance

26. Technician A says that a space saver tire is for use only as a spare in emergencies. Technician B says that a space saver tire can be rotated with the other tires. Who is right?
   (A) A only.
   (B) B only.
   (C) Both A and B.
   (D) Neither A nor B.

26. _____

27. Tire valves are always installed in the _____.

27. _____

28. Tire overinflation can cause _____.
   (A) casing breakage
   (B) hard ride or loss of traction
   (C) wear in tire center
   (D) All of the above.

28. _____

29. Tire underinflation can cause _____.
   (A) wear on outer tire edges
   (B) tire overheating
   (C) mushy steering
   (D) All of the above.

29. _____

30. The average vehicles' tires should be rotated about every

   _____.
   (A) 5,000 miles (8,000 km)
   (B) 2,500 miles (4,000 km)
   (C) three months
   (D) six months

30. _____

31. Technician A says that wheel runout is not as critical as tire runout. Technician B says that a tire can absorb some of its own runout. Who is right?
   (A) A only.
   (B) B only.
   (C) Both A and B.
   (D) Neither A nor B.

31. _____

32. Proper static balance is achieved when the _____.
   (A) weight mass is equal in both front tires
   (B) weight mass is in the same plane as the centerline of the wheel
   (C) weight mass is evenly distributed around the axis of rotation
   (D) None of the above.

32. _____

33. Proper dynamic balance is achieved when _____.
   (A) weight mass is equal in both front tires
   (B) weight mass is in the same plane as the centerline of the wheel
   (C) weight mass is evenly distributed around the axis of rotation
   (D) None of the above.

33. _____

34. High speeds and overloading produce excess _____.
    (A) heat
    (B) wear
    (C) noise
    (D) Both A and B.

34. _____

35. Identify the parts indicated in the illustration below.

    (A) _____

    (B) _____

    (C) _____

    (D) _____

    (E) _____

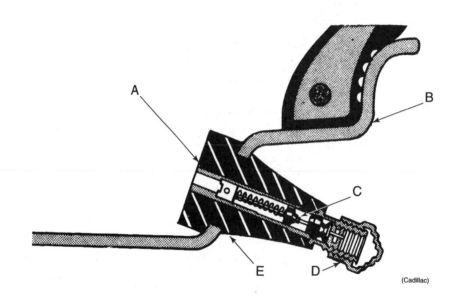

(Cadillac)

27

Wheel Alignment

Objectives: After studying Chapter 27 in the textbook, and completing this section of the workbook, you will be able to:

- Explain the purpose of wheel alignment.
- Identify the major wheel alignment angles.
- Identify the most common related wheel alignment angles.
- Identify vehicle alignment adjustment devices.
- Identify suspension, steering, and tire factors which could affect alignment.

Tech Talk: An automobile with its front wheels out of alignment will have reduced mileage, handle poorly, and wear out tires quickly. As an example, if a car's toe-in setting (distance between front of wheels compared to rear) is off only 1/4″ (6.4 mm), one mile of driving would be like skidding the tire sideways 22′ (6.7 m). Every 240 miles (384 km) of driving would skid the tires sideways for a full mile (1.6 km). Tire life could be reduced as much as 75%. As this example shows, it is very important to keep the steering system in proper adjustment and sound operating condition.

Instructions: Read the general instructions on pages 5–6 for answering the workbook questions. Then, as you study Chapter 27 of the text, answer the following questions in the spaces provided.

Purpose of Wheel Alignment

1. Wheel alignment is the process of measuring and correcting various _____ formed by the wheels.

1. _____

2. The wheels must be properly aligned to prevent _____.
   (A) excessive tire wear
   (B) poor handling
   (C) pulling and wandering
   (D) All of the above.

2. _____

3. A rear-wheel drive vehicle with an independent rear suspension will need a _____ wheel alignment.

3. _____

Caster

4. A furniture caster will always follow behind the _____ around which it swivels.

4. _____

5. Steering axis is formed by the _____.
   (A) upper and lower ball joints
   (B) lower ball joint and strut mount
   (C) lower ball joint and lower control arm
   (D) Either A or B.

5. _____

6. All of the following statements apply to positive caster, EXCEPT:
   (A) the axis centerline will be in front of where the tire touches the road.
   (B) it forces the wheels to travel straight ahead.
   (C) it makes it easier to turn.
   (D) there is a mild tipping effect when cornering.

6. _____

7. Negative caster makes the vehicle easier to _____.

7. _____

8. Technician A says that caster has little effect on tire wear. Technician B says that a vehicle will pull toward the side with the most positive caster. Who is right?
   (A) A only.
   (B) B only.
   (C) Both A and B.
   (D) Neither A nor B.

8. _____

9. Draw a line through the tire showing steering axis centerline when the wheel has positive caster.

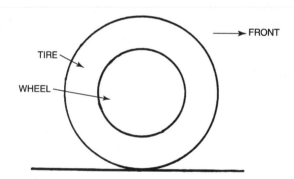

10. Draw a line through the tire showing steering axis centerline when the wheel has negative caster.

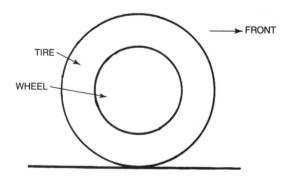

Camber

11. Modern camber angles are usually no more than _____ from zero.

11. _____

12. When viewing the vehicle from the front, positive camber causes the top of the wheel to be tipped _____.

12. _____

13. Tipping the tops of the front wheels inward provides _____.

13. _____

14. Technician A says that a wheel with too much negative camber will make the vehicle pull to the side with the excessive camber. Technician B says that too much positive camber will cause tire wear. Who is right?
    (A) A only.
    (B) B only.
    (C) Both A and B.
    (D) Neither A nor B.

14. _____

Steering Axis Inclination

15. All of the following statements about steering axis inclination (SAI) are true, EXCEPT:
    (A) SAI has an effect on the tendency of the tires to toe in or out.
    (B) correct SAI allows road shocks to be absorbed by the spindle and steering knuckle.
    (C) SAI makes it harder to return to the straight ahead position.
    (D) SAI is one component of included angle.

15. _____

16. Define *setback*. _____

    _____

    _____

17. The illustration below shows a front view of steering axis inclination. Identify the components indicated.

(A) _____

(B) _____

(C) _____

(D) _____

(E) _____

(F) _____

(G) _____

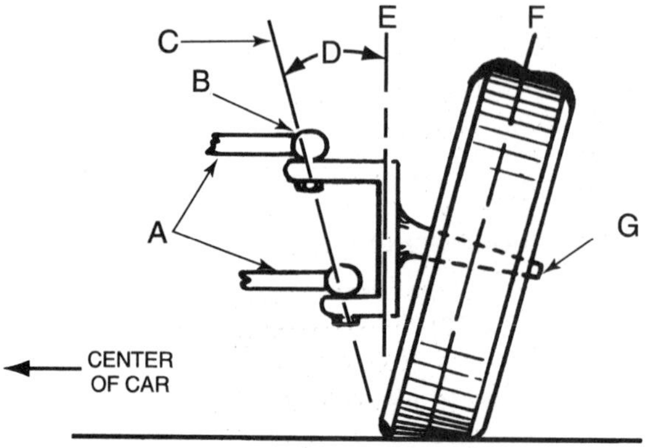

Toe

18. Rear-wheel drive vehicles are toed _____ to compensate for the road-to-friction that tends to force the wheels apart.

18. _____

19. Technician A says that toe adjustments compensate for play and wear in the steering linkage. Technician B says that toe compensates for wheel movement tendencies. Who is right?
(A) A only.
(B) B only.
(C) Both A and B.
(D) Neither A nor B.

19. _____

20. Excessive toe can cause a rapid tire wear condition called _____.

20. _____

21. Explain why the inner wheel must turn more sharply when the vehicle enters a turn. _____

_____

_____

22. Toe-out on turns is made possible by bending the _____.
(A) steering axis
(B) steering arms
(C) rear axle
(D) None of the above.

22. _____

23. Identify toe-in and toe-out.

    (A) _____

    (B) _____

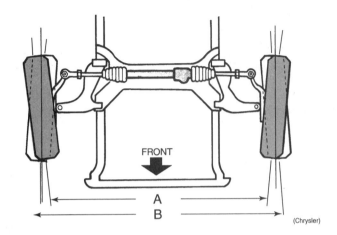

(Chrysler)

Steering Geometry

24. Slip angle can be reduced by _____.
    (A) adjusting camber
    (B) adjusting caster
    (C) adjusting toe
    (D) careful cornering

24. _____

25. Define *steering geometry*. _____

_____

26. The thrust angle is an imaginary line at _____ to the rear
    axle.
    (A) 30°
    (B) 60°
    (C) 90°
    (D) 120°

26. _____

27. If the vehicle follows the thrust angle when driving straight
    ahead, it is _____ correctly.

27. _____

28. Thrust angle setting is *easiest* on _____ vehicle designs.
    (A) rear-wheel drive
    (B) front-wheel drive
    (C) four-wheel drive
    (D) four-wheel steering

28. _____

29. Technician A says that moving the top of the MacPherson
    strut tower will change camber. Technician B says that
    moving the top of the MacPherson strut tower will change
    caster. Who is right?
    (A) A only.
    (B) B only.
    (C) Both A and B.
    (D) Neither A nor B.

29. _____

30. Caster and camber can be set on large rear-wheel drive   30. _____
    vehicles with _____.
    (A) shims at the control arms
    (B) slotted holes
    (C) eccentric cams
    (D) All of the above.

31. Front toe is set by adjusting the _____.   31. _____

32. Eccentric cams can be used to set all of the following,   32. _____
    EXCEPT:
    (A) front toe.
    (B) rear toe.
    (C) camber.
    (D) caster.

33. Rear wheel shims can be used to set _____.   33. _____
    (A) toe
    (B) camber
    (C) caster
    (D) Both A and B.

Tire Wear Patterns and Alignment

34. When performing a wheel alignment, which of the following   34. _____
    should be done *first*?
    (A) Check toe.
    (B) Check for worn steering and suspension parts.
    (C) Check caster.
    (D) Check camber.

35. How would you check for radial tire pull? _____

    _____

    _____

Name _____

Date _____ Period _____

Instructor _____

Score _____ Text Pages 531–554

28

Air Conditioning and Heating

Objectives: After studying Chapter 28 in the textbook, and completing this section of the workbook, you will be able to:

- Identify the three methods of heat transfer.
- Explain the principles of latent and sensible heat.
- Identify modern refrigerants.
- Explain the relationship between pressure and temperature in modern refrigerants.
- Identify the basic refrigeration cycle.
- Identify the basic parts of an air conditioning system.
- Describe the operation of each air conditioning system component.
- Explain the basic operation of the heater system.
- Compare differences in air conditioning control system design.
- State basic refrigerant safety rules.

Tech Talk: Although automobile air conditioning was once a luxury for many people, it has become so common that it is unusual to find late-model cars without air. Trucks and economy cars are also increasingly being equipped with air conditioners. The air conditioning system on a car greatly affects its overall performance so it is important that the technician fully understand its operation. Environmental concerns have caused the introduction of more environmentally friendly refrigerants. This, in turn, has complicated the service picture, and the technician must remain current on procedures for servicing and recycling. Study this chapter carefully for the latest information on air conditioning.

Instructions: Read the general instructions on pages 5–6 for answering the workbook questions. Then, as you study Chapter 28 of the text, answer the following questions in the spaces provided.

Principles of Refrigeration

1. Automobile air conditioning is a method whereby air entering the car is _____

_____ .

2. The air conditioning system makes use of the principles of   2. _____

_____ .

3. Define *cooling.* _____

_____

4. Conduction is the transfer of heat by _____ contact.   4. _____

5. Convection is the transfer of heat by the _____ air.

6. Heat in a object that does not cause a temperature rise is called _____ heat.

7. Heat that causes a rise in temperature is called _____ heat.

8. When a substance changes from a liquid to a gas (boils), it _____ heat.

9. Technician A says that when the pressure of a substance is raised, its boiling point is lowered. Technician B says that when the pressure of a substance is lowered, its boiling point is lowered. Who is right?
   (A) A only.
   (B) B only.
   (C) Both A and B.
   (D) Neither A nor B.

5. _____

6. _____

7. _____

8. _____

9. _____

10. Draw the missing lines and arrows showing heat transfer. On the blanks provided, explain the method of heat transfer.

_____

_____

_____

11. Draw the missing lines and arrows showing heat transfer. On the blanks provided, explain the method of heat transfer.

_____

_____

_____

12. Draw the missing lines and arrows showing heat transfer. On the blanks provided, explain the method of heat transfer.

_____

_____

_____

SUN

EARTH

Types of Refrigerant

13. The liquid used in the refrigeration system is referred to as _____.

13. _____

14. Why is R-12 being replaced by R-134a? _____

_____

_____

15. Technician A says that most new vehicle air conditioners use R-134a. Technician B says that R-134a and R-12 can be used interchangeably. Who is right?
(A) A only.
(B) B only.
(C) Both A and B.
(D) Neither A nor B.

15. _____

How the Refrigeration System Works

16. The basic difference between the two major types of automotive refrigeration systems is the design of the _____.

16. _____

17. Identify the air flow, refrigerant flow, and the parts indicated on the refrigeration system illustrated below.

(A) _____

(B) _____

(C) _____

(D) _____

(E) _____

(F) _____

(G) _____

(H) _____

(I) _____

(J) _____

(K) _____

(L) _____

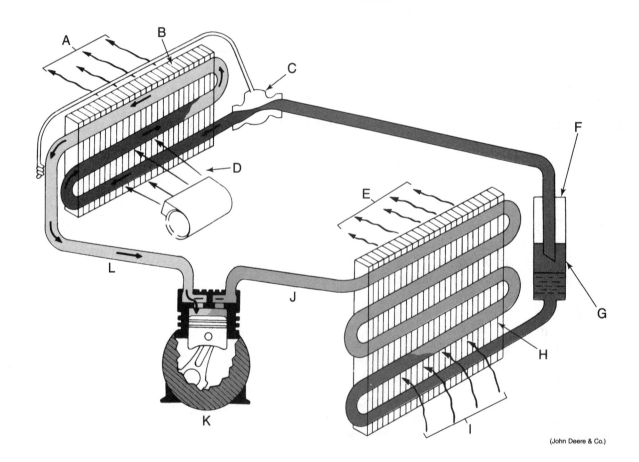

(John Deere & Co.)

Major Components of the Air Conditioning System

18. The air conditioning compressor is used to move and _____ the refrigerant.

18. _____

19. Most refrigerant compressors are _____ types.

19. _____

20. Technician A says that the radial compressor is a centrifugal compressor with no pistons. Technician B says that axial compressors have pistons that are parallel to the compressor crankshaft. Who is right?
    (A) A only.
    (B) B only.
    (C) Both A and B.
    (D) Neither A nor B.

20. _____

21. All of the following statements about compressor drive mechanisms are true, EXCEPT:
    (A) the compressor receives engine power through a belt.
    (B) the compressor clutch is operated by magnetism.
    (C) the compressor clutch is turned on and off to control condenser pressure.
    (D) the magnetic clutch coil does not revolve.

21. _____

22. Identify the parts indicated on the five-cylinder compressor illustrated below.

(A) _____

(B) _____

(C) _____

(D) _____

(E) _____

(F) _____

(G) _____

(H) _____

(I) _____

(J) _____

(K) _____

(L) _____

(M) _____

(N) _____

(O) _____

(P) _____

(Q) _____

(R) _____

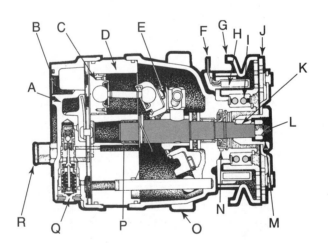

Condenser

23. The heated, high pressure _____ from the compressor is forced into the condenser.

23. _____

24. Condensers are commonly made of _____.
    (A) plastic
    (B) steel
    (C) aluminum
    (D) copper

24. _____

25. Identify the parts indicated on the illustration below.

(A) _____

(B) _____

(C) _____

(D) _____

(E) _____

(F) _____

(G) _____

(H) _____

(I) _____

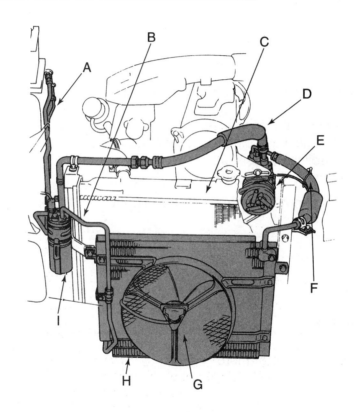

Refrigerant Flow Restrictor

26. The refrigerant arriving at the flow restrictor is in a _____ state.

26. _____

27. All of the following statements apply to the operation of the expansion valve, EXCEPT:
    (A) moves in relation to evaporator temperature.
    (B) has an internal spring.
    (C) used with a cycling compressor clutch.
    (D) has temperature sensitive bulb.

27. _____

28. When used as an expansion valve, the fixed orifice _____.
    (A) houses a fine screen
    (B) restricts the flow of refrigerant
    (C) can be made of plastic or metal
    (D) All of the above.

28. _____

Evaporator

29. The evaporator is a(n) _____ exchanger.

29. _____

30. As the refrigerant vaporizes, it absorbs _____ from the incoming air.

30. _____

31. Moisture in the incoming air _____ on the evaporator fins.

31. _____

32. A line connected to the bottom of the evaporator returns _____ to the compressor.

32. _____

Blower Motor

33. All of the following statements about blower motors are true, EXCEPT:
    (A) the blower forces air over the condenser.
    (B) the blower is usually called a squirrel cage blower.
    (C) blower speed is controlled by resistors.
    (D) the blower motor turns at high speed.

33. _____

34. Computer control systems on a blower motor eliminate the need for the _____.
    (A) sight glass
    (B) blower resistors
    (C) squirrel cage
    (D) None of the above.

34. _____

Lines, Hoses, and Mufflers

35. All air conditioner fittings use one or more _____.
    (A) tubes
    (B) O-rings
    (C) lines
    (D) None of the above.

35. _____

36. The muffler is _____.
    (A) used to reduce pumping noise
    (B) is placed between the compressor and condenser
    (C) used to reduce line vibrations
    (D) All of the above.

36. _____

Receiver-Dehydrator

37. The receiver-dehydrator is used only on systems with an _____.

37. _____

38. A desiccant is a _____ agent.

38. _____

39. Technician A says that a sight glass is always installed in the high-pressure side of the system. Technician B says that the sight glass has been eliminated from many vehicles not using expansion valves. Who is right?
    (A) A only.
    (B) B only.
    (C) Both A and B.
    (D) Neither A nor B.

39. _____

Accumulator

40. All of the following statements about accumulators are true, EXCEPT:
    (A) accumulators are used only on vehicles with fixed orifice tubes.
    (B) accumulators are installed between the condenser and evaporator.
    (C) the accumulator keeps liquid refrigerant from reaching the compressor.
    (D) the accumulator contains the desiccant.

40. _____

41. Identify the parts indicated on the accumulator illustrated below.

    (A) _____

    (B) _____

    (C) _____

    (D) _____

    (E) _____

    (F) _____

    (G) _____

    (H) _____

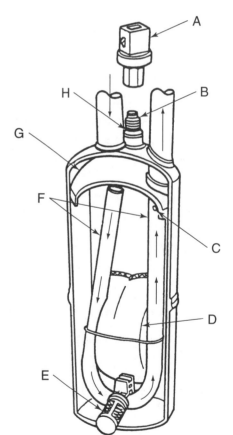

Evaporator Pressure Controls

42. What will happen if the evaporator pressure becomes too low? _____

_____

_____

43. All of the following evaporator pressure controls are obsolete, EXCEPT:
(A) hot gas valve.
(B) compressor cycling switch.
(C) suction throttling valve.
(D) pilot operated absolute valve.

43. _____

44. The compressor low pressure switch prevents compressor damage if the _____

_____.

45. Technician A says that a full throttle cut-out switch prevents dieseling when the engine is turned off. Technician B says that the ambient air temperature switch turns the compressor on when the temperature drops. Who is right?
(A) A only.
(B) B only.
(C) Both A and B.
(D) Neither A nor B.

45. _____

Service Valves

46. Air conditioner service valves _____.
(A) allow the refrigerant to be recovered
(B) allow the system to be filled with refrigerant
(C) allow pressure checking
(D) All of the above.

46. _____

47. R-134a systems use a(n) _____ valve.
(A) Schrader
(B) MacPherson
(C) Johnson
(D) quick-disconnect

47. _____

Refrigerant Oil

48. Refrigerant will form toxic gas if it contacts _____.
(A) oxygen
(B) nitrogen
(C) an open flame
(D) oil

48. _____

49. Liquid refrigerant can cause _____.

49. _____

50. Discharge of *any* kind of refrigerant into the atmosphere violates _____ law.
    (A) Federal
    (B) state
    (C) Both A and B.
    (D) Neither A nor B.

50. _____

51. Converting an R-12 air conditioning system to operate on R-134a is called _____.

51. _____

52. The heater core can be made of _____.
    (A) aluminum and plastic
    (B) aluminum
    (C) copper
    (D) All of the above.

52. _____

Air Distribution and Control

53. The blend door controls air flow through the _____.
    (A) heater core
    (B) evaporator
    (C) condenser
    (D) Both A and B.

53. _____

54. Most air control doors are operated by _____ diaphragms.

54. _____

55. Identify the parts of the air conditioning system illustrated below.

(A) _____

(B) _____

(C) _____

(D) _____

(E) _____

(F) _____

(G) _____

(H) _____

(I) _____

(J) _____

(K) _____

(L) _____

(M) _____

(N) _____

(O) _____

(P) _____

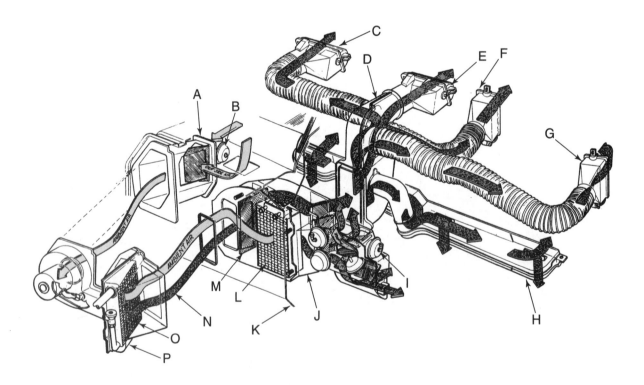

Name _____

Date _____ Period _____

Instructor _____

Score _____ Text Pages 555–560

29

ASE Certification

Objectives: After studying Chapter 29 in the textbook, and completing this section of the workbook, you will be able to:

- Explain why technician certification is necessary.
- Explain the process of registering for ASE tests.
- Explain how to take the ASE tests.
- Identify typical ASE test questions.
- Explain what is done with ASE test results.

Tech Talk: A technician without ASE certification is at a severe handicap. Some states are even considering legislation to make certification a requirement. ASE certification helps the technician keep current on the latest automotive technology. Study this chapter, and all other chapters, before taking the ASE tests.

Instructions: Read the general instructions on pages 5–6 for answering the workbook questions. Then, as you study Chapter 29 of the text, answer the following questions in the spaces provided.

Reasons for ASE Tests

1. The concept of setting standards of excellence for skilled workers dates from _____.
   (A) ancient times
   (B) labor unions
   (C) the aircraft industry
   (D) 1975

   1. _____

2. ASE was established to provide a _____ process for automobile technicians.

   2. _____

3. A test which is given to everyone throughout the United States is called a _____ test.

   3. _____

4. The public benefits from ASE certification because they have a way to identify _____.

   4. _____

5. ASE certification is _____.
   (A) not required by many repair shops.
   (B) not mandatory on a national level.
   (C) mandatory on a national level.
   (D) optional for many state vehicle inspector courses.

   5. _____

6. The ASE tests are given in _____.
   (A) January
   (B) May
   (C) November
   (D) Both B and C.

6. _____

Applying for the ASE Tests

7. To become certified in any area, you must pass the specific test and have _____ years working experience.

7. _____

8. In some cases, _____ courses or time spent in similar work may be substituted.
   (A) training
   (B) apprenticeship
   (C) Both A and B.
   (D) Neither A nor B.

8. _____

Taking the ASE Tests

9. List the three things that ASE tests are designed to measure. _____

_____

10. Why is it important to send in your application as soon as possible? _____

_____

11. All ASE test questions are _____ questions.
    (A) essay
    (B) multiple choice
    (C) matching
    (D) completion

11. _____

12. A test question with statements from technicians A and B is a _____ question.
    (A) one part
    (B) two part
    (C) negative
    (D) fill-in-the-blank

12. _____

13. A _____ question will have the word "EXCEPT."

13. _____

14. In most cases, you should recheck your answers _____ time(s).

14. _____

Test Results

15. The test questions are subdivided into _____ areas to help determine areas in which you need to study.

15. _____

16. ASE test scores are provided to the _____ only.
    (A) technician
    (B) employer
    (C) person who paid for the test
    (D) All of the above.

16. _____

17. You can take the certification test _____.
   (A) only once
   (B) twice
   (C) four times
   (D) any number of times

17. _____

18. The certified technician must take a recertification test every _____ years to keep his or her certification.

18. _____

19. Technician A says that a fee is charged for taking the recertification tests. Technician B says that the same form is used for recertification and first-time tests. Who is right?
   (A) A only.
   (B) B only.
   (C) Both A and B.
   (D) Neither A nor B.

19. _____

20. Fill out the ASE test form below. Pretend to be taking at least two tests in the areas in which you have the most confidence. In sections 13 and 14, list your actual experience. If you do not have any automotive experience yet, write down the jobs that you have had.

Registration Form—ASE Tests

Name _____

Date _____ Period _____

Instructor _____

Score _____ Text Pages 561–568

30

Career Opportunities

Objectives: After studying Chapter 30 in the textbook, and completing this section of the workbook, you will be able to:

- Describe the various types of careers available in automotive service.
- Compare the different types of specialized automotive technicians.
- Identify sources of training in automotive service.
- Explain why it is important to finish school before seeking a full-time job as a technician.

Tech Talk: Economical, technological, and the environmental concerns have converged to make it more important than ever for owners to rely on professional auto technicians to maintain and repair their vehicles. New cars are expensive investments and it's important that they be properly maintained and protected. Modern automobiles are also lasting longer because of improved quality so used vehicles are readily available and very popular. Well-maintained vehicles, both old and new, also pollute less and help the environment. The high-tech systems of modern automobiles also make it difficult for the average person to perform even the simplest maintenance and repair. The demand for well-trained, dependable auto technicians will increase with the increase in economic and environmental concerns and rapid technological advancements.

Instructions: Read the general instructions on pages 5–6 for answering the workbook questions. Then, as you study Chapter 30 of the text, answer the following questions in the spaces provided.

Types of Automotive Careers

1. Some service tasks that a light repair technician will do are
   _____.
   (A) replacing exhaust system components
   (B) overhauling an engine
   (C) aligning a vehicle after repairs
   (D) All of the above.

   1. _____

2. In the heavy repair department, you will be called on to _____

   _____

298 Auto Fundamentals Workbook

Areas of Specialization

3. It has become difficult for auto technicians to learn to repair the _____ vehicle and many auto technicians are turning to specialization which requires concentrated study in a specific area.

3. _____

4. Technician A says that the drivability technician isolates engine problems. Technician B says that the drivability technician may be involved with ignition and fuel system work. Who is right?
   (A) A only.
   (B) B only.
   (C) Both A and B.
   (D) Neither A nor B.

4. _____

5. The electrical/electronic technician handles work on all of the following, EXCEPT:
   (A) alternators.
   (B) transaxles.
   (C) starters.
   (D) tape players/CD systems.

5. _____

Automotive Careers

6. Advancement into a supervisory position depends upon _____

_____

7. The shop supervisor is in charge of _____

_____

8. The service manager is in charge of _____

_____

9. The service manager must see that customers get _____

_____

10. In the small shop, the technician may be called upon to _____.
    (A) make repairs
    (B) greet customers
    (C) prepare bills
    (D) All of the above.

10. _____

Working Conditions and Wages

11. When is the modern technician faced with outside weather conditions? _____

_____

12. What factors affect wages? _____

_____

13. Technician A says that the skilled technician will make more money than the inexperienced technician under the commission system. Technician B says that the wage system pays the technician for the number of hours that he or she is at the shop. Who is right?
    (A) A only.
    (B) B only.
    (C) Both A and B.
    (D) Neither A nor B.

13. _____

How Does a Person Become an Automotive Technician?

14. Which of the following require a high school diploma?
    (A) Automotive training courses.
    (B) Corporate training programs.
    (C) Manufacturer training courses.
    (D) All of the above.

14. _____

15. Why is it important to take language courses while in school? _____

_____

_____

16. Math is useful for taking _____, and for filling out _____.

16. _____

_____

17. The modern vehicle uses the principles of _____ and _____ in hundreds of ways.

17. _____

_____

Vocational Schools, Colleges, and Apprentice Programs

18. Vocational schools are sometimes called _____ or _____ schools.

18. _____

_____

19. Some colleges and vocational schools are operated by _____.
    (A) state governments
    (B) local governments
    (C) private institutions
    (D) All of the above.

19. _____

20. An apprentice program offers all of the following, EXCEPT:
    (A) on-the-job training.
    (B) related courses in math and science.
    (C) a guaranteed job upon finishing.
    (D) exposure to all areas of the trade.

20. _____

Name _____

Date _____ Period _____

Instructor _____

Job 1

Automotive Measurement

INTRODUCTION: One of the first steps toward becoming a skilled auto technician involves knowing when and how to measure automotive parts. Auto technicians frequently measure parts to determine if a part is worn. Mechanics measure everything from the tread wear on a tire to the amount of wear and taper in an engine cylinder. Whether you plan on becoming an amateur or a professional mechanic, you must master basic measuring skills.

OBJECTIVE: Given a ruler, your textbook, conversion charts, and the material in this job, you will learn to perform both English and metric measurements.

TOOLS AND EQUIPMENT: You will need a ruler, pencil, and your textbook.

INSTRUCTIONS: Use a ruler to measure the following twelve line lengths. Write your answer in the blank next each line. Refer to the examples as required. If you need help getting started, ask your instructor for assistance. This is very important!

RULER REVIEW

Two Times Actual Size

Actual Size

Length	Lines under one inch	Length	Lines over one inch
$\frac{1}{2}$	1. _____ Example	_____	7. _____
_____	2. _____	_____	8. _____
_____	3. ___	_____	9. _____
_____	4. _____	_____	10. _____
_____	5. _____	_____	11. _____
_____	6. _____	_____	12. _____

■Use your ruler to measure and label the sizes of the following parts. Also, study the various dimensions which are common to auto mechanics. Note, measure the parts—not the dimension lines.

PART DIMENSIONS

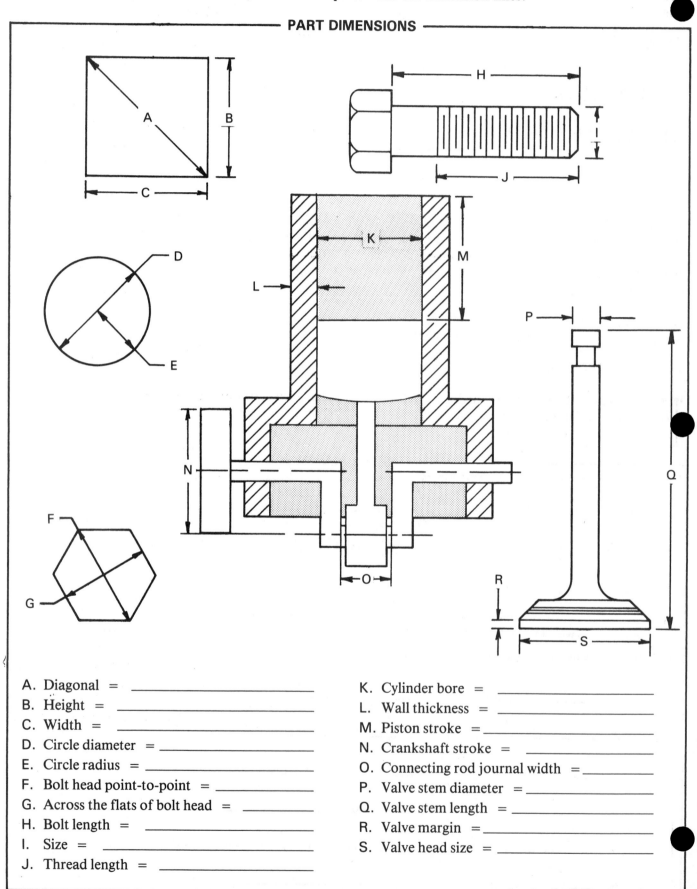

A. Diagonal = _____
B. Height = _____
C. Width = _____
D. Circle diameter = _____
E. Circle radius = _____
F. Bolt head point-to-point = _____
G. Across the flats of bolt head = _____
H. Bolt length = _____
I.   Size = _____
J. Thread length = _____

K. Cylinder bore = _____
L. Wall thickness = _____
M. Piston stroke =_____
N. Crankshaft stroke = _____
O. Connecting rod journal width =_____
P. Valve stem diameter =_____
Q. Valve stem length = _____
R. Valve margin =_____
S. Valve head size = _____

You have been measuring in fractions of an inch. When smaller than 1/64 of an inch precision is required, you should use the decimal system. Quite often, the auto mechanic must convert a fraction to a decimal or a decimal to a fraction. A conversion chart makes this change over easy.

■Turn to page 576 in your text. It has a conversion chart. Use this chart to convert the following fractions into decimals and decimals into fractions. Also, draw an arrow on each of the ruler scales to represent the two equal numbers. See number one which is an example.

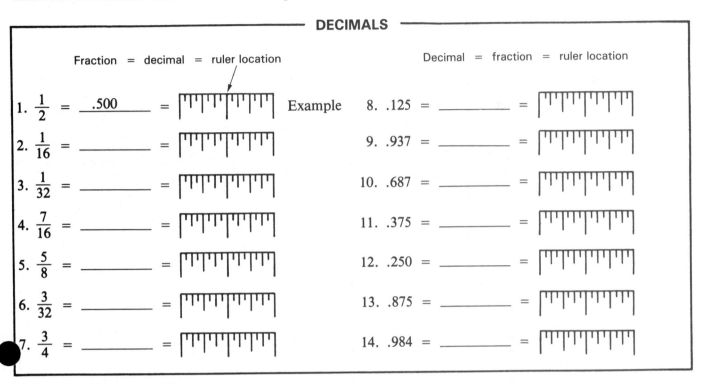

─── DECIMALS ───

Fraction = decimal = ruler location

Decimal = fraction = ruler location

1. $\frac{1}{2}$ = ___.500___ =   Example

2. $\frac{1}{16}$ = _____ =

3. $\frac{1}{32}$ = _____ =

4. $\frac{7}{16}$ = _____ =

5. $\frac{5}{8}$ = _____ =

6. $\frac{3}{32}$ = _____ =

7. $\frac{3}{4}$ = _____ =

8. .125 = _____ =

9. .937 = _____ =

10. .687 = _____ =

11. .375 = _____ =

12. .250 = _____ =

13. .875 = _____ =

14. .984 = _____ =

■Turn to page 569 in your textbook. Use the information on this page to list the following values.

─── EQUIVALENT VALUES ───

15. 36 inches = _____ yard
16. 1 mile = _____ feet
17. 1 pound = _____ ounces
18. 1 short ton = _____ pounds
19. 2240 pounds = _____ ton
20. 1 pint = _____ ounces

21. 4 quarts = _____ gallon
22. Water freezes at _____ F
23. Water freezes at _____ C
24. Water boils at _____ F
25. Water boils at _____ C
26. Room temperature _____ F

■Use your textbook to identify the following measuring tools and complete the statements that explain their function. Refer to text pages 81 through 100.

MEASURING TOOLS

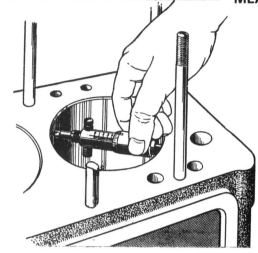

A. An _____ is commonly used to check cylinder _____ _____.

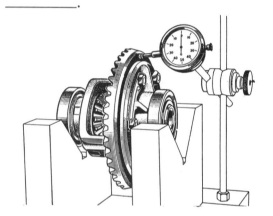

B. A _____ is commonly used to measure ring gear _____ (wobble), shaft _____ (side movement or clearance), gear teeth _____ _____ (teeth clearance), and _____ (camshaft) lift.

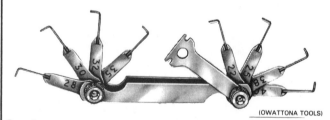

(OWATTONA TOOLS)

C. A _____ type _____ is frequently used when gapping spark plugs.

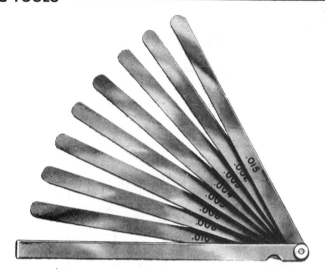

D. A flat type _____ can be used to check valve _____, piston ring _____, and ignition point gap.

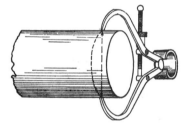

E. The diameter of this shaft is being measured with an _____.

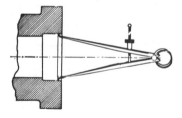

F. The _____ will measure the diameter of a counterbore.

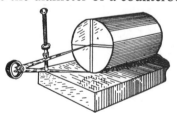

(SOUTH BEND LATHE)

G. _____ may be used to find the center of a shaft or to mark sheet metal before cutting.

■Using your text, identify the basic parts of this outside micrometer.

MICROMETER PARTS

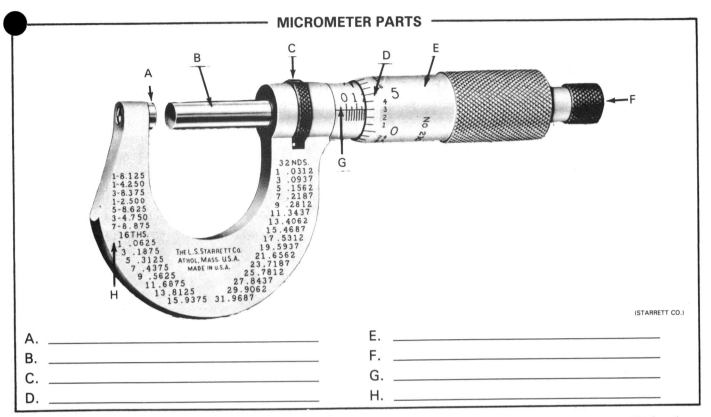

(STARRETT CO.)

A. _____   E. _____
B. _____   F. _____
C. _____   G. _____
D. _____   H. _____

■After your instructor reviews the steps for reading a micrometer, read the following micrometers. Write the values and the totals in the spaces provided.

READING A MICROMETER

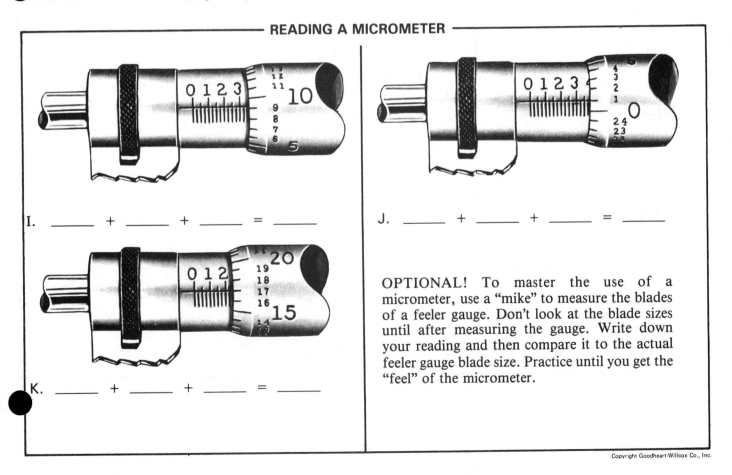

I. ____ + ____ + ____ = ____

J. ____ + ____ + ____ = ____

K. ____ + ____ + ____ = ____

OPTIONAL! To master the use of a micrometer, use a "mike" to measure the blades of a feeler gauge. Don't look at the blade sizes until after measuring the gauge. Write down your reading and then compare it to the actual feeler gauge blade size. Practice until you get the "feel" of the micrometer.

■Study the following Metric/U.S. Customary comparison chart. Memorize the three left columns of the chart and become familiar with the equivalents and automotive metric examples. The first step toward understanding metrics involves learning the basic "metric language."

MEASUREMENT	METRIC	SYMBOL	METRIC/U.S. CUSTOMARY	AUTOMOTIVE METRIC EXAMPLES
Length	Meter Millimeter	m mm	1 m = 39.4 in 1 mm = .04 in	Vehicle length = 4.5 m = 177.16 in Mileage = 24 000 km = 14,911 mi Ignition point gap = 0.4 mm = .016 in
Weight or Mass	Gram Kilogram	g kg	1 g = .035 oz 1 kg = 2.2lb	Piston weight = 750 g = 26.3 oz Vehicle weight = 1 500 kg = 3,300 lb AC refrigerant = 1.5 kb = 3.3 lb
Volume or Capacity	Liter Cubic centimeter	L cm³	1 L = .946 qt 1 cm³ = .061 in³	Gas tank capacity = 76 L = 20 gal Engine oil capacity = 4.7 L = 5 qts Engine size = 5.7 L = 350 in³
Temperature	Celsius	C	0 °C = 32 °F	Engine operating temperature = 85 °C = 185 °F Cylinder flame temperature = 1 092 °C = 1,998 °F
Area	Square centimeter	cm²	1 cm² = .155 in²	Brake lining area = 494 cm² = 76 in² Tire-to-road contact area = 387 cm² = 60 in²
Pressure	Kilopascal	kPa	1 kPa = .145 psi	Tire pressure = 205 kPa = 30 psi 250 kPa = 36 psi Air compressor line pressure = 689 kPa = 100 psi
Torque	Newton-meter	N·m	1 N·m = .737 lb-ft	Intake manifold bolt torque = 47.5 N·m = 35 lb-ft Cylinder head bolt torque = 135.6 N·m = 100 lb-ft

■Turn to page 569 in your textbook. Use the table on this page to list the ungiven metric units and abbreviations.

```
┌──── UNIT ──────── ABBREVIATION ─────── UNIT ──────── ABBREVIATION ────┐
│                                                                        │
│  1. _____  = km    5. _____ = mm      │
│  2. _____  = C      6. _____ = m       │
│  3. Centigram = _____               7. Liter = _____              │
│  4. _____  = g      8. Cubic centimeter = _____   │
│                                                                        │
└────────────────────────────────────────────────────────────────────────┘
```

■Turn to page 570 in your text. Use the measuring system chart to write the equivalents for the following values. In particular, note the prefixes (Kilo = 100, Milli = .001, etc.).

METRIC LENGTHS

9. 1 Kilometer = _____   12. 1 Decimeter = _____
10. 1 Hectometer = _____   13. 1 Centimeter = _____
11. 1 Dekameter = _____   14. 1 Millimeter = _____

METRIC WEIGHTS

15. 1000 Grams = _____   18. 1 Gram = _____
16. 100 Grams = _____   19. .01 Gram = _____
17. 10 Grams = _____   20. .001 Gram = _____

METRIC VOLUMES

21. 1 Dekaliter = _____   23. 1 Centiliter = _____
22. 1 Hectoliter = _____ 24. 1 Milliliter = _____

METRIC AREA

25. 1 Square meter = _____   26. 1 Hectare = _____

■Now, turn to page 573 in your textbook. Using the table, calculate the metric equivalent for the following U.S. Customary values. Write your answer in the blank.

U.S. CUSTOMARY — METRIC

27. 2 Inches = _____ mm   31. 5 Quarts = _____ L
28. 10 Yards = _____ m   32. 10 Gallons = _____ L
29. 5 Ounces = _____ g   33. 27 Square inches = _____ cm²
30. 100 Pounds = _____ kg   34. 195°F = _____ °C

Name _____

Date _____ Period _____

Instructor _____

Job 2

Auto Shop
Safety

INTRODUCTION: Thousands of technicians are injured or killed every year while on the job. Most of these technicians were breaking basic safety rules before their accidents. They learned to respect safety precautions the "hard way" — by experiencing a painful but instructive injury. Hopefully, you will know how to avoid accidents the easy way — by studying and abiding by shop safety rules.

OBJECTIVE: Given access to an auto shop, you will be able to locate the shop's fire extinguishers, fire exit, safety glasses, and other shop safety equipment. You will also learn the general safety rules of an auto shop.

TOOLS AND EQUIPMENT: You will need a floor jack, jack stand, and access to the auto shop facility.

INSTRUCTIONS: As you read the job instructions, answer the job questions and perform the job tasks. Print your answers neatly and use complete sentences. Ask your instructor for help as needed.

NOTE! You should have studied textbook Chapter 5, Tool Identification and Use. It will prepare you for some of the procedures in this job.

EYE SAFETY

1. Eye protection (safety glasses or goggles) should be worn during any operation that could injure your eyes. See Fig. 2-1. This includes, for example, hammering, drilling, grinding, sandblasting, using compressed air, carrying a battery, or working around a spinning engine fan.

   You must decide when your eyes are in danger and put on safety glasses or goggles.

2. Where are the safety glasses and goggles kept in your shop?_____

   _____

   _____

FIRE SAFETY

3. During a fire, a few seconds time can be a "life time!" Walk around the shop and locate all of the fire extinguishers, the fire exit, and fire alarms. This will help you during an emergency.

(HUNTER ENGINEERING COMPANY)

Fig. 2-1. This tecnician is wearing safety goggles to protect his eyes from flying debris.

Always take actions to prevent a fire. Store gasoline and oily rags in safety cans. Wipe up spilled gasoline and oil immediately. Hold a rag around the fitting when removing a car's fuel line.

Never siphon gasoline using your mouth and a section of hose. Use an approved hand pump and a safety can. Gasoline is poisonous and can be harmful or fatal if swallowed.

4. How many fire extinguishers and alarms are there in your shop? _____
_____

5. Where are the fire extinguishers located?
_____
_____
_____

6. Where are the fire alarms? _____
_____
_____

7. How do you leave the shop in case of a fire?
_____
_____
_____

BATTERY SAFETY

8. Automotive batteries can explode! Keep sparks and flames away from all batteries, especially when they are being charged. Hydrogen gas hovers around the top of batteries. If the gas is ignited, it can blow the battery case and acid into your face.

When connecting jumper cables to a battery, use industry-approved procedures. The final connection should always be made to the disabled vehicle's engine or frame, not to negative terminal of the dead battery. Then, if there is a spark, it will occur away from the battery.

When connecting a battery charger, make sure the charger is disconnected from the wall outlet. The area should also be well ventilated to prevent a buildup of hydrogen gas.

9. Why must you keep sparks away from the top of a battery? _____
_____
_____

10. What is the safe method of connecting jumper cables to a car's battery?
A. _____
_____
B. _____
_____
C. _____
_____
D. _____
_____

11. When connecting a battery charger, what safety precautions should you take?
_____
_____
_____

COMPRESSED AIR SAFETY

12. Use compressed air with caution! Shop air hoses can have in excess of 100 psi (689 kPa) air pressure in them. If abused, this is enough air pressure to blind, deafen, or even kill. Never point an air nozzle at yourself or anyone else.

13. What is the air pressure setting on your shop compressor? _____

SHOP CLEANLINESS

14. The floor of the auto shop must be kept clean at all times. Oil or water on the floor could cause a serious fall and injury. Wipe up or place quick dry (oil absorbant) on spilled oil or antifreeze. Use a squeegee and rags to remove spilled water.

Also, never leave tools, creepers, or car parts on the shop floor. Place them on, against, or under the work benches. Then, no one can trip and fall.

15. Can you find any unsafe condition on your shop floor?_____
_____

16. Always keep shop tools perfectly clean and organized. When your hands become oily or greasy, wash them off or wipe them dry with a clean rag. You can judge a technician by the condition of his or her tools and work area.

17. Are the shop tools clean and organized? _____ Explain. _____

_____

_____

_____

CLOTHING SAFETY

18. You should always dress like a technician. Loose clothing, jewelry, and long hair are very dangerous. They can get caught in drum lathes, wheel balancers, spinning engine fans, a drill press, drive shaft universal joints, and other spinning objects. Parts of your body can be pulled into the spinning equipment with deadly force.

    You should also wear protective shoes made of leather. Tennis shoes and sandals are NOT safe in an auto shop. If a heavy part (engine flywheel, brake drum, etc.) were dropped on an unprotected foot, a serious injury could result.

19. Are you dressed to work? _____ Explain. _____

_____

_____

_____

_____

CARBON MONOXIDE

20. When a car is running, a deadly gas blows out the exhaust pipe. The engine produces carbon monoxide, which is a colorless, odorless, toxic gas. Always install an ex-

(KENT-MOORE TOOLS)

Fig. 2-2. Technician is placing an exhaust hose over tail pipe of car before starting engine. This will prevent poisonous carbon monoxide from entering shop.

haust hose on the tail pipe of any car to be operated in the auto shop. See Fig. 2-2. Then, turn on the exhaust fan so that the hose will draw the fumes out of the shop.

21. Where are the exhaust hoses in your shop?

_____

_____

22. Where do you turn on the fan for the exhaust hoses? _____

_____

GRINDER AND DRILL PRESS SAFETY

23. An electric grinding wheel can cause serious injuries to your eyes, face, and hands when misused. Always keep the tool rest adjusted close to the grinding wheel. Hold small objects with vise-grip pliers. Wear goggles and keep the machine face shield in position. Also, be careful not to strike the grinding wheel. It can shatter and explode when spinning.

    Go to the electric grinder and inspect it closely. Locate the power switch. Observe the position of the tool rest and face shield. Also, check the condition of the grinding wheel.

24. Is the electric grinder in your shop safe? _____ Explain. _____

_____

_____

_____

25. When operating a drill press, use a portable vise or C-clamp to secure the workpiece to the worktable. When the drill bit is about to break through the workpiece, let up on the drilling pressure. This will keep the drill bit from catching in the hole.

    Also, NEVER leave the chuck key in the drill chuck. It could fly out and hit someone if the drill press is accidentally turned on.

    Locate and inspect the operation of your shop's drill press. Find the on/off button, feed lever, chuck, and other components.

26. If you had to use the drill press, how would you secure the workpiece? _____

_____

_____

FLOOR JACK AND JACK STAND SAFETY

27. Check out a floor jack and a set of jack stands, Fig. 2-3. The floor jack is only used to raise a car. The jack stands are for securing the car before working.

    Never work under a car only supported by a floor jack. If someone were to hit the jack handle or if a jack seal were to fail, the car could fall and crush you.

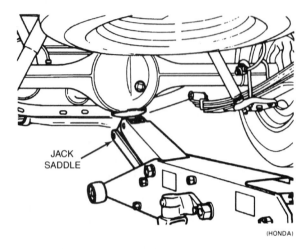

JACK
SADDLE

(HONDA)

Fig. 2-3. When raising a car, make sure saddle of floor jack is under a correct lift point. If positioned incorrectly, car could be damaged or fall. Place jack stands under car before working.

28. WITHOUT lifting a car, practice operating a floor jack. Close the valve on the jack handle. Pump the handle up and down to raise the jack. Then, lower the jack slowly. It is important that you know how to control the lowering action of the jack. This will help you lower a car off the jack stands safely when working.

29. In what direction must you turn the jack handle valve to raise the jack? _____
    To lower the jack? _____.

30. OPTIONAL! Use a floor jack to raise and secure a car on jack stands. Ask your instructor for permission before completing this part of the job. Your instructor may need to demonstrate the procedures to the class.

31. After getting your instructor's approval, place the jack under a proper lift point on the car (frame, rear axle housing, suspension arm, or reinforced section of the unibody).

If in doubt about where to position the jack, refer to a service manual for the particular car. Instructions will usually be given in one of the front sections of the manual.

32. To raise a car, place the transmission in neutral and release the emergency brake. This will let the car roll as the jack goes up. If the car cannot roll and the small wheels on the jack catch in the shop floor, the car could slide off the jack.

    As soon as the car is high enough, place jack stands under the suggested lift points. Lower the car onto the stands slowly. Check that they are safe. Then, remove the floor jack and block the wheels. It should now be safe to work under the car.

33. Raise the car. Remove the jack stands. Lower the car and return the equipment to the proper storage area.

34. Where did you position the floor jack when raising the car? _____

    _____

    _____

    _____

35. Where did you position the jack stands when securing the car? _____

    _____

    _____

    _____

WORK SAFETY

36. When in the auto shop, you must take full responsibility for your actions. A "joker" or "clown" in an auto shop is an accident just waiting to happen. Unknowingly, an unsafe worker is gambling with something of irreplaceable value—an eye, hand, face, or even a LIFE.

37. NOTE! Specialized safety rules are given throughout the textbook. They are printed in color. Pay close attention to these precautions.

38. Ask your instructor to sign this job before leaving class.

_____
INSTRUCTOR'S SIGNATURE

Job 3

Automotive Fasteners

INTRODUCTION: Auto technicians constantly use fasteners (bolts, nuts, screws, washers) when working on a car. A good technician realizes the importance of tightening certain bolts and nuts to factory specifications. If a bolt is undertightened or overtightened, vehicle breakdowns can result. Professional technicians always take the time to torque critical fasteners to their recommended torque values. They know that this can make the difference between a long lasting repair, and one that fails in a short period of time.

OBJECTIVE: Using the tools and equipment listed below, you will learn to use automotive fasteners, a degree scale, a torque wrench, a torque spec chart, and written instructions.

TOOLS AND EQUIPMENT: Check out a special bolt, washer, and nut assembly, a piece of chalk, torque wrench, socket, combination wrench, and an oil can.

INSTRUCTIONS: Follow the detailed procedures carefully. You will torque the bolt and nut assembly with a torque wrench while noting the rotation of the bolt. This will show you the relationship between the torque wrench reading and the tightness of the bolt. If you have trouble getting started, ask your instructor for help.

USING A TORQUE WRENCH

1. Clamp the large bolt and nut assembly in the vise as shown in Fig. 3-1. The vise jaws should clamp on the flats of the nut.

2. Unscrew the bolt from the nut. Place a few drops of oil on the bolt threads. Screw the bolt back into the nut.

3. Using the torque wrench, tighten the bolt to 1 foot-pound. This will give you a reference point for torquing the bolt to higher values.

4. With chalk or a pencil, draw an arrow on the head of the bolt as shown in Fig. 3-2. The arrow should run parallel to the vise jaws.

5. If you have a degree wheel designed for the job, place it over your nut. If not, draw reference lines on the vise as in Fig. 3-3. The lines should be approximately 45 degrees apart. Ask your instructor for help if you are having problems.

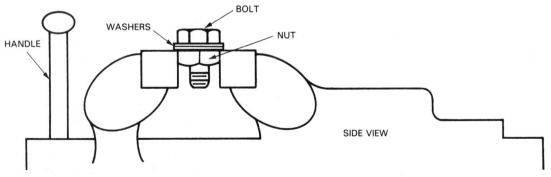

Fig. 3-1. Note how nut is clamped squarely in vise jaws. Tighten vise handle moderately.

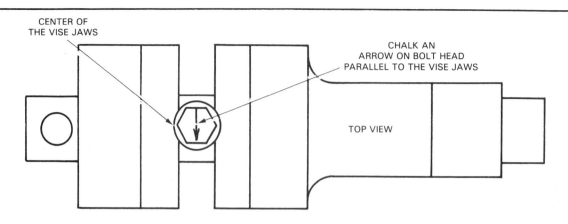

Fig. 3-2. Draw an arrow or line on bolt head as shown. Use a pencil or piece of chalk.

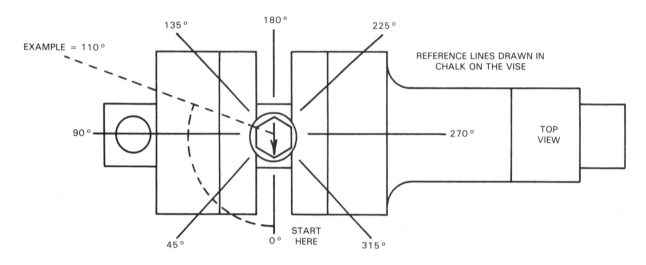

Fig. 3-3. If needed, mark lines on vise. These marks will tell you how far bolt turns when it is tightened.

Step	A	B	C	D	E	F	G	H	I	J
Torque value	5 ft-lb	10 ft-lb	15 ft-lb	20 ft-lb	25 ft-lb	30 ft-lb	35 ft-lb	40 ft-lb	45 ft-lb	50 ft-lb
Number of degrees bolt turned										

6. Now, tighten the bolt to the torque value given in step A of the chart above. This would be 5 foot-pounds.

7. With the bolt torqued to 5 ft-lb, note how far the bolt turned while tightening. Estimate the number of degrees the bolt rotated from zero. Refer back to Fig. 3-3.

8. Record the number of degrees the bolt turned in the chart under step A.

9. Now, loosen the bolt with your combination wrench. Turn the bolt until the arrow on the bolt head is aiming at zero again (parallel with vise jaws).

10. Repeat this procedure using the other torque values in the chart. Torque the bolt to 10, 15, 20, 25, through 50 ft-lb. Write down the number of degrees the bolt turned at each torque setting.

11. As you can see from this exercise, the more a bolt is tightened, the more the bolt will rotate in its hole. Also, as a bolt is tightened, it will stretch. A torque wrench assures that a bolt is not overtightened, overstretched, and possibly broken or stripped.

12. How many degrees did the bolt rotate at 20 ft-lb? _____

13. How many degrees did the bolt turn at 50 ft-lb? _____

14. Ask your instructor to sign this section of the job for credit. Then, if the class period is almost over, turn in your tools and equipment.

_____
INSTRUCTOR'S SIGNATURE

BOLT TORQUE SPECIFICATIONS

15. As you learned, a torque wrench measures the amount of twisting force applied to a fastener. It does this by registering the amount of flex or bend in the torque wrench handle. As you pull harder on the wrench, the handle bends more and indicates the torque on the bolt head.

   The torque wrench helps the mechanic tighten bolts and nuts to exact specifications. For example, if a bolt is overtightened, it can cause bolt breakage, thread damage, splitting of gaskets, part cracking, and other similar problems. If a bolt is undertightened, it can work free or fall out, cause oil or coolant leaks, and part breakage.

   Auto manufacturers commonly recommend that many bolts and nuts on a car be tightened with a torque wrench. For instance, a few engine parts that must be tightened with a torque wrench include: cylinder heads, intake and exhaust manifolds, connecting rod bearings, main bearings, and oil pump bolts.

16. What type of problems can occur if a bolt is improperly tightened? _____
_____
_____
_____

17. List a few engine parts that must be torqued.
_____
_____
_____

BOLT DIMENSIONS

18. The torque specification of a bolt is determined by the bolt's size (diameter of threads), thread pitch (number of threads per inch), and tensil strength (type and quality of metal in bolt).

   Bolt size is obtained by measuring the outside diameter of the bolt threads. See Fig. 3-4. Bolt length is the distance from the bottom of the bolt head to the end of the threads.

   Bolt size should not be confused with wrench size. Wrench size is the distance across the flats of the bolt head.

19. Using the information in step 18 of this job, identify the parts of the bolt in Fig. 3-4. Write the words in the blanks to finish the following statements.

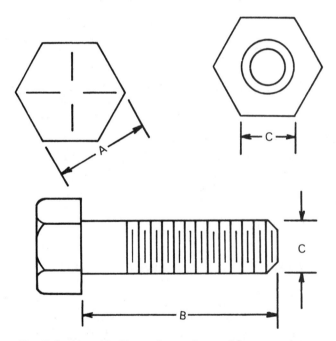

Fig. 3-4. Use this illustration and step 18 to complete statements in steps 20, 21, and 22 of job.

20. A in Fig. 3-4 would indicate the size of the _____needed for the bolt, or the distance across flats.

21. Dimension B in Fig. 3-4 would be the _____ of the bolt.

22. Dimension C in Fig. 3-4 is the bolt _____, which is the same as the diameter of the bolt _____.

BOLT THREADS

23. Basically, there are three types of bolt threads—fine, coarse, and metric. American made automobiles can use any of these three types of threads. Foreign cars commonly use metric threads on a majority of their bolts and nuts.

    It is very important that you do NOT mix thread types. For instance, if a metric bolt is forced into a fine thread hole, serious part and thread damage will occur. Always compare the threads on a bolt with its mating threads, especially if the bolt will not thread in easily by hand.

24. Compare the bolts shown in Fig. 3-5. Note the slight differences in the threads. Also, study the bolt designation numbers which identifies bolt size, thread type, and length.

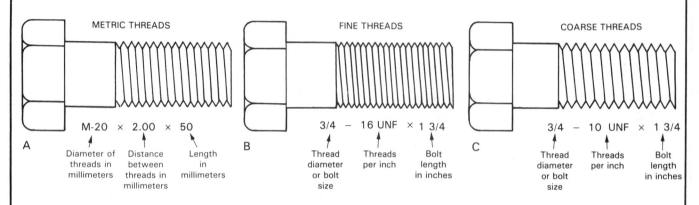

Fig. 3-5. Bolt drawings represent three thread types. Study letter-number designations. Designations are needed when selecting or buying bolts.

25. Refer to Fig. 3-5 to answer the next 6 questions.

26. How long is the metric bolt?_____

27. What is the size or diameter of the metric bolt? _____

28. How many threads per inch are there on the coarse thread bolt? _____

29. How many threads per inch are there on the fine bolt? _____

30. How long are the fine and coarse bolts?

_____

_____

_____

31. What is the size of the fine and coarse bolts?

_____

FASTENER TYPES

32. Now, study Fig. 3-6. It shows several common types of fasteners. Learn to identify each type and describe their usage.

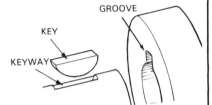

A. HEX NUT is the most common type nut used on an auto.

B. SLOTTED NUT AND COTTER PIN are used as a safety measure to prevent fasteners from loosening.

C. SNAP RING fits into a groove to hold a part on a shaft or in a hole.

D. KEY AND KEYWAY prevent a pulley or gear from turning on its shaft.

E. WING NUT is handy for fast nut removal by hand. It is used on air cleaners, for example.

F. LOCK WASHER is commonly used to prevent nut and washer from vibrating loose.

G. FLAT WASHER increases the clamping area of a bolt or nut to keep fastener from digging into part.

H. SPEED NUT is used with a screw to hold trim and body parts.

I. SET SCREW will hold small parts (knobs for example) on a shaft.

J. RIVET is sometimes used when a part must not be removed in normal service.

K. MACHINE SCREW is an inexpensive fastener. It is for low stress applications.

L. SHEET METAL SCREW is frequently used to hold thin metal or plastic parts.

Fig. 3-6. These are some of the most frequently used types of fasteners in auto mechanics.

BOLT TORQUE CHART

33. Look at the chart in Fig. 3-7. A bolt torque chart provides specifications on bolt sizes and bolt torques. When specification manuals are not available, chart can be used to determine how tight a bolt should be torqued.

    Note the bolt head markings in the chart. The more lines on a bolt head, the stronger the bolt. The head markings indicate tensile strength. A bolt with a higher tensile strength can take a higher torque value without damage.

BOLT SPECIFICATIONS AND TORQUING CHART

BOLT SIZE OR THREAD	DEC. EQUIV.	BOLT STRENGTH-GRADE MARKINGS SAE CLASSIFICATION			HEAD SIZE	NUT SIZE
		GRADE 1 OR 2 NO MARKS	GRADE 5 3 MARKS	GRADE 8 6 MARKS		
1/4	.250	6	7	11	3/8	7/16
5/16	.3125	10	14	22	1/2	9/16
3/8	.375	16	30	40	9/16	5/8
7/16	.4375	24	50	65	5/8	3/4
1/2	.500	37	75	100	3/4	13/16
9/16	.5625	53	105	135	7/8	7/8
5/8	.625	74	140	190	15/16	1
3/4	.750	120	175	220	1-1/8	1-1/8
7/8	.875	185	290	425	1-5/16	1-5/16
1	1.000	270	450	625	1-1/2	1-1/2

Fig. 3-7. Study use of this bolt torque chart. Note how torque values increase as size and strength of bolt increases.

34. Using the torque chart in Fig. 3-7, answer the following questions.

35. What is the normal head size for a 1/4 in. bolt? _____.

36. What is the normal size of a bolt requiring a 9/16 in. wrench? _____.

37. A 1/2 in. bolt, grade 5 (3 lines on head) should be torqued to _____.

38. A 1/4 in. bolt with 6 marks on its head should be torqued to _____.

39. A torque of 65 foot-pounds would be used on a _____ size bolt, grade _____.

40. When torquing bolts, make sure the threads are clean and in good condition. Also, a small drop of oil should be placed on the bolt threads. This will assure an accurate torque wrench reading.

Name _____

Date _____ Period _____

Instructor _____

Job 4

Checking Fluid Levels

INTRODUCTION: If a car's oils and fluids are not serviced properly, the useful life of the vehicle will be reduced. When a technician checks a fluid level (engine oil, coolant, power steering fluid, differential lubricant), it is a form of preventive maintenance.

Anytime a low fluid level, dirty oil, or other problem is found, it tells the technician something about the condition of the car. For example, an excessively low level may indicate a serious leak. Then, the technician would know to inspect other areas to find the source of the problem. This type maintenance can prevent costly on-the-road breakdowns.

OBJECTIVE: Given the tools and equipment listed below, you will learn to check the fluids in an automobile.

TOOLS AND EQUIPMENT: Check out a pair of safety glasses, standard screwdriver, set of hand wrenches, 3/8 in. drive ratchet, ruler, shop rag, battery hydrometer, antifreeze tester, and an automobile.

INSTRUCTIONS: Ask your instructor for any added details for the job. You may have to work on a shop owned car or an actual customer car.

BRAKE FLUID

1. Locate the brake master cylinder on your car. It is normally bolted to the firewall on the driver's side of the car.

2. Clean and remove the master cylinder cover. If spring clips are used, pry them off with a screwdriver. A wrench is needed if the cover is bolted in place.

3. Inspect the level and condition of the brake fluid. Typically, the brake fluid should NOT be more than 1/4 in. (6.4 mm) down in the reservoir. See Fig. 4-1.

   WARNING! Keep oil, dirt, and grease out of the brake fluid. Oil and grease can ruin the cups in a brake system.

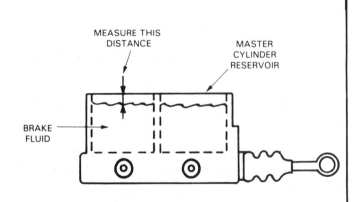

Fig. 4-1. Brake fluid must be kept at specified level for car to be in safe operating condition. Always refer to a service manual for exact specs on filling.

4. Is your master cylinder full or low? _____
   Explain. _____
   _____
   _____
   _____

OIL DIPSTICK SHOWS ALMOST 1/2 QUART LOW.

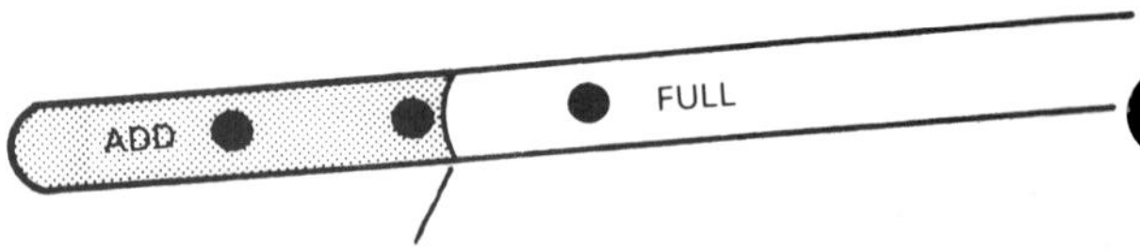

Fig. 4-2. When adding oil to an engine, only add enough to bring oil up to full mark on dipstick.

5. When the brake fluid becomes low in a short period of time, inspect the entire brake system for leaks. Check the wheel cylinders, brake lines, and back of the master cylinder for wetness. Brake fluid will show up as a dark, damp spot.

6. To improve your troubleshooting ability, memorize the smell of brake fluid. Then, if fluid leakage is found, you can quickly smell and identify the leak.

7. Inspect your brake system for leaks. Look behind the wheel backing plates, at the brake line fittings, and anywhere else a leak might occur.

8. Could you find any brake system leaks? _____ Explain. _____
   _____
   _____
   _____

9. NOTE! If you spill brake fluid, wipe it up immediately. Brake fluid can ruin the paint job on a car. It dissolves paint in a matter of minutes.

ENGINE OIL

10. With the engine off, find the engine oil dipstick. It should be on side or front of engine. Remove dipstick and wipe it off. Then, reinstall dipstick until fully seated.

11. Pull the dipstick back out and hold it over your shop rag. Inspect how far the oil is up on the stick. See Fig. 4-2. The oil should be between the full and add marks.
    Memorize the smell of engine oil. This will help you when diagnosing leaks.

12. When the oil level is even with the add mark on the dipstick, you usually need to add one quart of oil. If the oil is midway between the add and full marks, one-half quart is needed. Be careful never to add too much oil to an engine or oil foaming and other problems may result.

13. How was the level of oil in your engine? _____ Explain._____
    _____
    _____
    _____

14. If this is an actual customer car and oil is needed, remove the breather cap. The cap is usually on the valve cover. Pour in the correct type motor oil. Then, reinstall the breather cap.

15. Where would you add oil on this engine?
    _____
    _____
    _____
    _____

BATTERY

16. Inspect the battery. The top of the battery should be clean and dry. Moisture on the battery case top can cause battery leakage (current shorts from one cell to another across top of dirty battery). Also, check the condition of the battery terminals. They should be uncorroded, clean, and tight. Corroded terminals may keep the engine from cranking properly.

17. Describe the outer condition or cleanliness or your battery case and terminals. Could you find any other problems?

_____

_____

_____

_____

_____

18. What is battery leakage? _____

_____

_____

_____

ENGINE COOLANT

19. Determine whether your car has a closed or an open cooling system, Fig. 4-3. A closed system will have a plastic reservoir tank on one side of the radiator. The radiator cap may also be labeled – DO NOT OPEN.

   To check the coolant level in a closed system, inspect the amount of coolant in the plastic reservoir tank. Compare the level with the marks on the side of the tank.

   To check the coolant level in an open system, first make sure the radiator is cool. If warm, DO NOT remove the radiator cap. Hot coolant could blow into your face, causing serious injury. The coolant in an open system should be about one inch down in the radiator, Fig. 4-3.

   If either type cooling system needs coolant, add a mixture of 50% antifreeze. This is the most efficient mixture.

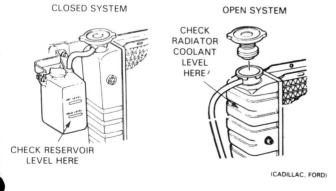

CLOSED SYSTEM   OPEN SYSTEM

CHECK RADIATOR COOLANT LEVEL HERE

CHECK RESERVOIR LEVEL HERE

(CADILLAC, FORD)

Fig. 4-3. Note the difference between closed and open cooling systems. You do not have to remove radiator cap to check coolant level in closed system.

20. How was the level of coolant in your cooling system? _____

_____

_____

_____

21. Check out an antifreeze tester. Draw coolant into the tester. Use the directions with the particular tester to determine the freeze-up protection of the coolant.

22. Also, inspect the coolant for rust or discoloration. After prolonged use, antifreeze can break down and become very corrosive. It can cause rapid rust formation and damage to the cooling system. For this reason, antifreeze must be drained and replaced at recommended intervals.

   A leak in a cooling system will usually be easy to see. The area around the leak will often be a bright, rust color or the color of the antifreeze.

23. To increase your troubleshooting skills, memorize the smell of antifreeze. Then, when a leak is found, the smell will tell you whether it is antifreeze or another fluid.

24. How much freeze-up protection does your coolant provide for the system? _____

_____

_____

_____

25. Is your coolant rusty or could you find any leaks? _____ Explain._____

_____

_____

_____

_____

POWER STEERING FLUID

26. Locate the power steering pump. It is normally on the lower front of the engine. With the engine off, remove the power steering pump cap and wipe off the dipstick. Reinsert dipstick and pull it back out. Holding it over your shop rag, inspect the level of fluid. The fluid should be between the full and add marks, as in Fig. 4-4.

If needed, add enough recommended power steering fluid (usually automatic transmission fluid) to fill to the add mark. Do NOT add too much, or fluid will blow out the pump after engine starting.

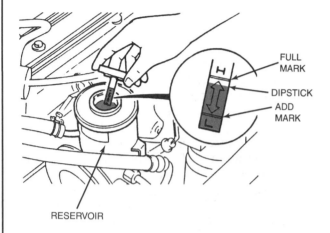

Fig. 4-4. Power steering fluid dipstick is normally attached to cap on pump. If needed, add recommended type fluid, usually automatic transmission fluid.

27. If the power steering pump is excessively low, check the power steering system for leaks. Look under the pump, around line fittings and any other component containing fluid.

28. Did your power steering fluid level check OK? Explain._____
_____
_____
_____
_____

AUTOMATIC TRANSMISSION FLUID

29. To check the automatic transmission fluid, start and warm the engine. Move the transmission selector through the gears. Apply the parking brake and then shift the transmission into park and block the wheels. Leave the engine running.

    Remove and wipe off the transmission dipstick. It will usually be at the rear of the engine on one side. Reinsert the dipstick and pull it back out. Hold it over your rag while you check the fluid level on the stick. Refer to Fig. 4-5.

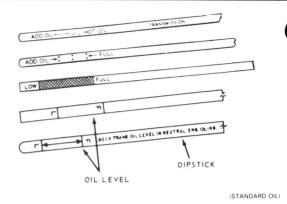

Fig. 4-5. Note different types of markings on these automatic transmission dipsticks. Some only show one pint from add to full, others show a quart from add to full. Only add enough to reach full mark.

30. When adding fluid to an automatic transmission, make sure you have the correct type of fluid. Different transmissions require different types. Always install the type fluid recommended by the manufacturer.

    Also, do NOT overfill the transmission. Overfilling can cause fluid foaming, poor transmission operation, and seal leakage.

31. Study the smell of automatic transmission fluid. If the fluid smells burned, then the bands or clutches inside the transmission may be worn and damaged.

32. Describe the condition and level of fluid in your automatic transmission. _____
_____
_____
_____
_____

DIFFERENTIAL LUBRICANT

33. OPTIONAL! Ask your instructor for approval before completing the last section of this job.

34. After getting your instructor's OK, raise the car on a lift or secure it on jack stands.

    Remove the differential filler plug, NOT the drain plug. The filler plug will be on the front or rear of the housing, about halfway up on the differential. This is pictured in Fig. 4-6.

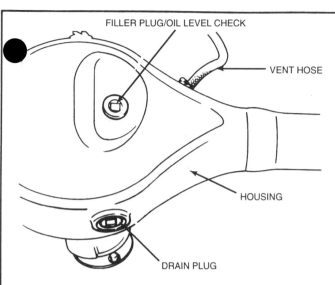

Fig. 4-6. Note locations of filler and drain plugs in this differential.

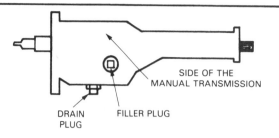

Fig. 4-7. Filler plug is on side of manual transmission. Drain plug will be on bottom. Only remove filler plug when checking level.

35. The differential fluid should be approximately 1/2 in. (12.7 mm) below the filler hole. This can vary with some cars so always refer to a service manual for an exact specification. Stick your finger in the filler hole to check the lubricant level.

If needed, add just enough recommended differential lubricant to meet factory recommendations. Memorize the smell of differential fluid so that you can quickly diagnose leaks.

36. Was the lubricant in your differential low? _____ Explain._____
_____
_____
_____

MANUAL TRANSMISSION LUBRICANT

37. OPTIONAL! Check the lubricant in a manual transmission. If your car has an automatic, you may need another car or a shop training unit.

Remove the filler plug on the side of the transmission. This is pictured in Fig. 4-7. Insert your finger into the hole. The lubricant should be slightly below or almost even with the filler hole.

If needed, add the recommended type gear oil for the particular transmission. Also, learn to identify the smell of gear oil.

38. How was the lubricant level in the manual transmission?_____
_____
_____
_____

39. OPTIONAL! Use the directions in a service manual to check the lubricant level in a manual steering gearbox.

40. Check the windshield washer solvent. It will be in a plastic reservoir on one side of the engine compartment. The solvent should be almost even with the full mark on the side of the container.

In cold weather, only add the recommended type solution to the windshield washer tank. If water is added, it could freeze and damage the windshield washer reservoir and pump.

41. Ask your instructor to sign this job for credit.

_____
INSTRUCTOR'S SIGNATURE

324   Auto Fundamentals Workbook

Name _____

Date _____ Period _____

Instructor _____

Job 5

Service
Manuals

INTRODUCTION: The service manual, also called shop manual or repair manual, is a book containing detailed directions on how to work on a car. It is an essential reference tool of the auto technician. When a technician must perform an unfamiliar or difficult repair, the service manual can be used to outline what must be done. It also provides specifications, capacities, and other useful information. In a sense, a service manual is like having an experienced technician standing ready to answer almost any of your questions.

OBJECTIVE: Supplied with service manuals and vehicle information, you will learn to use the index, contents, specifications, troubleshooting, and repair sections of a service manual.

TOOLS AND EQUIPMENT: You will need a service manual that covers your car or one covering all makes and models of cars.

INSTRUCTIONS: Use the service manual to look up and list the information requested in the job. Take your time. You may need more than one class period to fully grasp the use of a service manual.

INDEX AND CONTENTS SECTIONS

1. Ask your instructor for the following vehicle information. You may be able to look up data on a car of your choice or your instructor may assign a particular make and model car. Record this information in the following space. It will be used for the remainder of the job.

2. Car make_____ Car model_____
   Year car _____ Engine size _____
   Transmission type _____

3. Check out a service manual. Then, read the front section explaining how to use the manual. This information is normally inside the front cover or on first few pages of the book.

4. What is the title of the service manual you are using? _____
   _____

5. What model years does it cover? _____

6. Does your manual contain a table of contents? _____

7. Does your manual contain an index? _____
   Where is it located? _____

8. Are there small contents or index pages at the beginning of each repair section?_____

FINDING PAGE NUMBERS

9. On what page is the section covering the repair of your engine? The page number should be given in either the contents or the index. _____

10. List the service manual page numbers that explain the service and repair of the following engine parts. Also, read the instructions covering each area of repair.

AREA OF REPAIR	PAGE NUMBER
A. Engine assembly	_____
B. Valve lifters	_____
C. Connecting rods	_____
D. Main bearings	_____
E. Valve guides	_____
F. Timing chain, gears, or belt	_____
G. Pistons	_____
H. Camshaft	_____

BOLT TORQUE SPECIFICATIONS

11. Normally given under specifications, list the torque specs for the following engine components.

COMPONENT	TORQUE SPECS
A. Cylinder heads	_____
B. Main bearings	_____
C. Intake manifold	_____
D. Connecting rod bolts	_____
E. Flywheel bolts	_____
F. Exhaust manifold	_____

ENGINE TUNE-UP INFORMATION

12. Look up and list the following tune-up information for your engine.

TUNE-UP DATA	SPECIFICATION
A. Spark plug type	_____
B. Compression pressure	_____
C. Ignition timing	_____
D. Spark plug gap	_____
E. Fuel pump pressure	_____
F. Idle speed	_____

13. Most service manuals will have a simplified top view illustration of the engine. It gives information on engine firing order. The service manual illustration will usually show cylinder numbers, distributor cap numbers, direction of distributor rotation, timing marks, and spark plug firing order. It should be similar to Fig. 5-1. This type illustration may be needed when installing a distributor, spark plug wires, when adjusting ignition timing (finding number one cylinder), and other related type jobs.

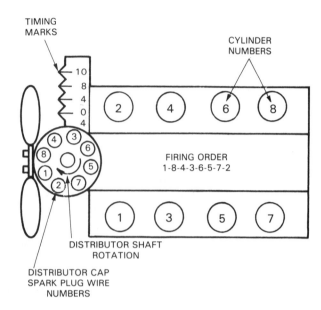

Fig. 5-1. This is an example of how a firing order-timing mark illustration in a service manual might look.

14. Locate the drawing in the service manual for your particular engine. Note how the manual illustration shows cylinder number and firing order information.

15. Draw your engine illustration in Fig. 5-2. Use a ruler to add the shape of the engine to the fan. Then, label the cylinder numbers, distributor cap, and any other data. Finally, draw lines (spark plug wires) from the distributor cap terminals to the correct cylinders.

Fig. 5-2. Draw shape of your engine. Then, add firing order, cylinder numbers, distributor shaft rotation, timing marks, and spark plug wires.

FOOTNOTES

16. When using a service manual, it is very important to pay close attention to footnotes. Footnotes are commonly used with specifications, for example. The footnote will give extra data or special procedures for complying with the specification.

    When a footnote is used, a symbol (@, 1, 2, 0, Δ, □) will be placed next to the specification. You must find another identical symbol elsewhere on the page. It will give the added details for the specification.

17. Find an example of a footnote in your service manual. What page is it on? _____ In your own words, explain the purpose of this footnote. _____

    _____

    _____

    _____

TROUBLESHOOTING CHARTS

18. Most service manuals have troubleshooting or diagnosis charts. They are helpful when a problem is difficult to locate or pinpoint. The troubleshooting chart will list common causes for particular problems, with needed corrections.

19. Can you find a troubleshooting chart or diagnosis information in your service manual? _____ On what page is it located? _____ In your own words, explain one problem and possible correction.

    _____

    _____

    _____

    _____

    _____

    _____

REVIEW OTHER SERVICE MANUALS

20. When you have spare time, thumb through different service manuals. Inspect the illustrations and repair procedures for various components. Also, compare the organization of one service manual to another.

21. Have your instructor sign this job for credit.

_____
INSTRUCTOR'S SIGNATURE

Name _____

Date _____ Period _____

Instructor _____

Job 6

Basic
Engine

INTRODUCTION: An automobile engine and a small lawn mower engine contain many of the same parts. They both have a crankshaft, piston, connecting rod, cylinder block, camshaft, cylinder head, valves, and other fundamental components. For this reason, a small gas engine can serve as an excellent "learning tool" for introducing the basic parts of an internal combustion engine.

OBJECTIVE: Given the tools and equipment listed below, you will learn to disassemble, identify, and reassemble the parts of a one-cylinder small gas engine.

TOOLS AND EQUIPMENT: You will need a set of basic hand tools, an inch-pound torque wrench, ring compressor, ring expander, compression gauge, valve spring compressor, oil can, ruler, dial caliper or feeler gauge, and possibly a set of micrometers.

INSTRUCTIONS: Follow the job instructions carefully. Only remove the engine parts mentioned in the job or by your instructor.

NOTE! If small engine service manuals are available, use them to obtain the exact specifications for your engine. This job lists very general specs which vary from engine to engine.

1. List the following information for your engine. This data is usually given on a metal tag attached to the engine.

   A. MAKE_____

   B. HORSEPOWER _____

   C. MODEL NUMBER _____

   D. SERIAL NUMBER _____

2. Check engine compression. If available, screw a compression gauge into the spark plug hole. Pull start the engine several times and read the pressure gauge. Compression pressure should be within specifications, typically above 60 to 80 psi (413 to 551 kPa).

   If you do not have a compression gauge, crank the engine over with the spark plug installed. Note how hard the engine kicks over on each compression stroke. If the engine spins freely, with little or no compression drag, something is wrong inside the engine. Compression pressure is leaking through a burned valve, worn piston rings, blown head gasket, or other component.

3. Describe the results of your compression test. _____
   _____
   _____
   _____

4. What did the compression test tell you about the general condition of the engine?
   _____
   _____
   _____
   _____

5. Make sure the gasoline and oil have been drained from the engine. Then, remove the air cleaner and blower housing, Fig. 6-1.

   Usually, the pull start mechanism can be removed while still bolted to the blower housing. Also unbolt and remove the screen on the flywheel, Fig. 6-1.

   Carefully note how the parts fit together. Keep your bolts organized.

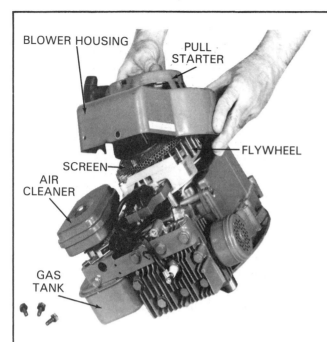

Fig. 6-1. Study the external engine parts that must be removed first.

6. If possible, unbolt and remove the carburetor and fuel tank as a single unit. As they are removed, note the location of the carburetor linkage rods and springs.

7. How many linkage rods are there on your engine? _____ What parts do they connect? _____
_____

8. Now, unbolt and remove the breather from the side of the engine. It is pointed out in Fig. 6-2. The breather is a small, rectangular cover over the valve springs and valve stems.

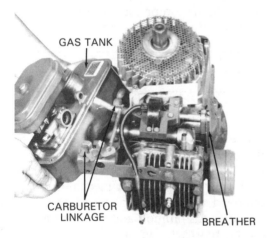

Fig. 6-2. As you lift fuel tank-carburetor assembly off, study how carburetor linkage and springs fit together. This will help you during reassembly.

9. Using a ratchet and socket, unscrew the cylinder head bolts, Fig. 6-3. As each bolt is removed, check the length and location of each head bolt. Quite often, the three bolts around the exhaust port are longer to help dissipate heat. You must reinstall these bolts in the correct holes or serious engine damage could result.

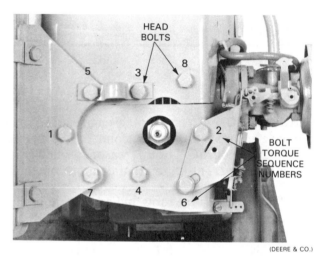

(DEERE & CO.)

Fig. 6-3. After you remove bolts, light taps with a mallet should free cylinder head from block. Number sequence in photo will be used during engine assembly.

10. After lifting the cylinder head off the engine, inspect the head and cylinder. Look for cracks, burned valves, scored cylinder wall, damaged piston head, or other problems that could upset engine operation.

11. Could you find any problems in the top end of your engine? _____
_____
_____
_____
_____
_____

12. You can now remove the valves from the engine. As in Fig. 6-4, use a small valve spring compressor to squeeze the valve springs. If a compressor is not handy, two large screwdrivers will usually work.

With the spring compressed, the keeper-retainer can be slid off of the valve stem. You may need to grasp the retainer with needle nose pliers.

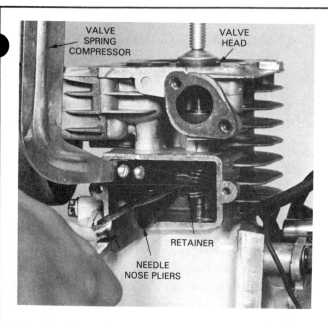

Fig. 6-4. Spring compressor holds valve head while compressing valve spring. This will let you pull retainer from stem.

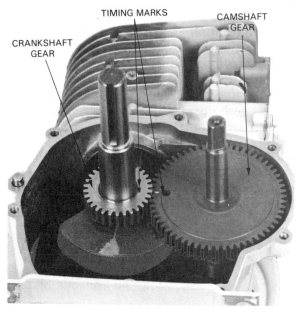

(DEERE & CO.)

Fig. 6-5. Check timing marks on crankshaft and camshaft gears. These marks are needed to time camshaft with crankshaft during assembly.

13. Make sure the crankshaft is clean and free of burrs. Then, unbolt and slide the crankcase cover off of the engine. This cover usually forms a portion of the engine block.

  Be careful not to pry on and dent the mating surfaces between the cover and block. The slightest knick or dent could cause an oil leak after assembly.

14. If used, remove the oil singer and governor assembly.

15. To prepare for camshaft removal, rotate the crankshaft until the valve timing marks line up. Look at Fig. 6-5. Dots or lines on the cam gear and crank gear should point to each other. When these marks align, the piston should be at TDC on the compression stroke.

16. What do the valve timing marks look like?

_____

_____

_____

17. How many teeth are there on the camshaft gear? _____

  How many teeth are there on the crankshaft gear? _____

18. Lay your engine on its side, as in Fig. 6-6. This will prevent the valve lifters (tappets) from falling out when the camshaft is removed.

  Pull the cam and the lifters out of the engine. Keep the lifters in order so that they can be installed in the same holes. If the lifters are mixed up, it could change the valve-to-lifter clearance.

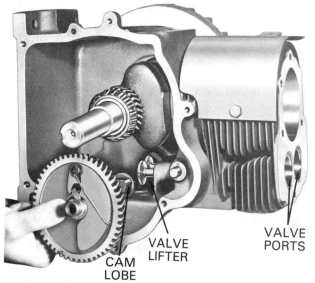

(WISCONSIN MOTOR CORP.)

Fig. 6-6. Position engine as shown to keep lifters from falling out and getting mixed up.

19. Pry down the bolt locks and unscrew the connecting rod bolts. Study how the rod is positioned in the block. Sometimes, there is a directional arrow or identifying bump or lip that shows connecting rod direction.

    You should place your own marks on the connecting rod if needed. Place a mark on the camshaft side of the rod. Then you will be sure to install the rod and piston correctly.

20. Inspect the top of the cylinder wall for a ring ridge (metal lip) or carbon build-up. These problems must be removed before the piston will slide out of the cylinder.

    If a ring ridge is excessive, a ridge reaming tool should be used. It will cut off the ridge and prevent piston damage.

21. Now, push the piston and rod out of the cylinder.

22. OPTIONAL! If your instructor has given approval, you can now remove the piston rings from the piston. As in Fig. 6-7, spread the rings using a ring expander. Be careful not to force the rings too wide or they will break. Compression rings are made of cast iron and are very brittle. Only open the rings enough for them to slide off the piston.

    As you remove each ring, look for identifying marks or differences in the inner edge. Sometimes, the inner edge is chamfered differently on the first and second compression rings.

    During this exercise, you will probably reuse the old piston rings. They should be kept right-side up and in order.

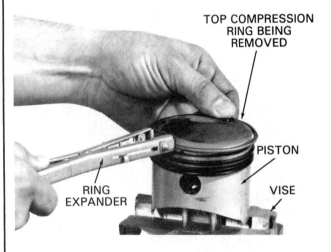

TOP COMPRESSION RING BEING REMOVED

PISTON

RING EXPANDER

VISE

(TECUMSEH PRODUCTS CO.)

Fig. 6-7 Do not overextend brittle rings or they will snap. Also, now how rod I-beam is clamped in vise. This holds piston and rod as you remove rings.

23. Now that the engine is disassembled, inspect all of the parts for wear or damage.

    During an actual engine rebuild, you would have to replace any part worn beyond specifications. A very thorough inspection and measurement process would be required.

24. To assure that you can identify all of the engine parts, measure and list the following dimensions. Use a ruler (estimate sizes), a caliper (general sizes), or a micrometer (accurate sizes).

PART	SIZE
A. Cylinder bore diameter	_____
B. Piston diameter	_____
C. Crankshaft journal diameter	_____
D. Intake valve stem diameter	_____
E. Camshaft journal diameter	_____
F. Compression ring thickness	_____
G. Exhaust valve head diameter	_____
H. Valve lifter length	_____

25. You are now ready to reassemble your engine. Wipe everything clean and place a few drops of oil on all friction surfaces.

26. Install the rings on the piston, Fig. 6-7. Stagger the ring gaps away from each other. Typically, the second compression ring should face one end of the piston pin. The top compression ring and oil ring should point at the other end of the piston pin. This provides a maximum distance between each ring gap which reduces pressure or combustion leakage.

27. Explain how you staggered your ring gaps.

    _____
    _____
    _____

28. Why must the ring gaps be staggered?_____

    _____
    _____
    _____

29. Squirt oil on the piston skirts and rings. Then, install a ring compressor on the piston. The edge of the compressor with small bumps or indentations must face down. Tighten the ring compressor while keeping it square on the piston, Fig. 6-8.

TIGHTENING WRENCH

HAMMER HANDLE

RING COMPRESSOR

PISTON HEAD

(KOHLER CO.)

Fig. 6-8. Ring compressor squeezes rings into their grooves for piston installation. This keeps rings from catching on cylinder wall. Piston can then be tapped into engine with a wooden hammer handle.

30. Turn the crankshaft to BDC. Fit the piston, connecting rod, and ring compressor into the top of the cylinder. Make sure the piston and connecting rod are facing the right direction. Check that the identifying marks on the rod are correct.

31. While using one hand to guide the connecting rod over the crankshaft, tap the piston into the engine with a hammer handle. Use light taps and stop if the rings catch on the cylinder. If the rings catch, remove the assembly and reinstall the compressor on the piston.

32. Install the connecting rod cap, locks, and bolts. Using a torque wrench, tighten the rod bolts to specification. A lawn mower engine should have a connecting rod bolt torque of approximately 5.5 foot-pounds or 65 inch-pounds.

33. WARNING! If you are going to start and run your engine, the connecting rod bolts must be torqued to an exact specification. Do NOT use the above value because it may not be accurate. If the connecting rod is under or overtorqued, the engine may "blow up" (throw a rod) when started.

34. After torquing the rod bolts, bend the locks over to keep the bolts from loosening.

35. Assemble the valves, springs, and retainers. If needed, ask your instructor for help. The retainers can be hard to fit into place.

36. Lay the engine on its side and slide the lifters into their correct holes. Rotate the crankshaft until the timing mark is pointing at the camshaft centerline.

Fit the camshaft into place so that the timing marks line up. Install an oil slinger if used.

37. Bolt the crankcase cover to the engine block. Make sure your gasket is in place. Tighten the cover bolts in a crisscross pattern. This will pull the cover down evenly.

38. Measure valve clearance. Turn the crankshaft until both of the valves are fully closed. Then, insert feeler gauge blades between the valve stems and lifters. The thickest blade size that fits between the two equals valve clearance.

39. What is your intake valve clearance? _____ What is your exhaust valve clearance?_____

40. Install the head gasket, cylinder head, and any brackets held by the head bolts. Run the head bolts down with your speed handle but do not tighten them. Make sure you have any long or short bolts in their correct holes.

41. Torque the cylinder head bolts to specifications, Fig. 6-9. Follow the crisscross sequence given in Fig. 6-3. First, tighten each bolt to about 4 foot-pounds (48 inch-pounds). Then, tighten the bolts to 8 foot-pounds (96 inch-pounds). Finally, torque the head bolts to their full specification, approximately 12 foot-pounds (144 inch-pounds).

42. CAUTION! Tighten the head bolts to manufacturer's specs if the engine is to be operated. The above torque is an average value and may not be correct for your engine.

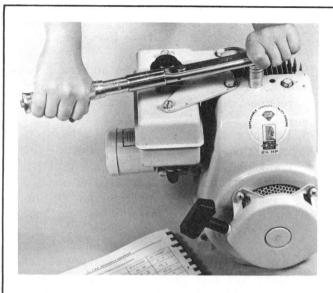

Fig. 6-9. When torquing head bolts, tighten each bolt a little at a time, using a crisscross sequence. This will compress head gasket evenly.

43. Install the remaining engine components in reverse order of disassembly. Note, be careful not to overtighten any of the fasteners. Most small gas engines are made of soft metal which can be damaged easily.

44. Clean your work area and get your instructor's signature on this job sheet.

INSTRUCTOR'S SIGNATURE

Name _____

Date _____ Period _____

Instructor _____

Job 7

Vehicle Safety Inspection

INTRODUCTION: Vehicle safety should be a concern to anyone entering a city street or traveling a highway. Thousands of auto related injuries and fatalities occur because drivers fail to keep their cars in a safe operating condition. It is up to you to inspect, report, and repair safety hazzards. Even when performing a tune-up, brake job, grease job, or other repair, keep an eye open for any condition that could endanger the passengers.

OBJECTIVE: Using this job, and an automobile, you will learn to perform a basic vehicle safety inspection.

TOOLS AND EQUIPMENT: Ask your instructor for details of the job. You may have to inspect your parents' car, your own car, a shop owned car, or a customer car.

INSTRUCTIONS: After inspecting the condition of each check point, place an X in the appropriate column. Identify whether the car passes or fails each check point. In the space for comments, sumarize why the car passed or failed the check point. Make sure you EXPLAIN the results for all 15 inspection points.
    NOTE! Before inspecting a car, obtain approval from your instructor. Ask your parents for written permission before inspecting their car.

VEHICLE SAFETY INSPECTION

1. List the following information for the car to be inspected.
    CAR MAKE _____ CAR MODEL _____ YEAR _____ COLOR _____
    OWNER _____ LICENSE NUMBER _____

	PASSED	FAILED	EXPLANATION
2. HORN. Horn should be audible at a distance of 200 ft. (61 m).			
3. GLASS. The windows should not be broken, cracked, or obstructed.			
4. MIRRORS. Mirrors should be unbroken, uncracked, clear, and in working condition.			
5. WINDSHIELD WIPERS. Check that the blades are not hardened or cracked. Make sure the wipers operate.			

	PASSED	FAILED	EXPLANATION
6. STEERING. There should not be excessive play in the steering wheel (1/4 in. or 6.35 mm maximum, engine running for power steering).			
7. BRAKES. The brake pedal should be full, solid, and the emergency brake should keep the car from rolling.			
8. TIRES. There should be a minimum of 1/16 in. (1.59 mm) of tread depth on all four tires. Wear pattern should also be even.			
9. HEADLIGHTS. Check that the high and the low beams operate.			
10. PARKING LIGHTS. Make sure all lights operate and lens are unbroken. Some cars have side lights and license plate lights.			
11. TURN SIGNALS. All turn signals should blink on and off at a reasonable speed.			
12. STOP LIGHTS. The brake lights should be visible at a distance of 500 ft. (152 m).			
13. EXHAUST SYSTEM. It should not leak. The tailpipe must not empty beneath the car.			
14. SHOCK ABSORBERS. Bounce each corner of the car. It should stop in one or two motions.			
15. SEAT BELTS. They should be anchored and working.			

Name _____

Date _____ Period _____

Instructor _____

Job 8

Oil Change, Grease Job

INTRODUCTION: Lubrication service is one of the most important and common maintenance operations performed on a car. Changing the engine oil, filter, and lubricating the various high friction points at prescribed intervals will prolong the useful life of an automobile. "You can pay now or you can pay later" is an automotive saying that relates to lubrication service. Anyone that fails to spend a few dollars to change their oil and have their car "lubed" will end up paying several hundred dollars for mechanical repairs.

OBJECTIVE: Given an automobile and the listed tools, you will learn to change the engine oil and filter and perform a grease job.

TOOLS AND EQUIPMENT: You will be needing an oil filter wrench, box end wrench, oil can spout, grease gun, oil squirt can, oil drain pan, some door latch lubricant, a few shop rags, and eye protection. If you are performing a live service, you should obtain the manufacturer designated type and amount of oil and an oil filter.

INSTRUCTIONS: Ask your instructor for details of the Job. Your instructor may want you to perform the Job on a customer car or just go through the motions on a shop owned auto or stand mounted engine.

DRAINING OIL

1. During an actual oil change, the engine should be warmed to operating temperature. Then, any dirt or contaminants will be picked up, suspended, and drained out of the engine with the oil.

2. Normally, you will have to raise the car on a lift or with a jack and then secure it on jack stands. In either case, the car should be level when raised to allow all of the oil to drain from the pan.

    To prevent accidental starting without oil in the pan, remove the key from the ignition switch.

3. Place your oil drain pan under the engine oil pan. Check that you are not looking at the transmission pan. Put the drain pan slightly to one side of the engine pan, as in Fig. 8-1.

4. With a box end wrench of the correct size, turn the oil drain plug counterclockwise and remove it, Fig. 8-2.

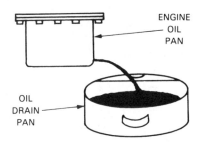

Fig. 8-1. Be careful, at first hot oil will pour out to one side of oil pan.

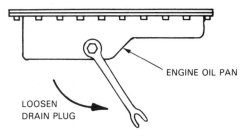

Fig. 8-2. An oil pan drain plug will strip easily. Looking at it from the front, turn plug counterclockwise for removal.

CAUTION! Keep your arm out of the way of the HOT OIL as is flows from the engine oil pan.

5. While the oil is draining for three or four minutes, inspect the drain plug. The plastic washer or seal should be uncracked and unsplit or it will leak. Check the threads for damage and wear.

   During an actual oil change, you would have to replace a damaged washer seal or drain plug.

6. What is the condition of your drain plug and seal? _____

   _____

7. Being extremely careful not to cross thread, overtighten, and strip its threads, install and snug the oil drain plug. Note! The drain plug only needs to be tight enough to slightly compress the plug seal. Overtightening will cause part damage and leakage.

8. Move the oil drain pan under the engine oil filter. Loosen the oil filter using your filter wrench, Fig. 8-3. Being careful not to let HOT OIL run down your arm, spin the filter the rest of the way off.

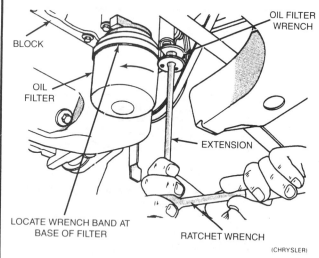

Fig. 8-3. Use oil filter wrench to unscrew old filter. Turn counterclockwise.

REPLACING OIL FILTER

9. Wipe off the mounting base for the oil filter to remove any dirt and contaminated oil, Fig. 8-4. Also, check that the old filter seal is NOT stuck on the engine.

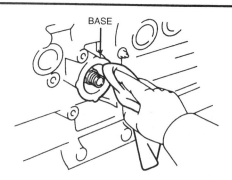

Fig. 8-4. After removing oil filter, clean off filter mounting base to help prevent leakage.

10. Make certain that your new filter is a proper replacement. Always check that the rubber O-ring seals are identical. The diameters of each should measure the same.

11. What is the measured diameter of your filter seal? _____

    _____

12. What is the measured diameter of the threaded hole in the filter? _____

    _____

13. If the filter fits on the engine upright, fill the new filter with oil. This prevents a temporary lack of oil pressure while the empty filter is filling.

14. How or at what angle is your oil filter mounted on the engine? _____

    _____

    _____

15. Wipe some clean engine oil on to the new oil filter rubber seal. This will assure proper tightening of the filter and help prevent leaks. See Fig. 8-5.

16. Without cross threading it, screw on and hand tighten the new oil filter (reuse old filter if an exercise). Your hands and the filter should be clean and dry. Look at Fig. 8-6.

    After the seal makes contact with the engine base, use a rag or towel to help turn the filter an additional 1/2 to 3/4 turn.

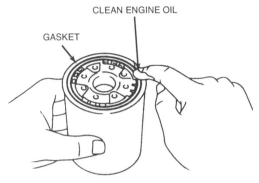

Fig. 8-5. Place some clean oil on seal of new filter. This will assure proper tightening.

Fig. 8-6. With your hands and filter free of oil, tighten filter by hand. Turn 1/2 to 3/4 turn after seal touches base.

17. Avoid tightening the filter with an oil filter wrench or the rubber seal can be smashed, causing a serious oil leak.

GREASE JOB

18. If you have your instructor's OK and a front end teaching unit or automobile, you can perform a grease job. Locate and lubricate the grease fittings on the upper and lower ball joints.

   Caution! Do not overfill the rubber boots or they can rupture. As soon as you see them swell a little — stop!

19. Look for other components needing lubrication. Sometimes tie rods ends, idler arm, or universal joints can be lubricated.

20. If the car has never been lubed, the small hex head screws will have to be removed so that fittings can be installed. Fig. 8-7 shows the most common location of grease fittings.

21. How many grease fittings did you find?

_____

22. Where were they located? _____

_____

_____

_____

23. Wipe up any spilled oil or grease and empty your oil drain pan.

   If this is a learning exercise on a shop owned engine, your instructor may want you to reinstall the same oil in the engine.

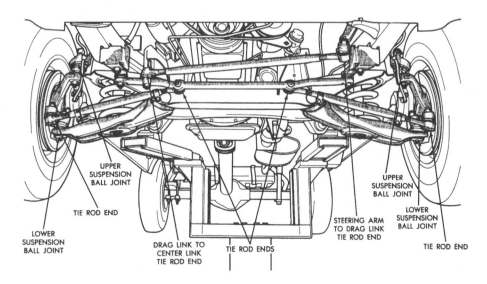

Fig. 8-7. Dots indicate possible grease fitting locations.

24. Lower the car to the ground and remove the filler cap. It is usually on valve cover.

INSTALLING OIL

25. Make sure that you have the right type, weight, and quantity of engine oil. Use the type oil recommended by the auto manufacturer or customer. Engine oil capacity (amount of oil sump will hold) can vary from only 4 quarts in small gasoline engines to 7 quarts in larger automotive diesel engines. If in doubt, refer to the specifications given in an owner's manual or service manual.

26. What type, weight, and brand of oil should be installed in this engine? _____

27. Push your oil fill spout into a can of oil. Wrap a rag or paper towel around the two to prevent drippage. Pour the oil into the filler opening in the engine. Repeat this operation until the engine is filled to the proper level.

28. How much oil does your engine require?

29. Replace the filler cap and wipe off any oil that you might have dripped on the engine, workbench, or floor.

30. Start the engine and watch the oil pressure indicator light or gauge. The oil warning light should go out within 15 or 20 seconds. A gauge should begin to register almost immediately. If not, SHUT OFF THE ENGINE and find the problem.

31. How long did it take for the engine to develop oil pressure? _____

LUBRICATE OTHER UNITS

32. Let the engine run for about 5 minutes while you CHECK FOR LEAKS under the engine. Also, lubricate other high friction and wear points (hinges, latches, etc.) on the car.

33. Did you find any leaks? _____

34. If this is actual service of a customer car, place a small amount of grease between the parts that rub on the hood hinges and hood latch. Squirt a small amount of oil on the door hinges and rub a little nonstain lubricant on the door latches and posts.

35. If this is an actual oil change, fill out a service sticker including the date, mileage, type, weight, and brand of oil. Stick it on the edge of the driver's door above the latch.

36. Shut off the engine. Wipe off the hood and fenders and have your instructor sign your job sheet for credit before leaving class.

INSTRUCTOR'S SIGNATURE

Job 9

Tire Change and Repair

INTRODUCTION: Changing, repairing, and balancing a tire are fundamental automotive service and repair operations. Damaged or improperly maintained tires frequently cause numerous drivability problems, such as wheel tramp, shimmy, vibration, hard steering, poor steering recovery, steering pull, steering wander, tire squeal, hard ride, tire wear, lowered gas mileage, and on-the-road breakdowns in the form of flats or blowouts. As you can see, anyone who plans on becoming a well qualified auto technician and problem troubleshooter should learn as much as possible about basic tire service.

OBJECTIVE: Given an old tire, a wheel, and the listed tools, you will learn to properly service and repair a wheel and tire assembly.

TOOLS AND EQUIPMENT: You will need a wheel and tubeless tire, tire changer, valve core tool, tire plugging tool kit, wheel weight pliers, small steel ruler, tread depth gauge or a Lincoln-head penny, soapy water, safety glasses, tire pressure gauge, diagonal cutting pliers, and shop rags or paper towels.

INSTRUCTIONS: Ask your instructor for the location of the particular tire and wheel to be used in the Job and for any other details. You should have seen a demonstration on the safe and proper use of your tire changer. Be sure to wear safety glasses, especially while inflating the tire.

REVIEW OF TIRE AND WHEEL

1. As a review and to help you better understand the procedures given in the Job, identify the parts of the cutaway tire, wheel, and valve stem assembly in Fig. 9-1. The parts that you cannot label from memory should be studied.

A. _____

B. _____

C. _____

D. _____

E. _____

F. _____

G. _____

H. _____

I. _____

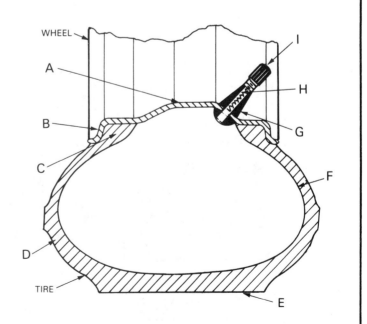

Fig. 9-1. Identify the parts of the wheel and tire assembly.

2. Check out the tools, equipment, tire, and wheel to be used for the Job.

3. From the information printed on the sidewall of the tire, fill in the following data on your tire.
   A. Brand name _____
   B. Wheel diameter _____
   C. Ply information _____
   D. Construction type _____
   E. Load range _____
   F. Maximum air pressure _____
   G. Maximum load _____
   H. DOT number _____

CHECK TIRE WEAR

4. As previously mentioned in your textbook, tire wear patterns are indicators of suspension, inflation, alignment, and driving problems. Compare your tire wear pattern to the ones given in Fig. 9-2. Diagnose the cause of any irregular tire wear.

5. What type of wear pattern does your tire have? _____

6. What was the most likely cause for the wear pattern? _____

7. Can you find any tire damage (cuts, cracks, etc.) other than wear? _____

8. As a rule of thumb, if the tread on a tire, at any point, is less than 1/16 in. (1.59 mm) deep, the tire is unsafe. It should be replaced.

9. A "trick of the trade" is to insert a Lincoln-head penny into the tire tread at various locations. If the top of Mr. Lincoln's head shows, then the tread is less than 1/16 in. (1.59 mm) deep and tire is unsafe for use. If the tread covers part of Lincoln's head, the tire is usually considered safe.

10. Use your depth gauge, steel rule, or Lincoln penny to measure the tread depth at its deepest and shallowest points.

11. What is the measured tread depth at its shallowest point? _____

12. What is the measured tread depth at its deepest point? _____

Fig. 9-2. Tread wear patterns indicative of pressure, alignment, or driving problems.

(DODGE)

13. Explain the tread condition of the tire. __

_____

_____

REMOVE TIRE

14. While wearing safety glasses, remove the valve stem core with your core tool. This will let the air out of the tire. Also, remove any wheel weights with your wheel weight pliers.

15. Use your tire changer to break or push the tire bead away from the lip or flange of the wheel. Follow the specific instructions provided with the tire changer.
Keep your fingers out of the way and follow all safety rules.
   If you are using a power tire changer, do not catch the bead breaker on the edge of the wheel. It can bend a steel wheel or break an alloy wheel.

16. Rub some special lubricant or soapy water on the tire bead and the wheel flange. This will ease tire removal. Then, use the proper end of the large steel bar of your tire changer to remove the tire from the wheel, Fig. 9-3.

Note, you must use one hand to HOLD THE TIRE DOWN into the drop center of the wheel while prying off the opposite side of the tire.
   Be careful not to cut or split the tire bead. If you run into difficulty, ask your instructor for help.

17. After the tire is off of the wheel, inspect the inside of the tire for splits, cracks, punctures, patches, or repairs.

REPAIRING A PUNCTURED TIRE

Note: In the past, tires were repaired by inserting a rubber plug in the puncture without demounting the tire. This practice is no longer acceptable. Tires must be repaired from the *inside* only. The following procedure is for repairing a puncture with a plug and a patch. If available, a one-piece head-type plug can be used. This type of plug eliminates the need for a separate patch. Follow the manufacturer's directions.

18. After removing the tire from the rim, remove the puncturing object and note the angle of penetration. Clean the area to be repaired.

19. From the inside of the tire, fill the puncture with a plug or a liquid sealer. After filling the hole, cut off the plug (if used) slightly above the tire's inside surface.

20. Scuff the inside surface of the tire well beyond the repair area. Clean the scuffed area thoroughly.

21. Apply cement to the scuffed area and place a patch over the damaged area. Use a stitcher to help bond the patch to the inner surface of the tire. See Fig. 9-4.

Fig. 9-3. When demounting a tire, work carefully and wear safety goggles.

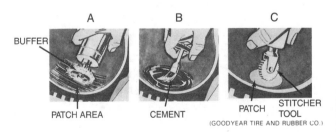

Fig. 9-4. Installing a tire patch. A — Buff an area slightly larger than the patch and clean the buffed area thoroughly. B — Apply the cement with a brush (allow for recommended drying time.) C — Install the patch. Use the stitcher tool to firmly roll the patch into contact with the cement. Roll over the entire surface of the patch.

22. Clean the outer pressure sealing edge of the wheel as needed. See Fig. 9-5. Wipe it off with your rags or towels or if rusted or dirty, clean it with steel wool.

STEEL
WOOL

Fig. 9-5. Clean and check rim before mounting tire. Remember rim is part of air chamber.

23. Check the condition of the valve stem. Bend it sideways and look for weather cracks or splits.

   If this were an actual repair, you would remove and replace a cracked or weathered valve stem. Unless instructed to do so, DO NOT remove the valve stem.

24. What is the condition of your valve stem?

_____

_____

_____

MOUNTING TIRE

25. To remount the tire, wipe soapy water on the tire bead and the flange of the wheel. Use the particular procedures for your tire changer to pry the tire back on the wheel.

   Remember! Push the tire bead (bead opposite the pry bar) down in the drop center of the wheel or the tire will NOT go on rim.

26. With the tire on the rim, pull up on the tire while twisting it. Try to get the tire to catch on the upper safety ridge. You want the upper tire bead to catch and hold on the upper flange of the rim. Then, the tire can be filled with air.

27. Inject air into the tire. If you can hear air rushing out of the tire, push IN lightly on the leaking part of the tire. When the tire begins to take air, do not over inflate it and loosen the wheel holddown cone. Be careful not to get your fingers caught between the tire and the wheel. Go to step 28 if your tire will not take air and expand.

28. If your tire will NOT hold enough air to expand and seal on the wheel, you may need to use a bead expander.

   Clamp the expander around the outside of the tire. This will push the tire bead against the wheel flange. Again inject air into the tire. DANGER! As soon as the tire begins to expand, RELEASE the bead expander. If not released immediately, the expander can break and fly off of the tire with unbelievable force.

29. While inflating the tire, lean away from the tire to prevent possible injury. The tire could blow out. DO NOT INFLATE THE TIRE OVER 40 TO 50 PSI! Check that the bead ridge on the sidewall of the tire is even or true with the wheel. If not, remount the tire on the wheel.

30. After the bead has popped over the safety ridges, screw in the valve core and·snug it up.

CHECKING TIRE PRESSURE

31. Use your pressure gauge to check tire pressure. The tire pressure should be a few pounds under the maximum pressure rating labeled on the sidewall of the tire. As a tire is operated, it can heat up. This may cause the pressure in the tire to go up.

32. What is the inflation pressure for your tire?

_____

33. To check for leaks, pour water over the tire beads, puncture repair, and valve stem. Watch for bubbles. Air bubbles indicate a leak.

34. Is your tire holding air? Why or why not?

_____

_____

35. Have your instructor sign this sheet for credit before leaving class.

_____

INSTRUCTOR'S SIGNATURE

Date _____ Period _____

Instructor _____

Job 10

Cooling System Service

INTRODUCTION: An automotive cooling system must be serviced periodically. The cooling system has the awesome task of removing around 30 percent of all of the heat energy produced by combustion. If unserviced, the cooling system can cause serious mechanical breakdowns in a short period of time. Deteriorated hoses and belts, system leaks, bad water pump, faulty radiator cap, and a stuck thermostat can all cause sudden and complete failure of the system. After extended service, antifreeze can break down, forming an acid that attacks and rusts the system. It is important that you know how to service a cooling system.

OBJECTIVE: Given the proper tools and equipment, you will learn to service an automotive cooling system.

TOOLS AND EQUIPMENT: Obtain a cooling system pressure tester, safety glasses, cooling system hydrometer or antifreeze tester, basic set of hand tools, and shop owned cooling system. For the out-of-car thermostat test, you will need a thermostat, a heat resistant container (beaker, pan, can), piece of mechanic's wire, and source of heat (oven or hot plate).

INSTRUCTIONS: Since this Job contains two sections, your instructor may want you to perform the thermostat test at home on a stove as a homework assignment. Ask about these details. The other, cooling system testing and inspecting portion of the Job will be performed in the shop on a school owned assembly.

REVIEW OF PARTS

1. As a quick review of cooling system parts, identify the parts in Fig. 10-1.

A. _____

B. _____

C. _____

D. _____

E. _____

F. _____

G. _____

H. _____

I. _____

Fig. 10-1. Can you name the components?

INSPECT COOLING SYSTEM

2. Visually inspect your cooling system. Squeeze the hoses to check for hardness, cracks, or softness. Look at Figs. 10-2 and 10-3.

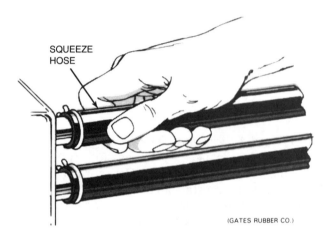

SQUEEZE HOSE

(GATES RUBBER CO.)

Fig. 10-2. Check hardness and condition of all hoses.

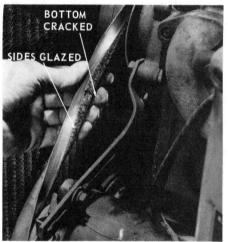

BOTTOM CRACKED

SIDES GLAZED

(GATES RUBBER CO.)

Fig. 10-3. Check belts for cracks, splits, glazing, low tension, and other problems.

3. If the system is cool, check the condition of the coolant. There should be no signs of rust and the system should be filled properly.

4. The percent of antifreeze should be appropriate. Measure the mixture or percentage of antifreeze with an antifreeze tester. Since testers vary, follow manufacturer's operating instructions.

5. Check that the radiator fins are free of leaves and bugs. The rubber seal on the radiator cap should be soft and unbroken.

6. Explain the condition (good, fair, replace) of each of the system check points in the spaces provided in the following chart.

CHECK POINT	CONDITION
Radiator Hoses	A. _____
Heater Hoses	B. _____
Water Pump Bearings	C. _____
Coolant Level	D. _____
Coolant Condition	E. _____
Antifreeze Protection	F. _____
Radiator Cap	G. _____
Radiator Fins	H. _____
Belt Condition	I. _____
Belt Tension	J. _____

REMOVE BELTS

7. Remove the belts from the engine by loosening the bracket bolts on the alternator, air conditioning compressor, power steering pump, or other unit. You may need a droplight so that you can find all of the bolts.

8. With your belts removed, measure and determine the length of each of the belts. If a tape measure or special belt scale is not available, use a ruler to get an estimate. Walk the ruler around the belt carefully keeping track of the total measurement.

9. What are the lengths of each of your belts?

_____

_____

_____

_____

10. Why did any of the cooling system check points fail in Step 6? _____

_____

_____

_____

_____

11. Reinstall your belts and adjust their tension. Special belt tension gauges are available that will measure exact tension. To adjust belts by hand, refer to Fig. 10-4. In general, a belt,

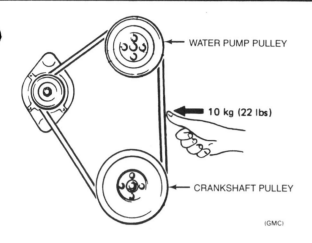

Fig. 10-4. Checking belt tension. A loose belt can cause slippage and overheating. An overtightened belt can cause premature bearing wear in water pump and alternator.

depending on length, should deflect about 1/2 to 5/8 in. (13 to 9.5 mm) with 25 pounds (11 Kg) of push applied.

12. Ideally, strive to adjust the belts as loose as possible without allowing them to slip, squeal, or flop in operation. This will lengthen the life of the alternator, A/C compressor, water pump, and power steering pump bearings.

   Note! The alternator bearings are NOT submerged in lubricant, as with the A/C compressor, water pump, and power steering pump. Thus, the alternator belt should NOT be tightened as much as the other belts.

13. List the types of belts (alternator, power steering) used on your engine. _____

_____

_____

_____

THERMOSTAT SERVICE

14. Now, remove your thermostat from under the top radiator hose fitting. This fitting is also called a thermostat housing. Scrape off all of the old gasket material from both the engine and the thermostat housing.

15. To make a new gasket, obtain a piece of gasket material, a pair of scissors, and a small ball peen hammer. Lay your thermostat housing over the gasket material and trace the outside shape of the housing with a pencil or pen. Cut out this shape with scissors.

Hold this pattern over the thermostat opening in the engine, Fig. 10-5. Then, to cut out the inside holes for the thermostat and bolts, tap lightly around the edge of the openings with the peen end of your hammer. Make sure that you do not shift the gasket while tapping or the holes will be misaligned.

After tapping and perforation, the inside of the gasket holes will easily tear out, Fig. 10-6.

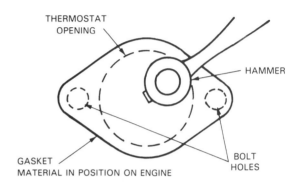

Fig. 10-5. Lay piece of gasket material over thermostat opening on engine and tap along hole edges (dotted lines) to cut out gasket.

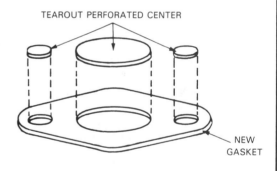

Fig. 10-6. After tapping with your hammer, tear out center of your holes.

16. Reinstall your thermostat, making sure that it is right-side up (pellet toward engine or pin pointing toward radiator) as shown in Fig. 10-7. Coat your sealing surfaces with non-hardening sealer and fit the gasket and housing into place.

   When tightening the thermostat housing bolts, be extremely careful not to overtighten the bolts. Snug them a little at a time to pull the housing down straight and prevent distortion. Overtightening the housing can cause breakage.

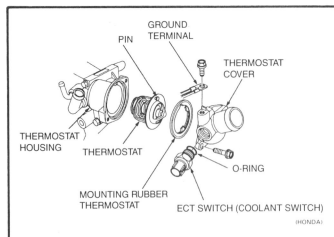

Fig. 10-7. Check that you are fitting thermostat into engine right-side up.

17. How do you know the thermostat is NOT installed backwards? _____

_____

_____

_____

PRESSURE TEST SYSTEM

18. Using a system pressure tester, check the condition of your radiator cap. Mount it on the tester as in Fig. 10-8. Pump up pressure until the pressure needle levels off at a specific pressure.

   A good radiator cap will hold the pressure listed on top of the cap and will not leak. A bad cap, besides leaking, may not hold pressure within specified limits (pressure high or low).

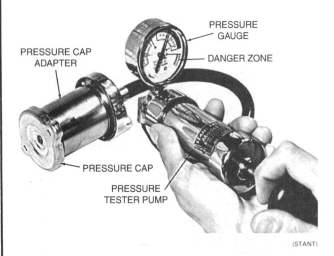

Fig. 10-8. A good radiator cap will hold specified pressure labeled on cap lid.

19. Explain the results of your pressure cap test.

_____

_____

_____

20. Again using your pressure tester, test for cooling system leaks by mounting the tester on the radiator. See Fig. 10-9. Pressurize the system to the pressure rating given on the top of the radiator cap (around 8 to 15 psi). If the pressure holds for two minutes without bleeding off, the system is not leaking. While waiting, always visually watch for leaks.

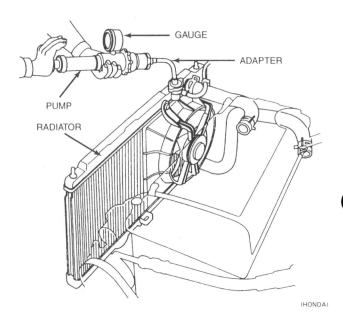

Fig. 10-9. Pump same amount of pressure as is listed on radiator cap and no more.

21. Explain the holding pressure and condition of your cooling system. _____

_____

_____

_____

22. Turn in all of your tools and equipment and have your teacher sign this job for credit. You may also need to ask about the details of the second portion of the Job on thermostat testing.

THERMOSTAT TESTING

23. First, visually inspect your thermostat. Hold it up to the light and check to see if there is a gap or opening around the edge of the sealing valve. If there is, then the thermostat may be defective and may require replacement. No matter what the condition, it will be tested.

24. What is the visual condition of your thermostat? _____

_____

_____

25. Mount your water or coolant filled container, thermostat, and thermometer as shown in Fig. 10-10. Stir the water gently while heating and watching the thermostat.

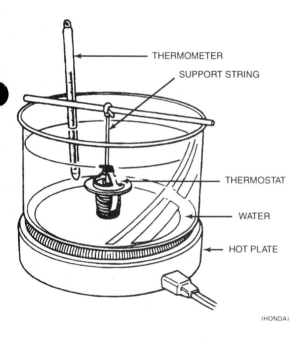

Fig. 10-10. Checking thermostat opening temperature. Note that both thermometer and thermostat are kept free of container sides and bottom.

26. Record whether the valve is closed, starting to open, or fully opened in the following chart. Write your answer next to the appropriate temperature.

   For example, the valve may be closed at 100°F (37.3°C) and open at 200°F (93.3°C). Watch very closely for the opening temperature when the valve first starts to open. It is important.

WATER TEMPERATURE	VALVE POSITION
100 °F.	A. _____
150 °F.	B. _____
170 °F.	C. _____
175 °F.	D. _____
180 °F.	E. _____
185 °F.	F. _____
190 °F.	G. _____
195 °F.	H. _____
200 °F.	I. _____
205 °F.	J. _____
210 °F.	K. _____
212 °F.	L. _____

27. At what temperature did your thermostat start to open? _____

_____

28. At what temperature did it fully open?

_____

_____

29. A good thermostat should start to open around 5 to 10° above or below the operating temperature stamped on the thermostat. It should be fully open at a temperature 20 to 25° above the opening temperature.

30. Explain the condition of your thermostat.

_____

_____

_____

_____

_____

31. Ask your instructor to sign this portion of the job for credit.

_____

INSTRUCTOR'S SIGNATURE